Advance Praise for ***PSI Spies***

"Jim Marrs' *PSI Spies* is the first, and still one of the best books ever written about the U.S. government's top-secret psychic warfare unit. Marrs introduces us to all of the main researchers and military viewers involved in this covert project and gives the reader a detailed view of the benefits and limitations of applied remote viewing. I highly recommend it to anyone wanting an accessible and cogent discussion of this fascinating and enigmatic subject."

—Simeon Hein, Ph. D., author of *Opening Minds*

"Jim Marrs uses his impressive investigative skills and impeccable research to delve into the shadowy world of remote viewing and psychic spying as a form of intelligence gathering. Marrs presents compelling and thorough documentation of the classified quest of the U.S. government to understand the mysterious world of "psi" and turn it to their military advantage. Both provocative and highly entertaining, *PSI Spies* proves that our government takes paranormal phenomena far more seriously than we've ever been led to believe. Another must-read book by an author who is never afraid to dig deep for, and expose, the truth."

—Marie D. Jones, author of *PSIence: How New Discoveries in Quantum Physics and New Science May Explain the Existence of Paranormal Phenomena*

High Praise for ***Crossfire***

"Compelling reading."

—***Washington Post***

"Raises profound and deeply troubling questions."

—***Cleveland Plain Dealer***

"Dallas journalist Marrs brings together under one cover diverse theories and facts advanced in many of these works. He points to the inconsistencies and unexplained elements embodied in the official versions as to what transpired in Dallas before, during, and after the president's death."

—***Library Journal***

"For its comprehensiveness alone, this would be the one book for anyone seeking a really thorough examination of the assassination. Marrs is sensible and straightforward, giving every side of disputed questions, though it is clear that for him, as for most thoughtful people, the Warren Commission's picture of Oswald as a lone assassin doesn't work."

—***Publishers Weekly***

High Praise for ***Alien Agenda***

"The most entertaining and complete overview of flying saucers and their crew published in years."

—***Publishers Weekly***

"You may find yourself watching the skies a little more intently, or even checking under the bed before you go to sleep."

—***Ft. Worth Star-Telegram***

PSI SPIES

The True Story of America's Psychic Warfare Program

Jim Marrs

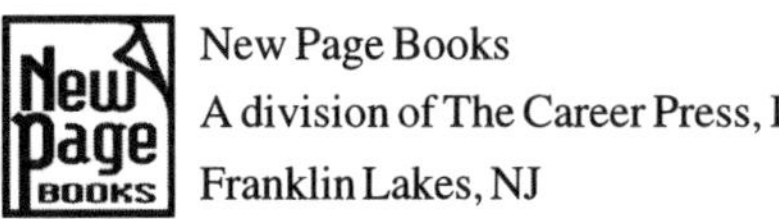

New Page Books
A division of The Career Press, Inc.
Franklin Lakes, NJ

Psi Spies

Edited by Jodi Brandon

Typeset by Michael Fitzgibbon

Cover design by Howard Grossman/12e Design

Printed in the U.S.A. by Book-mart Press

To order this title, please call toll-free 1-800-CAREER-1 (NJ and Canada: 201-848-0310) to order using VISA or MasterCard, or for further information on books from Career Press.

The Career Press, Inc., 3 Tice Road, PO Box 687,
Franklin Lakes, NJ 07417

www.careerpress.com
www.newpagebooks.com

Library of Congress Cataloging-in-Publication Data

Marrs, Jim.

Psi spies : the true story of America's psychic warfare program / by Jim Marrs.

p. cm.

Includes bibliographical references and index.

ISBN-13: 978-1-56414-960-2

ISBN-10: 1-56414-960-9

1. Parapsychology—Military aspects. 2. Remote viewing (Parasychology) 3. Government information—Miscellanea. I. Title.

BF1045.M55M33 2007

133.8--dc22

2007026647

CONTENTS

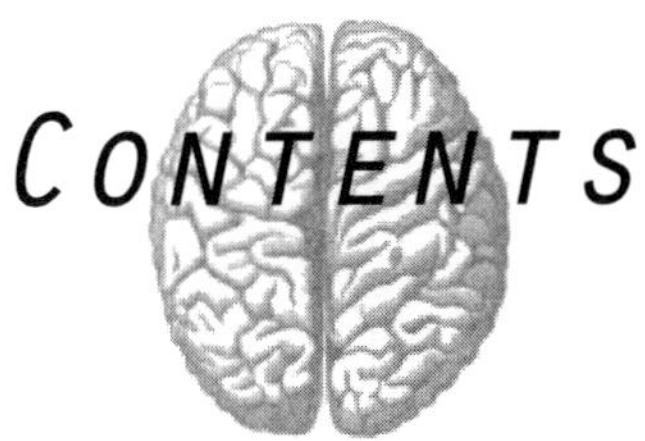

PREFACE

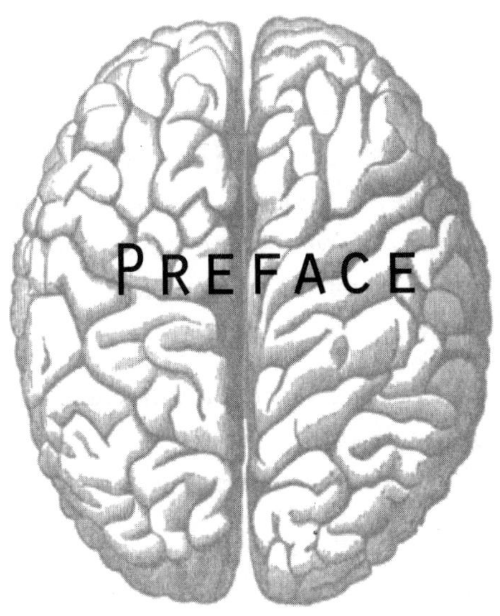

In 1992, following the success of my book *Crossfire: The Plot That Killed Kennedy,* I began to look for other dark secrets being hidden away by the federal government. What I found led me into an incredible journey through time, space, ESP, UFOs, censorship, and disinformation.

It began with my discovery of a psychic ability termed remote viewing, or RV. This phenomenon in the past had been called clairvoyance, prophecy, or soothsaying. Although recorded by all cultures throughout human history, it was believed to be simply an occult fantasy until scientific studies during the 20th century confirmed its existence.

Despite the fact that remote viewing was developed by various tax-supported government agencies including the CIA, the Defense Intelligence Agency, and even the U.S. Army, a majority of Americans still have never heard of this faculty.

But remote viewing forever changed the lives of the men and women employed in its use. This included people only tangentially connected to the government-funded RV programs.

This book became one of the casualties in the ongoing conflict between science and ESP, military secrecy and the public's right to know, as well as the never-ending intramural competition between government agencies and power-seeking individuals.

What you are about to read was suppressed in the summer of 1995, four months before the existence of government-sponsored remote viewing was publicly revealed by a CIA press release.

The story of remote viewing—then one of our government's most closely guarded secrets—now has filtered into certain aware segments of the public, where it continues to attract growing fascination and interest. Today, several experienced viewers are bringing this phenomenal technology to a wider audience. Others have spoken about it in books, articles, or public speeches. Even some entrepreneurs now advertise psychic readings reportedly accomplished through RV.

To understand this transition from top-secret government project to minor public fad, I invite the reader to follow my own experience with remote viewing.

As I traveled across the country on media tours and speaking engagements during 1991 and 1992, at every opportunity, I would ask, "What do you think is the next big secret government cover-up?"

The response was almost unanimous: I was told that people were curious about the UFO phenomenon. I realized that I was, too. Although I had been aware and curious about UFO stories since I was a young man in the 1950s, I was no further along than anyone else in learning the truth of the matter. I determined that I would research and write about the topic.

As I began to establish, and reestablish, contacts within the UFO research community, I was made aware of a speech presented by a military intelligence officer at a public conference in Atlanta in early 1992 (the Treat IV Conference). In a public speech, then-Army Captain Ed Dames spoke about UFOs, detailing in no uncertain terms what they were, where they came from, and where they were going.

His matter-of-fact tone intrigued me, for here was no starry-eyed New Age fanatic, but a decorated military intelligence officer. Furthermore, Dames was no loose cannon. During his talk, he was flanked by Col. John Alexander, a leading luminary in military nonlethal weapons research who moved freely between both military and intelligence programs, and Maj. Gen. Albert Stubblebine, former commander of the Army's Intelligence and Security Command.

Dames told his audience about the development of remote viewing, which he described as "this profound tool." He also spoke of flying "transport vehicles" used to "transport a type of resource, usually from Mars to Earth, sometimes through time." He spoke of giant inhabited underground caverns on Earth and hibernating Martians on Mars, even "transcendental" energy beings who could access our very minds.

Intrigued, I contacted Dames and soon learned the story of our military remote viewers. Dames said he and fellow Army officer David Morehouse were in touch with a New York literary agent. Both officers said the story of RV was too important to remain a military secret. They were willing to talk.

And I was willing to listen. To me this was a journalist's dream come true, for, if RV was fraudulent, it was a shameful waste of taxpayer money. If it proved true, it could well represent a leap forward in human evolution. Either way, it was a story I knew I had to pursue.

An agreement was reached: I would write about RV and its use by the military, and Dames and Morehouse would help supply facts, contacts, and information. In June 1993, I contracted to publish a book through Harmony Books, a subsidiary of Random House.

Beginning with my contact with Dames in the summer of 1992, I spent three years working on the remote viewing story. During that time, my research showed that the RV phenomenon was a reality that had been recorded throughout history. I was introduced to other military viewers, such as Lyn Buchanan and Mel Riley. I met members of the oversight committees that monitored the RV program, such as Dr. Paul Tyler and Col. Alexander. I interviewed Dr. Hal Puthoff and Ingo Swann, who, along with Russell Targ, were the men most responsible for the development of RV.

The work was arduous, particularly so because I was dealing with a subject most people wanted no part of—not to mention that it involved a top-secret government program. Many sources refused to be interviewed, and others demanded anonymity. Hard facts were difficult to come by.

In mid-1995, as the book was nearing publication and without consulting me, a Harmony editor paid a small sum to Morehouse to add some personal recollections to the manuscript. Morehouse had just resigned from the Army under contentious circumstances and gone to work for the New York agent.

The inclusion of Morehouse's experiences upset Dames, who apparently had come to view the book as his own personal biography, despite the fact that all concerned had initially agreed that it would be about remote viewing and the military unit rather than about any individual.

Dames, who by this time was claiming to be in contact with alien grays, sent a letter via an attorney to Harmony disavowing the book, even though he had previously signed an unprecedented release statement based on my completed manuscript (sans Morehouse's paragraphs). I found it most ironic that this obstruction came from the very person who had initiated the book in the first place, and nothing he had contributed had been altered or deleted. Some observers saw a darker purpose behind Dames's action.

This darker purpose seemed to have been confirmed by subsequent events. First, the book's editor was suddenly offered a job outside New York City and left the project. Interestingly, some months after the book was canceled, he returned to his old job. The senior legal counsel, who had approved publication of the book following a lengthy and thorough legal review, was suddenly no longer there.

The matter was turned over to a law firm previously unconnected to the publisher, and I was ordered not to contact or talk to the firm's attorney, who then decided the book had to be canceled because of the legal threats from Dames. I was told by the new book editor that, though she neither understood nor agreed with the course being taken, she was powerless to prevent the cancellation.

I was assured that the only reason for the cancellation was the possibility of legal action by Dames, yet when I explained that he was only one of many sources and could be deleted without affecting the book, I was told it would be canceled anyway.

Everyone involved with the book came to believe that the cancellation had been ordered by someone with great authority, perhaps within the government. Subsequent events only substantiated this belief.

The book was canceled in late July 1995, despite substantial orders from booksellers. On August 27, the story of RV broke in a London newspaper. The story, entitled "Tinker, Tailor, Soldier, Psi," was written by Jim Schnabel, who earlier that year had received a copy of my manuscript from Dames. Schnabel went on to publish a book on RV in 1997, which included much detail from insider sources.

By early September, the CIA was involved in a review of remote viewing by Ray Hyman and Jessica Utts. Considering that Hyman, a luminary of the Committee for the Scientific Investigation of Claims of the Paranormal (CSICOP), was biased against ESP to begin with, coupled with the fact that the review concentrated only on the weakest of the RV work, the outcome was never in doubt.

Their finished report, dated September 29, 1995, was a fascinating mixture of both support for and condemnation of

RV. The report concluded that, despite that fact that a "statistically significant effect" had been observed in laboratory RV experiments, "no compelling explanation has been provided for the observed effects...to say a phenomenon has been demonstrated we must know the reasons for its existence."[1]

In other words, we know it works but we don't know how, so therefore, it must not work. The report was a thinly disguised effort to restrict public interest in RV.

The report also stated that remote viewing "has not been shown to have value in intelligence operations."[2] The CIA concurrently announced that its RV work was unpromising and would be discontinued.

The story that the government had used psychics to spy on enemies first broke publicly in early October in a supermarket tabloid story headlined "How CIA's Psychic Spies Stole Russia's Star Wars Secrets." This tabloid treatment, obviously leaked by government sources, was a kiss of death to anyone in the mainstream media taking the subject seriously.

Remote viewing was officially acknowledged by a CIA news release dated November 28, 1995. The story received superficial and dismissive coverage in the *New York Times* and the *Washington Post,* which described the Psi Spies merely as "a trio of citizens with suspected paranormal powers who were located at a Maryland military base."[3] Even with this watered-down version, the story moved no farther than the East Coast. Nowhere was there any mention that remote viewing was simply dispersed to even more secret government agencies where its use continues today, according to several separate unofficial sources.

Also, in all the coverage of RV in the major media, it was never pointed out that this psychic program had been funded for more than quarter of a century under four separate administrations, half Republican and half Democrat, indicating that someone felt the government was getting its money's worth.

In 1996, Morehouse's own book, *Psychic Warrior,* was published by St. Martin's Press and was well received by readers. But the book's revelations incurred the lasting animosity of the military authorities who were already angered by Morehouse's whistle-blowing on other secret operations. This animosity spread to Morehouse's former comrades-in-arms, causing deep divisions between the former military remote viewers.

Morehouse suffered greatly for his part in exposing the RV story. Charged with taking a typewriter without permission and adultery with another soldier's wife (they both were separated at the time), Morehouse was ordered before a court martial and was later admitted to a psychiatric ward within Walter Reed Army Medical Center. On the occasions when I visited him there, he was so heavily drugged that he could barely lift his head.

Charges were quietly dropped after Morehouse agreed to resign his commission and accept a less-than-honorable discharge from the Army, thus losing all benefits, not to mention the damage to his credibility.

On the other hand, Dames, who had initiated the exposure of the Psi Spies, suffered no retaliation and, in fact, maintained control over the private company that he and Morehouse had created (PSI TECH). He soon devoted himself to teaching RV.

A frequent guest on late-night radio, Dames remained popular despite a continuing loss of credibility. In a 1993 magazine interview, Dames said he wanted a "face-to-face" meeting with Martians hibernating underground in New Mexico, adding, "If we don't have it by the end of August, we're getting out of the UFO game."[4] Neither happened.

Prior to the arrival of the Hale-Bopp Comet in 1997, Dames told a *Coast to Coast* radio audience that his remote viewing had revealed that a container filled with plant-killing pathogens was accompanying Hale-Bopp. He said spores from the companion would blanket the Earth, killing most of the population. He also predicted massive breakdowns in the human immunization system, widespread death from exotic plagues, and nuclear power plant disasters. Either Dames's RV accuracy had worsened since leaving the military or he was pursuing another agenda.

Meanwhile, the American public was left to only study the available bits and pieces of information on remote viewing. Some information came from former Psi Spies, more from scientific and government documents, and some from persons with suspect motives.

In 2000, this book was published in a limited edition. This present incarnation is an effort to provide readers with my account of the remote viewing story. Here then is the original *Psi Spies,* updated and expanded.

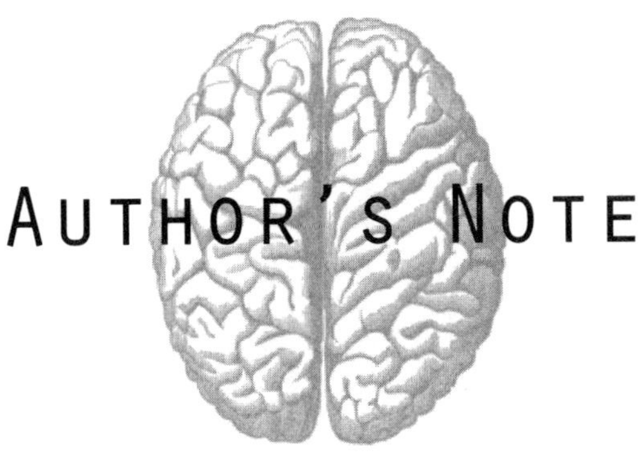

Author's Note

Please note when reading *PSI Spies* that I have cited interviews with an endnote only on the first quotation by an interviewed source. After that, readers can assume that quotations attributed to a person but not cited come from that same interview previously noted. I chose to note only the first instance in order to prevent the book from becoming cumbersome with endnotes. All relevant information is included in the Notes (beginning on page 299) with the first mention from each source throughout the book.

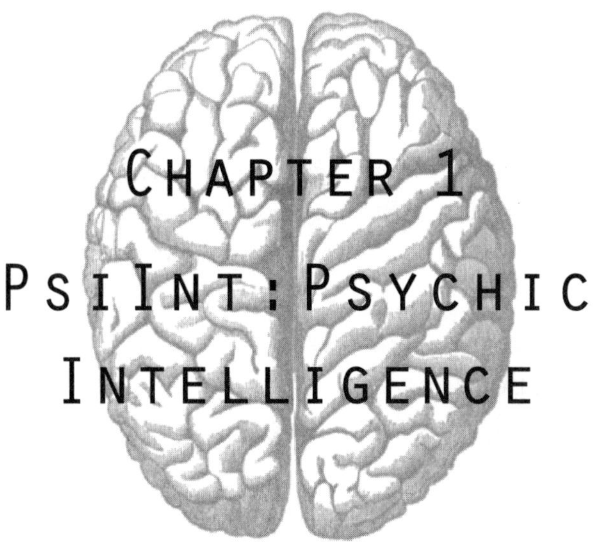

Chapter 1
PsiInt: Psychic Intelligence

U.S. Army Captain David Morehouse should never have told his unit psychologist about his out-of-body experience. He didn't think it was any big deal, but the incident had stayed on his mind, and he wanted to share it with someone.

His sharing set him on a course that completely altered his life, bringing him face to face with the most fundamental questions of life on Earth and its place in the universe.

It all began one morning in early 1988. As Morehouse drove to his job with a top-level military intelligence unit, he felt he had it made. The unit was an odd mixture of Special Forces soldiers, intelligence officers, military pilots, communications experts, and even some Marines. Morehouse felt slightly out of place as, for the past 10 years of his career, he had been an infantry officer first commanding a Ranger company in Panama, then serving as a staff officer at battalion level.

He and his wife, son, and two daughters were living in a two-story Colonial home in Bowie, Maryland. Although he didn't have the kind of close family life he might have desired, they were living comfortably.

Each morning, Morehouse made the same drive from his home to the Kingman Building outside Fort Belvoir where he worked in the enclosed offices of a unit known only as ROYAL CAPE.

This "special access" unit was housed in modular offices, which had been constructed inside an existing building. Armed guards, key-card locks, and electronic fields protected the entire unit.

Entering the main hallway that morning in 1988, Morehouse nodded to the armed guards in their glass-encased room. To his left was the office of the unit psychologist, Lt. Col. Ennis Cole (a pseudonym, as he still works for the government), a tall, slender man with a thick head of blondish-brown hair.

Morehouse knew Col. Cole's work within the unit was critical. ROYAL CAPE's responsibilities included the handling of operatives in foreign countries. Such operatives had to be extremely stable people. And yet the people that chose to do such work were almost always inherently unstable.

He knew that it was a fine line in these agents' psychological profile that decided which would go and which would stay. It was the unit psychologist that would ultimately make the decision. Then there was the fact that no one in the special access unit was hired without thorough testing by Col. Cole. He probably knew more about the unit members than their own families.

Morehouse looked to his right, into his commanding officer's office, to see if anything seemed out of the ordinary. Once he saw that everything appeared routine, he veered left into his own office. The small cubicle was depressing. It had no windows and nothing hung on the walls—no photos, no pictures, no posters, nothing. A few weeks earlier, Morehouse had tried to bring the room to life by mounting his military awards, plaques, and trophies on the wall, but one of his superiors had ordered the removal of this self-aggrandizing museum.

Sadly, Morehouse had removed the items, all except for the Kevlar helmet he had brought back from his tour in Jordan the year before. The bullet hole from a 7.62-millimeter slug was still prominent on that helmet. The shot to his head had been deflected by the helmet, but the shock of the bullet strike had opened doors into his mind he had never known existed. The incident had begun a series of strange experiences.

Morehouse had no more than settled into the chair behind his large wooden desk when he made his decision: He decided to see the psychologist and talk about his experiences.

He walked down the hallway and entered Cole's office. The psychologist was sitting behind his desk with his head buried in a stack of papers.

Cole pushed the stack aside, looked up, and said, "Hi, Dave. What's up? Are you still concerned about that last man we checked?"

"No, I have a little personal matter I want to talk with you about," replied Morehouse.

Cole straightened in his chair and leaned forward. "Oh?" he said, suddenly interested.

Morehouse began to have second thoughts about his decision to share his latest experience with Cole. It was pretty outlandish-sounding, and he himself had never put much stock in stories of the paranormal. But, over time, he had developed a certain trust in Cole.

He squirmed in his seat a moment and was about to rise to leave when Cole said, "Well, what is it, Dave? You know that you can tell me anything and it will be held in the strictest confidence."

"Yeah, I know, but this is pretty wild," replied Morehouse.

When Cole didn't say anything, Morehouse sighed, settled in his chair, and began recounting his story.

"Well, it was last weekend. Something happened while I was on a camping trip with my son and his Boy Scout troop as one of the adult supervisors."

Cole nodded and sat quietly as Morehouse continued.

"It was really cold and the snow was quite deep. It had been a big struggle to get to the camping spot and set up camp. We were all pretty tired and went to bed early. I really enjoy being with my son and his friends in the outdoors, but this time was special for me. It was a strange outing."

"What do you mean, strange?"

"I somehow felt closer to everyone and everything, as if I was tuned in to a different frequency or something. Once I looked into my son's eyes and almost started crying. I felt I could see into his life, into his future. There was this jumble of visions. I couldn't make any sense out of it. I know that sounds crazy, but that's what happened."

Cole nodded. "Well, I think—"

Morehouse interrupted. "There's more. When we all went to bed, I slept outside the tent, alone in my bedroll in the snow. It was about midnight and there was a full moon and a bright starry sky. I just lay there, taking it all in. I was in that Alpha State, you know, not quite asleep but not wide awake.

"Suddenly I felt myself rising slowly off the ground. I wasn't frightened. In fact I was oddly calm. I felt weightless and free as I passed nearby tree branches. Looking down to my left, I saw a dark body lying in the snow and I knew it was me.

"I wasn't scared, just intrigued by it all, as if I knew it was going to happen. Almost as if I had done this before.

"I remember coming straight up out of my sleeping bag. I mean I shot straight up into the sky. It seemed like I went up more than 1,000 feet. I was really moving. I saw the moon and the clouds and, more importantly, I felt all this. It was no dream. I was speeding toward the moon so fast it made me physically ill. I actually felt my stomach roll from the acceleration.

"I stopped high above the Earth and looked at everything around me. I could see for miles in the moonlight; the snow-covered hills, the forests, and the lights in the homes."

"Then I was moving along and before long I was above the house of a close friend of mine. I dropped through the roof and was seeing the inside of the house, moving from room to room."[1]

Morehouse sat staring at the wall, captivated by the memory of the incident.

Cole finally broke the silence. "Yes, well, then what happened?" he asked quietly.

Morehouse shook his head. "I woke up," he said.

Noting Cole's quizzical look, Morehouse quickly added, "Well, I didn't exactly wake up, you see, because I had never really been asleep. I guess you could say I just came to.

"I remember feeling that this was the end of the journey as I slowly descended back to where my body was. I watched myself all the way down but I lost everything just before I became me again. Then I was back in my sleeping bag as if nothing had happened."

Morehouse sat looking at the psychologist, as if waiting for word of a death sentence.

Cole smiled and said, "Dave, I can see your question coming. No, you're not going crazy."

"Well, that's a relief," he said. "But you have to admit that this is not normal."

Cole rose to his feet and began pacing his small office.

"I would say, from what you've told me, that you've had an out-of-body experience. And understand that this is not an uncommon occurrence."

"Really?" Morehouse was somewhat amazed. Because he had never really looked into the subject, he had always thought that stories about psychic insights and leaving the body were only for the supermarket tabloids.

"The psychological literature is full of such accounts," Cole said seriously. "Usually this phenomenon is connected to some life-threatening situation. Combat soldiers, in extreme danger, have often reported out-of-body experiences.

"Most of the material on these events is strictly anecdotal but there have been some successful scientific tests also. Under lab conditions, test subjects have been able to induce an out-of-body experience and have retrieved data that was not available through normal means. In fact, the army has been making a study of such things."

After rummaging in a filing cabinet, the psychologist put some papers together. Cole handed them to Morehouse, saying, "Here, I want you to read through this and tell me what you think."

"All right," said Morehouse absently as he thumbed through the material.

After returning to his office, Morehouse studied the material more closely.

It included some reports from the Army's Intelligence and Security Command's Golden Sphere program designed to enhance human performance. Some were stamped "Secret" and carried the strange acronym "GRILL FLAME." The reports addressed such topics as sleep-assisted learning, biofeedback, and stress management. There were also references to parapsychology and something called "remote viewing."

Parapsychology? Morehouse thought to himself. *I can't believe they are talking seriously here about clairvoyance and ESP.*

But his interest was aroused, and with his camping trip experience still fresh in his mind, Morehouse found he was more willing to look at the material with an open mind.

Two days later, Morehouse finally asked Cole the questions that had been plaguing him. "I want to know more about that material you gave me. There was a lot of talk about psychic abilities. Can that really exist? Is the Army seriously studying stuff like that? Can people really leave their bodies?" he asked seriously.

"What do you think?" Cole countered his questions with a question.

Morehouse sat quietly for a moment, then said slowly, "I used to think that all that was a bunch of bunk. But, now, after my experience, I'm not so sure."

Cole perched himself on the desk and leaned toward Morehouse. "What if I told you there were people doing those very things in the Army right now?" he said.

Morehouse was shocked. "You mean leaving their bodies and seeing with their minds?" he asked incredulously.

Cole nodded.

Morehouse sat for a moment thinking of the implications of what he had just been told. "How could I get in on something like that?" he finally asked.

Cole only smiled and said, "We'll talk later."

The next day Cole started dropping off folders for Morehouse to read. They were stamped "SECRET" and "GRILL

FLAME" and were filled with what appeared to be interrogations or interviews. Though they didn't seem to make sense, the reports in the folders continued to arouse his interest. Statements such as "now move forward through the wall," "move through the closed door," and "I'm reaching for the lock but it keeps passing through my hand" caught his attention.

After all, this was the United States Army, and military officers, particularly the unit psychologist, didn't make jokes about classified material.

Morehouse continued to meet with Col. Cole, both inside and outside the office. Cole shared information and articles on paranormal studies.

In time, he slowly revealed the secrets of GRILL FLAME.

A small, select group of soldiers, the colonel explained, were having out-of-body experiences. They were leaving their physical bodies, going to distant targets, and describing the targets. "They call this remote viewing," Cole explained.

Morehouse still couldn't quite believe this was real, yet here was his unit psychologist, a man with serious rank and credentials, telling him that people were sending their minds out of their bodies to view faraway persons and places.

It began to dawn on Morehouse that he was being let in on a very big secret, a secret that went outside the boundaries of his conventional upbringing. "What the hell am I getting myself involved in?" he thought, thinking back on his background.

Raised a "military brat," young Morehouse was shuffled from one home to another, sometimes in rough neighborhoods.

"I remember stomp fights," he recalled. "That's where one guy would stomp the other until someone fell down and then they would stomp his face—and that was just the third grade!"

The Morehouse family, practicing Mormons, finally settled in San Clemente, California. The beaches, surfers, and sun-baked beauties made Morehouse feel he was in heaven. He was a cheerleader while attending Mira Costa College, and in 1974 was voted "Mr. Cheer, USA" in national competition. But he also proved he was no wimp by placing fourth place in a statewide wrestling competition, a feat that earned him a scholarship to Brigham Young University.

It was at BYU that Morehouse gained both a wife and an obsession with becoming a soldier as his father, who had served in both World War II and Korea, was. He was soon on an ROTC scholarship.

Following stints at the U.S. Army's airborne and Ranger schools at Fort Benning, Georgia, Morehouse began his active duty, which included his ill-fated assignment to Jordan, where a stray bullet punctured his helmet provoking expanded mental abilities.[2]

One rainy spring morning, Col. Cole breezed into Morehouse's office. "Come with me. I've got some people I want you to meet."

Nothing further was said, but Morehouse was of the definite opinion that he was about to meet the Army's remote viewers, psychic operatives—the Psi Spies.

Morehouse was deep in thought as the Chrysler K car driven by Col. Cole turned off Maryland's Highway 5 into the front entrance of Fort Meade.

He pondered what might lie in store for him with a psychic unit. *I'm just an infantry officer, and now I'm literally off to see the wizard,* he thought to himself.

The blue Chrysler passed Burba Park, but before reaching the base hospital, Cole turned off into a dead-end street where two long, low, wooden buildings were nestled in a grove of trees. The buildings appeared deserted.

The easternmost building, marked only with the number 2560, was an old World War II-era barracks. The other building was marked 2561. They were apparently the only such structures still standing. All the others were long gone.

Morehouse surveyed the buildings and was not impressed. Paint was peeling off the sides, and the tall metal chimneys obviously had not been used for some time. Walking up onto a small wooden porch, he noticed the front door was green-painted steel with a modern high-security lock. Morehouse laughed to himself. *A second-year karate student could kick his way through this building with his bare feet, yet the front door is secured with a high-tech lock,* he thought, wondering what secrets the lock protected.

He didn't have long to wonder, as the door was quickly opened by a short, thickset woman.

"Morning, Jeanie," Cole said cheerfully.

Peering around the colonel, the woman studied Morehouse. "And who have you brought with you?"

"This is the man I've been telling you about," Cole replied, striding through the doorway.

The woman waved Morehouse inside. "Come right in," she said with a smile that Morehouse could have pictured on the face of a cat who had just caught a canary.

As Jeanie went off to announce their arrival, Cole explained that she was the wife of a retired Army colonel who had been a civilian employee at Fort Meade before joining the psychic unit as a secretary.

As Morehouse's eyes became accustomed to the dim interior he gave a small gasp. Having been in the spit-and-polish Army for so long now, he was taken aback by the dark and cluttered office. A mural stretched along one wall depicting a star field with a swath across it representing a red galaxy. Gazing at the painting, he felt as if he had stepped onto the set of a *Star Trek* movie.

The office itself contained an odd assortment of old wooden desks, chairs, and other accessories. Notes, news clippings, and memos were pinned or pasted onto the walls. Everywhere were stacks of papers, files, and books, as well as an incongruous array of potted plants.

The office's occupants did nothing to dispel the idea that this was merely a college research facility. Next to a coffee machine, an older man with a bit of gray in his hair stood in his stocking feet. Beside him was a shorter, younger man whose hair was combed forward and cut in bangs. Both wore civilian clothes.

It resembled nothing Morehouse had experienced in his service career.

Cole seemed at ease in this disheveled environment. He obviously had been here many times. He guided Morehouse to the pair standing by the coffee machine.

He introduced them as Master Sgt. Mel Riley and Capt. Ed Dames. The two nodded cordially, but were obviously more concerned with their conversation than with Morehouse. Morehouse noted that Riley had a wise and relaxed appearance; Dames, though short, was trim and muscular, with a boyish grin on his face.

Cole pulled Morehouse away from the men and guided him past the receptionist's desk to a small cubicle where a large man sat staring at a computer screen. Noticing Cole, the man extracted himself carefully from one of those back-saving computer chairs and shook hands. Morehouse noticed he too was not wearing shoes. Morehouse was thus introduced to Lyn Buchanan. A large man with graying hair and fatherly eyes, he seemed to be a kind and caring fellow. Morehouse liked him immediately.

Continuing his tour, Morehouse was presented to the other members of the remote viewing unit.

Paul Smith waved hello from behind piles of papers and books on an old desk. A hefty intellectual-looking fellow, Smith was surrounded by a clutter of plants, books, paintings, and food. A computer printer was spitting out a barrage of paper onto the floor of his cubicle.

Gabriella Pettingale, an attractive blonde with a sincere smile, leaned in from an adjoining cubicle. Gesturing at Smith's desk space, she said with an apologetic look, "And I made him clean it up just this morning. It was spilling across the floor into my space."

A man introduced as Major Ed May seemed the only person there with a military bearing, despite his lack of a uniform.

Morehouse was soon pulled away by Cole, who said, "Come on. Here's the man I want you to meet."

Morehouse found himself in a small side office. Looking down, he noticed that the floor was covered with squares of carpet material all pieced together. It looked to be a collection of carpet samples, none of which matched. There were two big old chairs facing a large desk. Around the small office were potted plants in various stages of decay. Some sort of dry tacking was hanging off of the wilting leaves and stems. Morehouse had never seen such a collection of unkempt plants. He hoped these people cared more for their business than they did for their plants.

The man behind the desk stood and extended his hand. Morehouse was introduced to Fernand Gauvin, a civilian General Service Administration(GSA) employee who headed the small unit. His eyes sparkled with intelligence and enthusiasm as he was introduced to Morehouse.

"Welcome, Captain Morehouse," he said warmly. Gauvin was of medium height and build and looked to be in his early 50s. His dark, thinning hair was combed straight back, and his dark eyes and olive complexion indicated a Mediterranean heritage.

"I guess you are wondering why you've been brought here." It was really not a question but more the opening of a prepared speech.

Apparently Cole had heard the speech before. He made his apologies and quickly left the room.

Gauvin and Morehouse looked at each other in silence. Finally, Gauvin sat back in his chair, crossed his legs, and put his hands straight out in front of him, locking his fingers.

Looking slightly down his nose at Morehouse, Gauvin said, "I am constantly amazed that young people such as yourself are still willing to sacrifice their careers to be part of an organization like this."

This guy knows everything about me, thought Morehouse. *He must know that I am to be part of this unit. Why else would he start a conversation in the middle like this? Perhaps he thought that I would tell him, "I'm not sacrificing anything. This is all just a job!" and walk out.*

"I don't understand," said Morehouse.

"Oh, I think you do," replied Gauvin. "You know that if you get mixed up with some unconventional and controversial unit like this, you can probably kiss your advancements goodbye."

Morehouse slowly replied, "That may be so, but I'm fascinated by all of this."

To this point no one had mentioned the kind of work being done in the office.

Seeing that he had not unnerved Morehouse with his opening statement, Gauvin relaxed somewhat and said, "Well then, we are going to give you a limited read-out, tell you a bit about what we do here."

He got up from his chair and walked to the office door.

"Jean, bring me the forms he needs to sign," he called out.

After the secrecy forms were signed, Gauvin returned to his desk and took a sip of coffee.

Leaning slightly forward, he looked Morehouse squarely in the eyes.

"What we do here is train people to transcend time and space to view persons, places, or things, and to report accurately on what they see about each of those targets I just mentioned." The words were spoken low and slow, with no trace of amusement.

Gauvin stood and looked down at Morehouse. "Are you interested in doing that?"

Morehouse's mind was in a whirl. *Do I want to do that? Transcend time and space? This is fascinating. He's really talking to me about something like this? And he's serious?*

He jumped to his feet, his composure forgotten. "Hell, yes, I'm interested! Can I start yesterday? How about today?" Catching himself, Morehouse said, "Uh, sorry, sir, what I meant is that I would like to start as soon as possible. Tomorrow morning, if possible."

Gauvin smiled broadly. He knew he had an eager recruit. Leaning back in his chair, he savored his control over the situation. Finally he said matter-of-factly, "We'll get back to you."

"But sir," stammered Morehouse. "After what I've been told about your work, and here you are, a GS-14, standing here telling me that this really exists, that what these people do is for real. How can I go back to what I was doing? I want to start right away."

"I understand that," said Gauvin, "but I need to talk with Col. Cole a little bit more about you. We have some things we need to look at. We'll get back to you."

In other words, don't call us, we'll call you, thought Morehouse. He felt disappointment setting in that he couldn't immediately learn more about this unusual group. He almost missed the rest of Gauvin's remarks.

"We have some more forms and other things for you to fill out," Gauvin was saying. "Just so I can get a better idea about what kind of person you are, whether or not you will be good at what we do."

Walking around the desk, Gauvin handed Morehouse another form. "Right now, I want you to go outside and sign this. It just says you promise not to talk about what I have just told you," he said.

After Morehouse left the office and was the signing the form, Cole suddenly appeared. He and Gauvin closed the office door and began an earnest conversation, obviously concerning Morehouse.

As he stood there trying to digest all that had just happened, the man introduced as Paul Smith walked up and spoke softly, "Look, you're going to be asked to fill out some questionnaires like this." He handed Morehouse some papers.

"What I want you to do is fill these out, and when you answer the questions, answer them as though you were the person you would like to be, not the person you are."

Morehouse didn't understand what he meant until he had a chance to go through the papers. They were full of questions and obviously were meant to prepare a psychological profile on the respondent. There were about 250 questions, all requiring a lengthy answer. Most were questions about what he would do in a given situation.

When the meeting with Gauvin ended, Col. Cole motioned to Morehouse, and soon the pair were making the return trip to Washington. Nothing much was said on the long drive, which was fine with Morehouse. His mind was filled with the idea of transcending time and space. *How can you do that? Can I really do this? Is this whole thing some sort of gigantic gag? Why is the Army doing something like this? Does it really work? Does it involve electronics or drugs?*

The questions kept coming and he had no answers. Not yet.

During the next few days, Morehouse had difficulty keeping his mind on his work. All he could think about was the odd assortment of people at Fort Meade and their work transcending time and space. And that he was going to be part of it. His thoughts alternated between fascination and skepticism.

One afternoon he heard loud voices across the hall. They were coming from his commander's office. Suddenly Morehouse's ears perked up. He had heard his name mentioned.

Easing his way to his door, he strained to hear.

His commander, Col. Tony Lackey, was arguing with Cole. Morehouse could not make out everything that was said, but it was obvious that his commander did not want to lose him. As he listened, it also became obvious that Cole was using every trick in the book to gain his reassignment.

Morehouse ducked back behind his office door as Cole barged from the commander's office and stalked back to his own.

Moments later Morehouse was summoned before Lackey.

His commander sat looking at him for some time and finally said, "Is it true that you wish to join a certain unit as Col. Cole has suggested?"

"Yes, sir, I do," replied Morehouse.

"Do you know that this unit is highly controversial?"

"Yes, sir, I do."

"Do you know that it's highly experimental?"

"Yes, sir, I do."

"Do you realize you could be jeopardizing your military career by participating in something like this?"

"Yes, sir, I do." Morehouse tried to ignore all of the small bits of hesitation and doubt that remained circling in the back of his mind. His curiosity had overcome his skepticism.

Standing up, Lackey said sternly, "That unit has a bad reputation, do you know that?"

Morehouse shrugged his shoulders. He had not heard that but at the moment he was so intrigued that it didn't seem to matter.

"You realize you're making a bad choice here?"

Morehouse did not reply.

Finally, Lackey let loose. "Damn it, man. You're a fine officer and we need you here."

Morehouse took a moment and then said quietly, "Thank you, sir. But if any part of what I've already learned about this unit is true, I would never forgive myself for not learning more. I'm really excited, sir. This move could change my whole life."

"Yeah, but maybe not for the better," groused Lackey. Suddenly his shoulders slumped. He breathed a heavy sigh and sank back into his chair.

"Oh, hell, son. It's your life. If you want to go, go. I'll approve your permanent change of station order."

Lackey looked up at the enthusiasm on Morehouse's face and growled menacingly, "Now get the hell out of my office!"

It was just a few days later, after completing the lengthy psychological profile, that Morehouse again found himself sitting across the desk from Fern Gauvin.

"I see your new orders have been cut," Gauvin said, glancing over some papers in his hand. "I guess a hearty welcome is in order. Now let me explain some things."

Gauvin began by outlining the unit's training process. He said it would take between 12 and 18 months before Morehouse would be considered operational.

"It takes that long," Gauvin said, "because there's testing and lectures and other things. But it might not actually take that long. We are constantly finding ways to shorten the training period. You know, one thing leads to another. We're getting faster and faster."

Then, leaning across the desk toward Morehouse, Gauvin became quite serious.

"You have to understand that, once you enter this work, your life will change and you will never be the same again," he said. "You will never look at the world the same way again. You'll never look at your friends, your loved ones in the same way again. You will have a better understanding of life and of the universe and it will, in essence, change you forever.

"You'll never be the same person again. When you look back at what you are now, you'll know that you will never be that way again because you'll know too much. Your life will never be the same."

With that introduction, Army Capt. Morehouse, a self-styled "shaved-head, high-and-tight, grunt Ranger," became a psychic spy for the U.S. government.

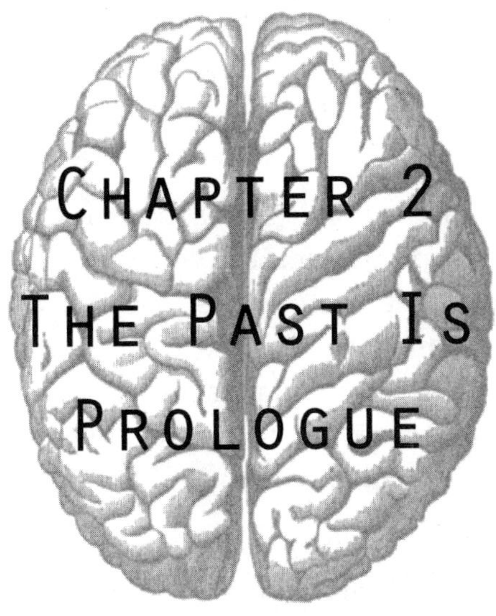

Chapter 2 The Past Is Prologue

Answers began to come to Morehouse with his acceptance into the remote viewing unit.

Once his training began, Morehouse found that remote viewing apparently has been with us throughout history. It simply has gone by different names. From the earliest writings there have been accounts of visions, prophesy, soothsaying, and divination. And careful study shows clearly that the same phenomenon appears to be working in each of these activities.

In the Vedas, the most ancient written record of man, there are references to supernatural powers called "siddhis." According to the venerable Hindu scriptures, these were unwanted paranormal side effects of meditation that tended to distract the meditator.[1]

Dr. Richard Broughton, director of research at the Institute for Parapsychology in Durham, North Carolina, has quoted from Patanjali's Yoga Sutras, written some 3,500 years ago. His descriptions of Patanjali's yoga meditation techniques sound remarkably similar to the techniques developed for remote viewing:

> [Y]oga meditation... [is] a succession of stages in which outside distractions are reduced.... In the stages of the meditational process—termed Samyana—paranormal phenomena may be produced, most commonly a feeling of clairvoyant omniscience, but sometimes including physical effects such as levitation, object movements, and healing.[2]

Up until very recently, mankind's record of psychic phenomena has been inextricably intertwined with religion. So what does religion tell us about such things?

All of the world's religions, from the Bible to the Koran to Oriental mysticism, contain a wealth of stories involving prophecy, visions, and spiritual instruction. And all seem to involve visual input.

The Biblical book of Isaiah opens with the statement, "These are the messages that came to Isaiah, son of Amoz, in the visions he saw during the reigns of King Uzziah, King Jotham, King Ahaz and King Hezakiah—all kings of Judah."

Another Biblical prophet, Ezekiel, appears to be more than a starry-eyed dreamer. He exhibits the attributes of a good journalist when, rather than simply state "Once I had a vision," he instead cites the day, the year, and the month in Ezekiel 1:1, "In the thirtieth year, in the fourth month, on the fifth day of the month, as I was among the exiles by the river Chebar, the heavens were opened and I saw visions of God."

According to the *Holman Bible Dictionary,* early Biblical prophets influenced almost every institution of Israel, despite the fact that they often were viewed with contempt, locked up, ignored, and persecuted. Prophets formed guilds or schools, and their assistants recorded their words for posterity.[3]

Biblical prophecy was not limited to men. In the Old Testament book of Judges, we find that a "prophetess" named Deborah provided the Israelite leader Barak with information about the military disposition of Sisera, the commander of the forces of Jabin, the King of Canaan. Sisera's forces were routed and thus Deborah, using psychic intelligence, played a pivotal role in the conquest of the Promised Land. She might rightly be called the world's first military remote viewer (Judges 4:4–16).

Even in the New Testament, prophesy and visions played an important role as the messianic plan unfolded.

St. Paul offered some advice on prophesy that modern people might well take to heart. "Do not scoff at those who prophesy, but test everything that is said to be sure if it is true, and if it is, then accept it," he wrote to church members in Thessalonica (1 Thessalonians 5:20–21).

According to the Greek historian Herodotus, King Croesus desired to learn strategic military information from the available prophets and oracles. But he wanted to make sure that their information was correct. So about the year 550 B.C., Croesus conducted the first recorded test of psychic abilities. He sent messengers to the top seven oracles of his day with instructions to approach the oracles exactly 100 days after their departure. They were to ask the oracles to describe what the king was doing on that day.

On the appointed day, Croesus chose an unkingly activity. Using a bronze kettle, he cooked up a stew of lamb and tortoise. Only the oracle at Delphi correctly reported the king's activity, stating:

Can I not number all the grains of sand,

and measure all the water in the sea?

Tho' a man speak not I can understand;

Nor are the thoughts of dumb men hid from me.

A tortoise boiling with a lamb I smell:

Bronze underlies and covers them as well.

But then King Croesus learned another lesson: Do not place blind faith in psychics.

It seems that Croesus, having satisfied himself of the Delphic oracle's powers, asked if he should cross the Halys Mountains and attack Cyrus of Persia. The oracle replied, "When Croesus has the Halys crossed, a mighty empire will be lost." Croesus, thinking his plans were promised success, attacked Cyrus. But Croesus was defeated and it was his "mighty empire" that was lost.[4]

This experience attests to both the problem of correctly interpreting psychic information and correctly relaying that information. Of course, because it was the Greek habit of that time to kill messengers bringing bad news, perhaps the ambiguous nature of the oracle's reply is understandable.

Accounts of paranormal powers abound in all of human history, from the African witch doctor to the Fiji Shaman.

The powerful spiritual system of Huna found in the Polynesian Islands contends that each human being consists of three souls or spirits. The "Unihipili" and the "Uhane" are related to the conscious and the subconscious, whereas the "Aumakau" seems to be a higher self related to psychology's "superconsciousness."

According to paranormal author Brad Steiger, ancient Kahuna priests were able to contact this higher self through the use of a prayer rite known as "Ha." This rite entailed quieting the mind, eliminating extraneous thoughts or mental noise, deep breathing, and repetition of techniques, not unlike the techniques of remote viewing.

Steiger wrote:

> [T]his rite can be used by anyone who earnestly desires to establish this type of contact. If you correctly follow this format and practice it, you will be able to accomplish the same kind of feats of telepathy, clairvoyance and healing that the Kahunas did regularly in earlier times—and still do in secret today.[5]

American Indians have a rich heritage of belief in powers beyond the five senses. This heritage of visions and prophecy is typified by a story told by Mathew King, a traditionalist spokesman for the Lakota people. ("Don't call us Sioux, that's the White Man's name for us.") According to King, he once went up on a mountain and prayed to God for a cure for diabetes. He reported:

> And while I was there, somebody said, "Turn around!" So I turned around and there was the most

> beautiful Indian woman I'd ever seen. She had long black hair and the most wonderful face. She was holding something out to me in her hand. It was those little berries of the cedar, the dark blue berries on cedar trees. She held them out but before I could reach out my hand she disappeared....Later on when I got diabetes, I forgot about the berries. They sent me to White Man's doctors. They gave me pills. Every morning I had to take insulin. I spent a lot of time in the hospital. Then I remembered White Buffalo Calf Woman and those little blue berries. I picked some, boiled them, strained the juice and drank it. It's so bitter it took the sugar right out of my body. The doctors checked me and were amazed. They said the diabetes was gone. I didn't have to take insulin anymore. They asked me how I did it, but I didn't say. God gave us medicine to share with people, but if the White Man gets his hands on it he'll charge you a great price and will let you die if you don't have it. God's medicine is free.[6]

Many other writers have documented the mysticism and belief in the paranormal that form an integral part of Native American lore.

After describing how ancient Indians used sheets of mica or quartz to send heliograms over considerable distances, author Arthur C. Parker went on to say, "Marvelous as these methods of signaling may seem, there were medicine men who claimed that they could send their thoughts through the air and make things come to pass from afar. Others could send their mind's eyes to distance places and discover what was happening."[7]

In one study of native North American spirituality, the story was repeated of a Penobscot Indian who went on a hunting trip with his wife, son, and daughter-in-law. The women stayed behind at a hunting camp while the men went off, promising to return within three days.

After four or five days, the women became anxious about the men's safety. One night the Penobscot wife told the daughter-in-law that she was going to sleep and would dream about the men. After a long time, during which the younger woman believed she saw a "ball of fire" exit and enter the wife's body, the wife finally stirred and said, "Don't worry, they will be back tomorrow. They had good luck and are bringing lots of game. I just saw them sitting by their fire eating supper." The next day the hunters returned loaded with an abundance of game.[8]

There are even bits of information relating to Indian lore that suggest that their psychic travels may have penetrated beyond this world.

In the early 20th century an Osage, Playful Calf, told anthropologist Francis La Flesche about his studies with tribal elders, called No-ho-zhi-ga. He said:

> My son, the ancient No-ho-zhi-ga have handed down to us, in songs, wi-gi-e, ceremonial forms and symbols the many things they learned of the mysteries that surround us on all sides. All these things they learned through their power of wa-thi-gtho, the power to search with the mind. They speak of the mysteries of the light of day by which the earth and all living things that dwell thereon are influenced; of the mysteries of the darkness

> of night that reveal to us all the great bodies of the upper world, each of which forever travels in a circle upon its own path, unimpeded by the others. They searched, for a long period of time, for the source of life and at last came to the thought that it issues from in invisible creative power to which they applied the name Wa-Ko-da."[9]

In Mexico it has been well documented that, for at least four generations before the arrival of the Spanish, prophecies abounded that one day strange bearded men would arrive from across the sea wearing "caskets" on their heads. According to the legends, these men, armed with sharp swords, would overrun Mexico and destroy the Aztec gods.[10]

Stories such as these abound and some reach right up to modern times.

Stephan A. Schwartz, who pioneered psychic archaeology in his book, *The Secret Vaults of Time,* wrote of a researcher in the late 1950s who described how Indians would contact relatives through long-distance extrasensory perception. According to the researcher, "certain members of the Montagnais habitually repair to the woods, set up a log shelter about the size of a telephone booth, get inside and, when the power is sufficiently strong, make contact with a friend or relative who may be hundreds of miles away."[11]

Just as the Indians routinely practiced meditation techniques both as a means of communication as well as to view future events, prophecy and soothsaying likewise were common practices in ancient Rome, despite being frowned upon officially. Both in history and in literature it is well recorded that Julius Caesar was forewarned of his assassination in the Roman senate during the "Ides of March."

One of the most remarkable of the Roman "seers" was Apollonius of Tyana. During a speech to a crowd in Ephesus, Apollonius suddenly broke off his talk and cried in a loud voice, "Ephesians, it is done. At this moment, the tyrant has fallen and I see Rome acclaiming its liberty." A few days later word arrived in Ephesus that the Roman Emperor Domitian had been stabbed to death by his wife's servants.

Apollonius, who was well traveled and well versed in both Eastern and Western philosophy, said renunciation of material things resulted in "the opening of the eyes upon the infinite world of immortal essences" and the ability to "measure all time with a glance, to embrace all things in one thought."[12] Years before the events, Apollonius correctly foretold the destiny of the seven Roman emperors who reigned between A.D. 68 and 96.

The time of the Middle Ages was replete with soothsayers and diviners such as Hermes Trismegistus, Albertus Magnus, Pico (Count of Mirandola), Porta, and Roger Bacon.

Bacon, a Franciscan friar born into a well-to-do English family, was educated at both Oxford and the University of Paris. He studied all medieval sciences—alchemy, astronomy, astrology, optics, and mathematics—but Bacon is best remembered for his unerring predictions. In *Epistola de Secretis,* written in 1268, he wrote of "chariots...that will move with incredible rapidity without the help of animals," "an engine [in the sense of a device, in this instance an uncanny description of the elevator]...whereby a man may ascend or descend any walls," and "vessels might be made to move without oars or rowers, so that ships of great size might move on sea or on river...."[13]

Bacon described modern explosives so well that for many years, Westerners attributed him with the invention of gunpowder. Bacon wrote:

> Sounds like thunder can be made in the air but more terrifying than those which occur in nature; for an appropriate material in moderate quantity, as big as a man's thumb, makes a horrible noise and shows a violent flash; and this can be done in many ways by which a whole town or army may be destroyed.[14]

Near the end of the 14th century the French prophetess Marie d'Avignon had visions of "a maid who should restore France." Of course, she foresaw one of history's most famous figures: Joan of Arc. Saint Joan herself was a visionary and diviner who used her power of supernatural sight to great advantage during her battles to liberate France from the English.[15]

Once, according to her confessor Jean Pasquerel, Joan passed a horseman who cursed her. Joan told the man, "In God's name, do you swear, and you so near your death?" Within the hour, the man fell into the moat of Castle Chinon and was drowned.

On March 1, 1431, during her trial for heresy at the hands of the French clerics who sympathized with the English, Joan stated, "I know that before seven years are passed the English will lose a greater stake than they did at Orleans, and that they will lose all they hold in France." The English lost Normandy, their last foothold in France, at the battle of Formigny in 1439, only one year later than Joan's prediction.[16]

But the visions of Saint Joan and Bacon pale when compared to the most famous of medieval seers. During his training,

Morehouse studied the prophecies of Michel de Nostredame, better known to history as simply Nostradamus.

Nostradamus, already well respected in his own time as a physician and scientist, assured his place in history as a prophet by the publication of his book, *Centuries,* in 1555.

Due to the zeal of the Inquisition, Nostradamus was forced to used a skillful combination of puns, anagrams, and scientific and astrological jargon to prevent his arrest as a practitioner of witchcraft. Actually, Nostradamus, whose family included men educated in both the Christian and Jewish traditions, became a devout Christian and always attributed his prophetic insight to powers given by God.[17]

Though many of the four-line quatrains in *Centuries* are obscure and defy interpretation, others are astoundingly clear. For example, in Century II: Quatrain 51, he wrote, "The blood of the just will be demanded of London burnt by fire in three times twenty plus six. The ancient Dame will fall from her high position and many of the same denomination will be killed."[18]

There can be little debate that Nostradamus was referring to the Great Fire of London in 1666, as he named both the place and the date. The "ancient Dame" refers to the statute of the Virgin Mary, which fell from the roof of St. Paul's Cathedral during the fire that consumed many innocent Christians.

Although most of Nostradamus's writings described events in Europe and near to his own time, many seem to have a bearing on more modern times. His descriptions of the Emperor Napoleon are particularly convincing and, in Century VIII:Quatrain 1, he even named this "Emperor...born near Italy [who] will cost his empire dearly" as one "PAU, NAY, LORON," a fairly obvious anagram for NAPAULON ROY, Napoleon the King.[19] The spelling of Napoleon in Corsician is Napauleone.

Century IV: 75 appears to be a good description of Napoleon's defeat and retreat from snow-bound Russia: "He who was ready to fight will desert, the chief adversary will win the victory. The rear guard will make a defense, those faltering, dying in a white country."[20]

In Century IX: 16, Nostradamus again names the person he foresees: "From Castille Franco will bring out the assembly, the ambassadors will not agree and cause a schism. The people of Riviera will be in the crowd and the great man will be denied entry to the Gulf."[21] According to interpreter Erika Cheetham, "Franco" refers to Spain's Francisco Franco, and "Riviera" may well refer to the dictator Primo de Rivera, who was deposed by Franco. The last line well describes Franco's exile when he was not allowed to cross the Mediterranean to his native Spain.

Nostradamus wrote in Century IV: 68: "At a nearby place not far from Venus, the two greatest ones of Asia and Africa will be said to have come from the Rhine and Hister; cries and tears at Malta and the Ligurian coast."[22] Cheetham has written that this verse hinges on the word *Venus,* which she sees as actually meaning Venice. Thus the verse refers to the meeting at the Brenner Pass (near Venice) of Musssolini, Hitler (Hister), and the Japanese to sign the Tripartite Pact. "Africa" refers to Mussolini's attempts to seize Ethiopia, and the last line describes the ensuing combat in the Mediterranean between British and Axis forces.

Century III:35 again seems to be referring to Hitler: "From the deepest part of Western Europe, a young child will be born to poor parents; who by his speech will seduce a great multitude, his reputation will increase in the Kingdom of the East."[23] Hitler, born of poor parents in Austria, used his oratory powers to seduce the German nation and boost his reputation in Japan, which became his Axis partner.

Writers have described how Nostradamus foresaw events ranging from the assassinations of John and Robert Kennedy to the fall of Communism. Some even claim that Nostradamus foresaw the 1986 space shuttle *Challenger* disaster when he wrote in Century I:81, "Nine will be set apart from the Human flock, separated from judgment and advice. Their fate is to be decided as they depart. The unripe fruit will be a scandal, [they] dead, banished and scattered."[24]

Admittedly there is no certain interpretation of Nostradamus's writings, though his predictions have been uncannily correct in many instances, enough so that everyone who has studied the French seer at any length has realized that his accuracy rating goes far beyond any simple trick or ingenious interpretation.

How did Nostradamus gain his prophetic insights? He provided the answer in Century I:1–2:

> Being seated by night in secret study, alone resting on the brass tripod. A slight flame comes out of the emptiness and makes successful that which should not be believed in vain. With rod in hand set in the midst of the three branches, with water he wets both limb and foot; with fearful voice, trembling in his clothes, Divine splendor. The divine sits nearby.[25]

Although certain variations of translation of this passage exist, the overall meaning is clear: Nostradamus would closet himself at night in his secret study and place a cup of water on a brass tripod. This method of divining was described by 4th-century neo-Platonist Iamblichus in his 1547 book, *De Mysteriiss Egyptorum,* and most probably was read by Nostradamus.

After quieting his mind, Nostradamus would stare into the water until, acquiring a meditative state, he would see visions of the future. Again this methodology is strikingly similar to that devised for remote viewing.

During the reign of England's Queen Elizabeth I, court astrologer John Dee became another early psi spy when he claimed to have received a psychic message that Spanish agents were plotting to burn the forests that provided wood for the English fleet. Precautions were taken and history records how a well-fitted, if outnumbered, British navy defeated the Spanish Armada in 1588, thus establishing England as a world power.[26] (It is interesting to note that John Dee became Her Majesty's first "James Bond," as he signed his reports with the code numbers "007."[27])

As the 19th century approached, much of the advances in parapsychology can be attributed to Franz Anton Mesmer, whose name became synonymous with mesmerism or hypnotism. Mesmer was an Austrian-born scientist and philosopher.

According to British author and paranormal expert Colin Wilson, Mesmer developed ideas that are "virtually the intellectual cornerstone of modern psychology." Wilson wrote:

> ...Mesmer [developed] the notion that the universe is permeated by some "magnetic fluid," and that the

> stars and the planets cause "tides" in this fluid.... Mesmer believed that these "tides" cause sickness and health in human beings, for we are also full of a kind of magnetic fluid generated by the nerves. When this fluid becomes blocked or stagnant, we become ill. When it is unblocked—by magnets, or by the doctor's own "animal magnetism"—we become well again.[28]

After moving to Paris in 1778, Mesmer's odd claims caused such an uproar that a Royal Commission of Inquiry was convened to look into the matter. This commission, which included the American ambassador, Benjamin Franklin, concluded that Mesmer's claims of healing through magnetism were most probably caused by suggestion. However, despite this report and the chaos of the French Revolution, interest in Mesmer's claims continued.

In 1826, the French Academies of the Sciences and of Medicine created a second commission to study Mesmer's methods. Skeptics fully expected a report as dismissive as the first. However, they were startled by the commission's conclusions.

According to Richard Broughton:

> The Commission acknowledged that they could not precisely identify what the trance state was but that they were convinced that it was genuine. Moreover, they felt it could give rise to "new faculties which have been designated by the terms clairvoyance, intuition, interior prevision." Finally they urged the academies to encourage further research into "magnetism," which they regarded as a "very curious branch of psychological and natural history." The leaders of the academies

were not pleased with the report and did nothing to follow the commission's recommendation.[29]

After many years of controversy in the scientific and medical communities, Mesmer's ideas were finally refined into what we know today as hypnotism.

Also during the 19th century, public notice was drawn to an Englishman named William Denton, who documented some of the earliest pure remote viewing. As a young man, Denton converted to Methodism, moved to the United States, and married a Cincinnati woman. By the mid-1800s, Denton was professor of geology at the University of Boston.

At the time, clairvoyance went by the name of psychometry, and Denton became very involved in the study of viewing far-off locations by means of holding some object connected to the particular place. He found a very excellent psychometric subject in the person of his wife, Elizabeth.[30]

According to Wilson:

> ...Denton took a precaution which reveals that he was a genuine scientist, determined to rule out all possibility of auto-suggestion. He tried wrapping several specimens [of rock] in separate sheets of paper, then mixing them up, so he had no idea which was which. Then he handed his wife one of them. She had a vision of a volcano, with molten lava flowing down its side. "The specimen must be lava," said Mrs. Denton, and she was right.[31]

Mrs. Denton's success record of "seeing" by touching objects was remarkable and well documented. As she became more skilled, she was even able to discern different periods of history in the specimens.

On one occasion Denton handed his wife a fragment of mosaic pavement that had been excavated from the villa of the Roman orator Cicero. Denton, hoping to hear a description of the famous Roman, asked his wife to describe what impressions she got from the fragment.

Mrs. Denton described a Roman scene, complete with a large columned villa and heavy velvet drapes. She also saw lines of helmeted soldiers and described their leader as "a fleshy man with a broad face and blue eyes. He is majestic, yet has a good deal of geniality about him too," she said. "He regards himself as superior, and withdraws from others."[32]

Denton was disappointed. His wife's description did not appear to match that of Cicero, who was tall and thin. Yet some time later Denton discovered that the Roman dictator Sulla had been the previous owner of Cicero's house. Sulla was a convivial man who was fond of his friends and called "lucky Sulla" by his troops. Thus, it must have been Sulla that Denton's wife saw in her vision, a clear indication that Denton's own expectations had little or no influence on her psychic voyage.[33]

In a book published in 1873, Denton tried to describe what his wife experienced as she remote viewed other planes of existence:

> The question is often asked, where are all these things that the psychometer sees? The following, unexpectedly seen by Mrs. Denton, may shed some light upon this question. Can this be the realm into which the spirit is ushered at death? Or is there a still more interior

realm, from which we receive echoes occasionally, but of which we still know so little? [Mrs. Denton stated] "I am in a different realm from any I have ever before observed.... Yet it appears to be a realm of real, substantial existences, stretching back, and backward still, almost interminably, into both time and space. I see forms—people and the results of their labors; even the very efforts that produced the results. At first I thought it a species of mirage. It seemed like a picture of all that had ever been; yet now it seems to me that I could step from this planet upon that world—I can call it nothing else—and travel back through all the scenes that have ever transpired in this. What a difference between that which we recognize as matter here and that which seems like matter there! In the one, the elements are so coarse and so angular, I wonder that we can endure it all, much more that we can desire to continue our present relations to it: In the other, all the elements are so refined, they are so free from those great, rough angularities which characterize the elements here, that I can but regard that as, by so much more than this, the real existence."[34]

Denton wrote, "I have good reason to believe that trained psychometers will be able to travel from planet to planet and read their present condition minutely, and their past history."[35]

The Psi Spies claim the visions of Mrs. Denton match exactly the experience of remote viewers who have ventured into planes of existence other than our own.

Mesmer's hypnotism and Denton's psychometry were joined by spiritualism and mediumship to create a great public interest in psychic phenomena during the latter 19th century and early 20th century. And as with any topic of public interest, charlatans and hoaxers abounded.

Paranormal research moved into the realm of modern science in 1882 when a group of scientists and scholars met in London to form the Society for Psychical Research (SPR).

For the first time, the techniques of modern science—standardized descriptions and methodology, disciplined experiments, and so forth—were applied to psychic phenomena.

Among the accomplishments of the SPR was the exposure of fraudulent mediums and spiritualists. In 1884, following an investigation of Elena Hahn, better known as Madame Blavatsky, founder of the mystical Theosophical Society, the SPR caustically termed her "one of the most accomplished, ingenious, and interesting impostors in history."[36]

But the SPR did much more than chase hoaxes. Its research into psychic experiences was prodigious and laid the foundation for all psychical study to follow.

One of the SPR's more notable researchers was Charles Richet, professor of physiology at the University of Paris medical school and a future Nobel Prize winner. Richet studied clairvoyance by having subjects identify playing cards placed in opaque envelopes, thus pioneering the methods that were later used by the well-known psychic researcher J.B. Rhine.[37]

Joseph Banks Rhine (always known to his friends as simply J.B.) and Louisa Weckesser had been companions since their teenage years, and both had completed Ph.D. degrees in botany at the University of Chicago in the early 1920s. After their marriage, it appeared both Rhines would pursue a career in botany, but this was all changed by a chance encounter with the famous author Sir Arthur Conan Doyle, creator of Sherlock Holmes and himself an ardent student of psychic phenomena. After hearing Doyle speak on psychical research, J.B. turned his attention to this fledgling science.

Soon both Rhines were heavily involved in psychic research at Duke University in Durham, North Carolina. According to Broughton, "While scholars regard the founding of the SPR in 1882 as the start of psychical research as a science, they consider the arrival of the Rhines at Duke University in September 1927 as the start of its *professionalization* [emphasis in original]."[38]

The thrust of the Rhines' experimentation was initially statistical. Using specially designed cards, hundreds of subjects would try and guess which card would come up next. By 1932, Rhine and his associates had clearly demonstrated the existence of psychic phenomena. Rhine applied the term *extrasensory perception* (ESP)to his findings. But, perhaps more importantly, he had demonstrated that ESP involved natural relationships in the same manner as ordinary psychological phenomena.

In 1933, a young man approached J.B. Rhine and claimed that when he gambled he could influence the roll of the dice simply by concentrating on them. Previously Rhine had only studied ESP. Causing a physical reaction with the mind is known as psychokinesis (PK). Rhine's curiosity was piqued and he promptly turned his statistical procedures to dice-tossing.

Wilson wrote, "Rhine's experiments showed the gambler was correct; he could, to some extent, influence the dice to turn up sixes. Since then, there have been thousands of similar experiments, and the evidence for PK is regarded as overwhelming."[39]

Broughton noted that, although the man was able to produce results that supported his claim, "even more interesting for Rhine was that some of his ESP subjects were similarly able to influence the fall of dice. Even Rhine himself had some success at it."[40]

From 1927 until J.B. Rhine's death in 1970, the husband and wife team produced a prodigious amount of scientific papers demonstrating the existence of both ESP and PK. This exciting research into psychic phenomena was presented in dry publications with titles such as "Experiments Bearing on the Precognition Hypothesis: Pre-shuffling Card Calling" and "A Review of the Pearce-Pratt Distance Series of ESP Tests."

The Rhines did acquire their fair share of critics. Yet through the years they quietly, yet steadfastly, answered every criticism that came up. In 1940, the Rhines, along with other parapsychologists, produced a book entitled *Extra-Sensory Perception After Sixty Years,* a compendium of psychical research since the founding of the SPR in 1882. The research presented in this book was so careful and scientific that the book became assigned reading for introductory psychology classes at Harvard for the 1940–41 academic year.[41]

Even the most cursory look back over the historical record of psychic phenomena should convince the most steadfast skeptic that there is definitely something beyond the five human senses at work here.

As late as World War II, sensitive military information was being received by psychic means, and in England, this meant jail time for an otherwise nondescript Scottish housewife.

Helen Duncan had spent a quiet life raising a number of children and occasionally demonstrating her psychic talent through local séances. But in wartime Britain, she quickly came to the attention of the authorities after twice reportedly telling of ships sinking before the news was made public. In January 1944, Duncan was arrested during a Portsmouth psychic reading and charged with vagrancy. Fearful that she might talk about the upcoming plans for the invasion of France, British authorities whisked her off to stand trial in Old Bailey and upgraded the charge against her to conspiracy to violate a 1735 law against witchcraft.

Despite numerous witnesses who testified to the reality and accuracy of her psychic powers, and representatives of the law societies in both Scotland and England terming her trial a travesty of justice, Duncan was found guilty and served a nine-month prison term, keeping her under wraps until long after D-Day.

Even Prime Minister Winston Churchill futilely tried to intercede for Mrs. Duncan. In his memoirs written years later, Churchill credited psychic guidance in leading him to a friendly home during his escape as a prisoner during the Boer War.

In late 1956, Duncan was again seized by police and died less than a month later, many believed as a direct result of the trauma of her arrest. In 1998, the British news media reported continued efforts to have Mrs. Duncan pardoned posthumously.[42]

"Until this very day, psychic viewing is looked on by the British establishment with horror," noted Tim Rifat in his 1999 book *Remote Viewing*. "A country such as the UK, obsessed with secrecy, cannot allow remote viewing to become public knowledge...."[43]

After many hours studying the history of the remote viewing experience, David Morehouse grew anxious to try his hand at it.

One day after a brief lunch, Morehouse found himself in one of the small viewing rooms in Building 2562 with the pretty Gabriella Pettingale acting as instructor. The room was painted a dull gray with gray carpets and a gray table in the center. Track lights on the ceiling ran the length of the table. Pettingale sat on one end and Morehouse on the other.

Looking around, Morehouse muttered, "This place looks like some prison interrogation cell."

Pettingale explained that the drabness was necessary to keep the surroundings aesthetically bland during a remote viewing session so there would be no distractions.

"Just adjust your chair any way you want," said Pettingale congenially.

"Shit," Morehouse muttered to himself. "I've never done this before. I don't know if I want the damn thing lying back, sitting up straight, or jacked up higher than the table."

As Morehouse fumbled with his chair, Pettingale handed him a stack of white, blank paper, placing one sheet in front of him.

"Here's what we call an 'Ingo pen,'" she said, handing him a black ball-point pen with a broad tip. He learned it was named after the man who was instrumental in developing much of the methodology for remote viewing: Ingo Swann.

"You'll find a rheostat under the table," she said, resuming her seat. "Adjust the lights any way you like." Morehouse dimmed the lights slightly, thinking, *Under other circumstances this could be romantic. But here I am in a top secret military unit in a dim room with a pretty woman and I don't have a clue about what I'm supposed to do.*

It had been explained that he would be given a set of coordinates, just some numbers, and that he was supposed to draw an ideogram and then interpret it. An ideogram was described as simply a mark on the paper that represented the main concept of the target of his mental search.

He had learned these fundamentals already, but had no idea how it was all supposed to work.

Placing his pen on the sheet of paper, Morehouse waited expectantly as Pettingale read out the coordinates. There was a long period of silence. Morehouse stared at his hand. Nothing happened.

His mind was racing. *Okay, something is supposed to happen here. It's supposed to move.* But nothing happened.

Pettingale declared a break in the session. Morehouse didn't want a break; he wanted something to happen. Later he learned that taking a break was an important part of the remote viewing discipline.

A few minutes later, they began again. Pettingale read out the coordinates and Morehouse sat staring at his hand. It didn't move.

"Let's take another break," Pettingale declared. After a moment, she looked at Morehouse and said, "Look, David, it's not like something is going to grab your hand and drag it across the paper for you. When you hear the coordinate, just allow your hand to move across the paper."

Morehouse was feeling very incompetent. *Great,* he thought. *How do I allow my hand to move across the paper? I mean, you're talking to a grunt soldier here.*

Pettingale took a deep breath and repeated the coordinates again.

Without his thinking or willing it, Morehouse's hand began to move across the paper. It moved slightly across and then move sharply upwards and back down.

Morehouse looked up with a grin of relief and accomplishment. Pettingale was not smiling. "Now decode it. Describe how it felt."

"I feel it rising sharply upwards," Morehouse said confidently.

"Fine. Now touch the ideogram with your pen point and tell me what you feel."

Morehouse was again perplexed. He did as he was told and mumbled, "I feel a pen-point touching the paper."

Pressing him, Pettingale said, "No, open up, relax, close your eyes, feel what it is."

His anxiety level was increasing. He had no idea what he was supposed to be getting. Was he supposed to be feeling something through the paper, or was some small voice supposed to say something to him? Morehouse, the highly trained combat soldier, was at a loss.

Suddenly Pettingale's voice cut through his mental turmoil. "Does it feel man-made?"

Morehouse's mind focused on her question. Somehow, from somewhere deep inside of him, he knew the answer. There was nothing analytical about it, simply an undefined gut feeling.

"No, it doesn't feel man-made."

"Well then. What is it?"

"It's rising up sharply. It's natural." He was just verbalizing his thoughts as they came. "It's a mountain," he blurted out, surprised at the conviction in his voice.

"Very good," said Pettingale. "That's all for now. Write 'end session' at the bottom of your paper."

Walking over to Morehouse, she handed him a manila folder. "Here's your feedback," she said with a broad smile on her face. She turned and walked out.

Looking inside the folder, Morehouse was stunned to find a photograph of Japan's Mount Fuji. It was indeed a mountain.

Morehouse sat in the room for a long time, thinking. He felt like a kid again, full of awe and excitement. *Holy shit! It really works. And I can do it!*

He felt as if a whole new world had just opened up for him.

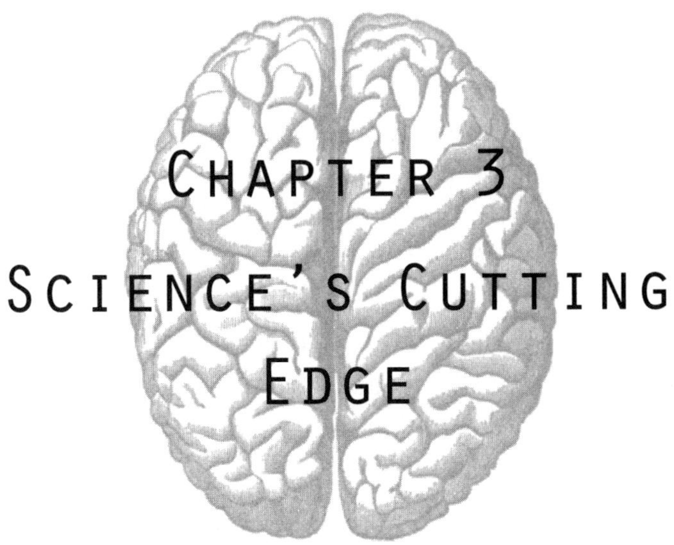

Chapter 3

Science's Cutting Edge

After his success with viewing Mount Fuji, Morehouse was brimming with excitement. Still, he harbored some doubts he couldn't entirely shake. Had it been simply beginners luck? A fluke?

Whatever it had been, his curiosity about remote viewing was soaring, and he was more than ready to return to the lengthy studies of psychic history.

He learned there had never been a slowdown in parapsychological research, there was simply a tremendous lag in the public's perception. This was due to the ongoing controversy between psychical evidence and steadfast debunkers in the scientific and medical communities. Because of the controversy, writers in the news media tended to report from one extreme or the other—either uncritically recounting stories of amazing psychic powers or passing off psychic accounts in a dismissive manner.

Despite the impressive historical record and the ever-growing body of scientific evidence for the existence of psychic phenomena, the battle between believers and skeptics continues unabated. However, two recent developments in the field of parapsychology may present a definitive answer to the question of the reality of psychic abilities. These are the Ganzfeld Technique and meta-analysis.

Ganzfeld, from the German for "whole field," refers to ESP experiments in which the human subject is placed in a mild state of sensory deprivation so as to exclude any possibility that outside influences may be affecting psychic testing. In some cases light, sound, and color are used to block the subject's normal senses and create a soothing environment with nothing to distract the subject.

This type of experiment first began in the early 1960s at the Maimonides Dream Laboratory, an adjunct of the Maimonides Medical Center in Brooklyn, New York. The dream studies produced impressive results. In one 1970 test, a young English psychic named Malcolm Bessent described his prophetic dream by describing various types of birds. "I just have a feeling the next target material will be about birds," Bessent told the experimenters.

The next day, a lab member who had not been in contact with Bessent randomly selected the next dream target: a slide show with a soundtrack devoted to a variety of birds. Just as a control condition, Bessent was told to try and dream about birds, but none appeared in his dreams.[1]

The Maimonides Dream Lab closed in 1978 due to lack of funding, but the results of experiments there are still being studied. One such study was described by Richard Broughton:

> In 1988, Alan Vaughan, one of the participants in the dream project, and Jessica Utts, a University of California statistician, performed a statistical appraisal of the entire project. Using the Maimonides definition of a hit as a mean ranking by the judges that fell in the upper half of the possible range, Vaughan and Utts found there were a total of 233 hits in 379 trials, or an accuracy rate of 83.5 percent (where chance would be 50 percent). The odds against chance for this are better than a quarter of a million to one. Psychic dreams—about the present and the future—had been brought into the laboratory.[2]

It was from the Maimonides experiments that one team member, Charles Honorton, a former student of J.B. Rhine, developed an interest not only in dreams, but in altered states of consciousness. Honorton theorized that ESP signals might be overwhelmed by signals from our conventional senses. After studying the historical record, he came to believe that one must achieve "a quietness," almost a meditative state, to produce psychic results on demand.

During a period of years, Honorton developed Ganzfeld Techniques including the placement of ping-pong ball halves over the subject's eyes and earphones over the ears, and sitting the subject in a soft reclining chair and ridding the test environment of any distracting noises.[3]

While Honorton was perfecting his Ganzfeld Technique, a second technique was being developed that has brought parapsychology much closer to scientific acceptability.

Meta-analysis is a term coined by University of Colorado psychologist Gene Glass to describe a technique of gaining an overview of any particular subject by combining separate experiments into one.

Harvard University's Robert Rosenthal used meta-analysis effectively in his studies of interpersonal expectancy effects, which is the tendency for investigators in psychological studies to unconsciously bias a subject's responses. In other words, an investigator may gain the answer he or she seeks by the way a question is presented.

Meta-analysis has been applied to both the historical record and to the many psychic experiments of recent years.[4] And although most effects of these experiments appear to be weak—recall that researchers have long stated that psi signals are easily drown out by our strong sensory signals—nevertheless meta-analysis gives support to the psychic experience. Broughton wrote, "[S]everal lines of parapsychological research are undoubtedly producing consistent, reliable effects that cannot be attributed to chance, poor methodology, or the vagaries of a few experimenters or unusual studies."[5]

It was meta-analysis that, in 1985, enabled Honorton to overcome the arguments of one of his chief critics, psychologist Ray Hyman. That year, in a debate sponsored by the *Journal of Parapsychology,* Hyman attacked Honorton's database of the success rate for ESP research. Claiming Honorton's figures were a gross overestimate of the success rate, Hyman presented his own statistical analysis, which purported to show that the Ganzfeld experiments with the greatest flaws were the very ones exhibiting the best ESP scores.

For his part, Honorton focused on 28 studies comprising 835 Ganzfeld sessions in 10 different laboratories. Significant results were obtained in 43 percent of these studies. "The odds against that result arising by chance are greater than one billion to one," reported Broughton.[6]

After further rounds of attack and counterattack across the meta-analysis battlefield by both Hyman and Honorton and their associates, both sides drew closer together. In a surprising "Joint Communique," both Hyman and Honorton agreed that the effects demonstrated in the Ganzfeld database "cannot reasonably be explained by selective reporting or multiple analyses."[7] In other words, there were significant effects in the studies. But, of course, neither Hyman nor Honorton could agree on what caused these effects. Interestingly enough, it was Hyman who, in 1995, was selected by the CIA to coproduce a dismissive report on remote viewing.

British mathematician and psi skeptic Christopher Scott was prompted to term Honorton's presentation "the most convincing argument for the existence of ESP that I have yet encountered," and even meta-analysis pioneer Rosenthal indicated he felt the Ganzfeld studies had demonstrated some effect.[8]

After reviewing the Ganzfeld debate issue, Broughton, a former president of the International Parapsychological Association, wrote:

> Meta-analysis has shown that these impressive ESP results are consistent across experiments and experimenters. They are not just statistical flukes—or possibly suspicious results—associated with one

> experimenter or just a few series. While it would be rash to say that anyone can run a successful Ganzfeld experiment, there can be no doubt that, *in the hands of a competent experimenter,* the Ganzfeld-ESP *is* a repeatable experiment. [Emphasis in original.][9]

Harold E. Puthoff, one of the pioneers of remote viewing, agreed that with more modern methodolgy, such as meta-analysis, more acceptance has been gained in the scientific community. He said:

> Early on there was a relative degree of nonacceptance except by people who were predisposed to believe that there might be something to it. So the big change in the intervening years since I finished working in that area is that experiments have continued to be replicated by various laboratories. I would say that things have changed. Scientists are more willing to take an objective look today. There is a broader climate of acceptance.[10]

It was into this "climate of acceptance" that remote viewing was first introduced.

But to trace the development of remote viewing, one must first trace the development of the one man most responsible for today's understanding and use of the phenomenon: Ingo Swann.

Swann is a remarkable person. Generally soft-spoken, he sits with cigar and wine glass in hand in his 19th-century brick office/studio/home in New York City, impressing visitors with his paintings, his knowledge of science and history, and his descriptions of psychic travels.

Scattered about his home are various filing cabinets and drawers filled with scientific literature spanning several decades. "I don't like to be referred to as a 'psychic,'" groused Swann. "I was trained in biology and I consider myself first and foremost a scientist." As such, Swann has performed ESP research only under the most stringent laboratory conditions.

"My life-long interest has focused on studies of creativity and the various kinds of creative processes and abilities of which I feel psi phenomena are adjunct and contributing parts. My views on psi thus often differ from parapsychological approaches I feel isolate the psi phenomenon away from holistic human phenomena and functional creative processes," he has stated.[11]

Theses regarding his laboratory work in parapsychology earned Swann a master of humanities degree in 1990 and a doctor of humanities degree in 1991 from The International College of Spiritual and Psychic Sciences in Montreal.

Scientist though he may be, Swann's experiences in the paranormal date back to his childhood.

Born Ingo Douglas Swan on September 14, 1933, in Telluride, Colorado, Swann was a free-spirited youth who spent much of his time in the outdoors. He came from solid Swedish stock. His parents, who immigrated to the United States, brought with them the virtues of frugality, hard work, and obedience to authority.

Just as the Rockies nurtured his spirit, his intellect was nurtured by reading. Swann claimed that by age 3 he read a dictionary from cover to cover, and between the ages of 4 and 7, he read the entire *Encyclopedia Britannica.*

One particular incident at age 2 has stayed with Swann throughout his life. He was taken to a hospital for a tonsillectomy. Frightened by the experience, young Swann fought with the nurses and the doctor.

Suddenly a nurse appeared with a half-filled balloon. "I bet you can't blow this up further," she said. Taking the challenge, Swann began blowing on the balloon and quickly realized he had been tricked. The balloon was filled with ether, and each inhalation brought him closer to unconsciousness.

An ether mask was finally placed over his face, but the enraged youth found his mind slipping into a different viewpoint. As he looked down on the operation as an observer, he saw the doctor place a cutting instrument down his throat and heard him mutter, "Shit!" when he accidentally cut Swann's tongue. He saw the doctor take his two small tonsils from his mouth and place them in a small bottle, which a nurse placed behind some rolls of tissues on a counter.

He was aware as the doctor sewed up the slice in his tongue and as he began to regain consciousness, he said, "I want my tonsils."

A nurse told him that his tonsils had already been thrown away. Young Swann replied emphatically, "No, you didn't." Pointing to the rolls of tissue, he astounded everyone present by proclaiming, "You put them behind those over there. Give them to me. Mama, the doctor said 'Shit!' when he cut my tongue."[12]

Swann's psychic experiences also included the remembrance of past lives. But all this was pushed into the back of his mind as he grew to manhood.

At age 14, his family moved to Utah, where he eventually studied biology and art at Westminster College. He received a bachelor of arts in biology in 1955.

Joining the U.S. Army, Swann served in Korea and Japan as a secretary and an aide on the staff of the Commander of Pacific Forces.

In 1958, Swann left the military and joined the international civil service, working for the United Nations in New York. "The UN was a wonderfully broadening experience," he recalled. During the 11 years he worked at the UN, Swann rubbed elbows with world leaders such as Golda Meir and Indira Gandhi.

But Swann said he eventually became disillusioned with the politics and machinations within the UN and resigned in 1969. He added an extra "n" to his surname and pursued a career in painting. "I immediately began starving to death," he recalled with a laugh. "No one wanted my paintings and I refused to paint what everyone wanted."

Then one cold afternoon in the spring of 1970, Swann walked past a pet store on Greenwich Avenue and noticed "something I had never seen before." He discovered that the object of his interest was a chinchilla, and within two weeks, he had purchased the pet and brought him home.

Mercenary, the name selected by Swann for his pet, was given the run of Swann's apartment until he noticed that the chinchilla's appetite included "books, pencils, typewriter ribbons, furniture, wood, and the telephone cord."

Thereafter, Swann began locking the nocturnal animal in a cage each evening. Shortly, he noticed something that once more brought him into the field of psychic phenomena.

Mercenary quickly began to equate bedtime with being locked in his cage, and each night he would make himself as scarce as possible. It became a nightly ritual: to spend at least 30 minutes searching for and capturing Mercenary. One night, though, an amazing incident occurred as Swann sat watching television. Mercenary was perched on his knee and Swann idly scratched his ears. Bored with the program, Swann thought to himself that it was time to lock Mercenary in his cage and go to bed. Mercenary immediately bolted from the room. "I had not moved at all when the thought of putting him in his cage occurred," said Swann. "It came as a stunning recognition, therefore, when...I realized that he had obviously picked up my thought."[13]

Swann spent the next several days testing this phenomenon. He would place Mercenary in his cage at unlikely times. "The effect was superb," stated Swann. "After what appears to have been a brief learning period, he refused to react but would sit back on his hind legs, his eyes blazing, his tail switching back and forth, while he mentally probed my mind to find out if I meant it or if this was just another testing sequence."[14] Mercenary soon escaped Swann's apartment and disappeared into the greater world of New York City.

But for Swann, even while mourning the loss of his pet, there was but one overriding consideration: "Mercenary could perceive and apprehend my thoughts," Swann concluded. "[H]is perception of my thoughts could not exist unless a similar potential existed within me, since this obviously was an interaction, a *meeting* [emphasis in original] of mind, and not a cause-effect situation."[15]

His interest and scientific curiosity aroused, Swann began to move into the circles of those studying psychic phenomena.

First he made contact with Cleve Backster, a New York polygraph (lie detector) operator who, in 1966, had made the amazing discovery that plants hooked up to the polygraph machine registered responses to outside stimuli just as humans did.

His find, now termed the "Backster Effect," was the object of an immensely popular 1973 book entitled *The Secret Life of Plants,* which sold more than 100,000 hardcover copies.

After finding that any living tissue, including even the bacilli of yogurt, exhibited reactions on his graphs, Backster concluded, "Sentience does not seem to stop at the cellular level. It may go down to the molecular, the atomic, and even the subatomic. All sorts of things which have been conventionally considered to be inanimate may have to be reevaluated."[16]

Swann worked in Backster's lab for about a year. Backster's work, verified and augmented by other scientists around the world, convinced Swann that his experience with Mercenary had not been a fluke. Something very real was transpiring on the psychic level.

By the end of 1971, Swann was engaged in psychic experimentation with Dr. Karlis Osis and his assistant, Janet Mitchell, at the American Society for Psychical Research (ASPR) in New York. This work was done under the auspices of Dr. Gertrude Schmeidler of the Department of Psychology at the City College of the City University of New York, and a board member of ASPR.

Time-Life Books described the experiments:

> In the Osis experiments, Swann would sit in an easy chair in a room illuminated by a soft overhead light, virtually immobilized by wires that hooked him up to a polygraph machine, which monitored his brain waves, respiration and blood pressure. Puffing away on his cigar, he would, as he put it, "liberate his mind"; then he would be asked to describe or draw his impression of objects that were set out of sight in a box on a platform suspended from the ceiling.[17]

The results of this experimentation were generally good, with more "hits" than "misses." On at least two occasions, though, the tests resulted in something quite extraordinary.

On March 3, 1972, the target box had been lined with white paper, and Swann reported that there was printing on a portion of the paper. The tester commented that this test was a "miss" because there was not printing on the paper.

"To everyone's chagrin, when the box was taken down and inspected, there was the printing just as I felt I had seen," remarked Swann.[18] The person lining the box had simply not noticed the printing.

In another instance, Swann was valiantly trying to view the inside of a lighted box, but all he perceived was darkness.

"The goddamned light is out over the target," he shouted to the testers, who replied, "Impossible!" However, when one of the monitors climbed a tall ladder to reach the target box, it was discovered that the light had indeed gone out, just as Swann had perceived.[19]

With results such as this, Swann's psychic ability began to flower and the concept of remote viewing drew that much nearer.

"I went to the ASPR two or three days a week for many months and tried to identify an endless series of targets—while strapped into a chair with my brain waves being monitored on an EEG machine by Janet Mitchell. At first I was not very good at this kind of 'perceiving,' but as the months wore on, I got better at it," Swann later explained.[20]

It was during this work for Dr. Schmeidler and Dr. Osis that the term *remote viewing* was first used by Swann and Mitchell. "It was coined to identify a particular kind of experiment—not a particular kind of psi ability," Swann later wrote.[21]

The experiments revolved around out-of-body experiences that, in earlier times, had been called clairvoyance, ecsomatic experiences, bi-location, or astral projection.

Swann recalled:

> Janet Mitchell and I devised a playing-around experiment in which I would try to "see" the weather conditions in distant cities. Since some kind of feedback was absolutely necessary to determine what was "seen," after my distant weather impressions had been given and recorded, Janet, or someone else, could immediately telephone the weather information number in the distant city and find out what the weather was doing. The cities we were to play around with "seeing" were selected by third parties. So unless I had somehow memorized all of the weather conditions in a large number of cities, it is reasonable to conclude that a "distant seeing" had taken place if the response was fed back as correct.[22]

Swann told of the occasion when he sensed heavy rain in a particular city. "Impossible," retorted the testers. "The city in question is Phoenix, where it's hot and dry." However, a quick check with the Phoenix weather bureau confirmed heavy thunderstorms in the city that day.[23]

"I suggested that we call [these experiments] 'remote-sensing,'" said Swann. "Shortly, though, it became clear that I didn't just sense the sites, but experienced mental-image pictures of them in a visualizing kind of way.

"Without at all thinking much about it, and before the end of 1971, we began referring to the long-distance experiments as remote-viewing ones, since this term seemed the most suitable."[24]

It was also during this time that Swann happened to be in Cleve Backster's lab and learned of a proposal by physicist Dr. Harold E. Puthoff.

"At that time, I had submitted a proposal to Research Corporation, which was handling a laser patent for me, to obtain funds for some basic research into quantum biology," Puthoff recalled. "This proposal was widely circulated and a copy was sent to Cleve Backster in New York."[25]

Swann said Backster encouraged him to write to Puthoff. He did on March 30, 1972, and a series of letters and phone calls back and forth ensued.

Puthoff, a pleasant and studious man with a soft, controlled voice, said that early on he was never particularly interested in ESP or other psychic phenomena at all.

As a young man, Puthoff had served as a Navy officer for three years after obtaining a master's degree. He recalled:

> I was one of the lucky people. I had been in the reserves and went to Officers Candidate School while I was still in college. I was slated to get my commission in 1958. But in the summer of 1957, *Sputnik* went up and Congress passed a law that anyone in a technical field who was slated to go on active duty could remain in graduate school. So I went to a year and a half of graduate school and got my Lieutenant Junior Grade by the time I went on active duty. In three years, I went to Lieutenant.

Puthoff said he spent his military service working in a research laboratory for the National Security Agency (NSA), a government agency he had never heard of before going to active duty. It may have been here that Puthoff made the military contacts he was to successfully utilize in later years during his psychic research.

After leaving the military, Puthoff earned his Ph.D. degree in electrical engineering and physics from Stanford University. "I worked on lasers and quantum electronics and other things," he said, "a very standard sort of engineering and physics background."

Then one day, Puthoff was reading the popular book *Psychic Discoveries Behind the Iron Curtain,* when he read about the "Backster Effect," the ability of plants to communicate and make a polygraph machine register their galvanic changes. He said:

> It occurred to me that an interesting experiment to do would be to take some algae cultures, separate them by several miles, and then send out a laser signal to one culture to see if the sister culture responded before

> the laser signal got there. If the laser signal felt loss of life, and since tachyons [particles that theoretically travel faster than the speed of light] would travel faster than the laser, then that would determine if there [were]tachyonic connections. So it was purely a physics experiment. I sent it around to various people and they came back and said, "This sounds like you're talking about psychic effects." They suggested that that I should just study psychics directly.

In communications between the two, Swann hesitated to participate until Puthoff had assured him that the strictest scientific protocols would be enforced during the experimentation. "So, on a lark more than anything else, I invited him to come out and do some experiments," said Puthoff, who by this time was working for the prestigious "think tank" Stanford Research Institute (SRI) in Menlo Park, California. His proposal had been funded in April 1972, by Science Unlimited Research Foundation of San Antonio, Texas, though not specifically for parapsychological research.

As for Swann, his decision to work with SRI turned his life onto a new track. "I had no idea that this would result in a 19-year career," he said years later.

Puthoff recalled that, once his SRI associates learned of Swann's impending visit, they warned him that "all those people are frauds and charlatans." They told Puthoff, "You'd better have some experiment that you know they can't fake."

Taking his suspicious colleagues at their word, Puthoff looked around and located a superconducting magnetometer, sort of a supersensitive magnetic compass needle that can register magnetic fields down to one millionth of the Earth's field. This particular magnetometer had been devised along with other multi-million-dollar equipment to detect quarks, the theoretical building blocks of matter. Stability and dependability were absolute necessities in this work.

Puthoff found Swann to be a thoughtful and knowledgeable man—and one who wanted to be an integral part of any experiment. "I was to find out what has now been reported to me from other labs, that Ingo would often be the first to discount an apparent success, pointing out some potential loophole in a protocol or possible misinterpretation of the data," recalled Puthoff.[26]

On June 6, 1972, Swann was taken to the basement of Stanford University's Varian Physics Building, where the magnetometer was housed. There, as somewhat amused observers, were Dr. Arthur Hebard, who had agreed to Puthoff's use of the magnetometer, Dr. Martin Lee, a physicist at the Stanford Linear Accelerator Center, and an assortment of physics students.

Swann was initially taken aback. He had expected the usual array of electrodes, boxes with targets inside, and so on. Here he found, to his dismay, that he was to try to affect a small needle on a magnetic probe located in a vault beneath the basement floor that was shielded by a magnetic shield, an aluminum container, copper shielding, and a superconducting shield—one of the best shielding known to man.

As Puthoff explained, a decaying magnetic field had been set up inside the magnetometer, which provided a steady background calibration signal expressed as oscillating lines on a chart recorder. Swann was asked to mentally affect the magnetic field, which should then be expressed by a change on the lines of the chart recorder.

"This made me mad," recalled Swann. "How was I expected to produce results if I did not know what the experiment entailed?"

Swann said that, after the initial shock wore off, he began mentally probing the inside of the magnetometer, even to the extent of "seeing" how the mechanism looked.

"I sketched it out and asked, 'Is this it?'" he said.

"Yes, that's it," he was told. "So now that we had gotten the experiment straightened out," Swann said, "I took a look at this thing."

Within seconds, the oscillation of the recorder doubled for about 30 seconds.

"Everyone stopped breathing," recalled Swann.

According to Puthoff, Dr. Hebard, the physicist in charge of the magnetometer, "looked startled," as his own work was greatly dependent on the undisturbed operation of this equipment.

Despite the fact that the magnetometer had been working smoothly prior to Swann's attempt at mental manipulation, Hebard immediately suspected that something must have gone wrong with the machine. He suggested he would be more impressed if Swann could stop the magnetometer's field output altogether. Swann agreed to try.

Puthoff described the results: "[I]n about five seconds [Swann] apparently proceeded to do just that...for a period of roughly 45 seconds. At the end of the period, he said that he couldn't "hold it any longer" and immediately "let go" at which time the output returned to normal.... I was absolutely amazed."[27]

His amazement was heightened when, in discussions after the test, Swann explained that he had experienced direct vision of the insides of the magnetometer. Apparently the mere act of internal observation had resulted in affecting the machine as reflected in the recorder graph.

"On the way out, I asked Dr. Hebard to continue monitoring and recording so that we could determine whether the apparatus was behaving erratically," Puthoff later wrote. "He agreed and the apparatus was run for over an hour with no trace of noise or nonuniform acitvity."[28]

But the next day, a shaken Dr. Hebard said further testing was useless as the magnetometer was "behaving erratically."[29]

Swann recalled that researchers were denied further access to the magnetometer because it was torn down in an attempt to discover if anything was wrong with it. "They rebuilt the machine," Swann recalled with a laugh, "and they wouldn't let me back in the building."

Puthoff later criticized his own test for not arranging multiple recordings, thus not being able to objectively validate that the machine's interruption occurred internally. He said that it took two years for the SRI lab to duplicate Swann's magnetometer test using another subject. "We were able to set up more complete protocols," Puthoff said. "Swann's case was a pilot observation, and later we had a controlled experiment, but with the same results."

The apparent success of Swann's battle of mind vs. machine so impressed Puthoff that it was the beginning of a decade-long study of this type of phenomenon at SRI, which resulted in the development of remote viewing.

But successful experiments of projecting a person's mind to a distant target were not the sole property of SRI. At about the same time as the SRI experiments, Dr. Robert Morris, director of research at the Psychical Research Foundation in Durham, North Carolina, was conducting tests on a Duke University student named Keith Harary. As Swann did, Harary reported having out-of-body experiences since childhood.

Researchers would place Harary in one building and have him guess the identity of large cardboard letters some distance away in another building. The results were varied, sometimes incredibly accurate but other times poor. On one occasion, while Harary failed to correctly identify the letter, he nevertheless reported that a second assistant was in the room with the letters. It was a correct insight as a second volunteer had entered the target room unbeknownst to the experimenters.[30]

Morris concluded that psychics, at least Harary in particular, may respond better to people than to things. So a test was devised in which Harary was placed in isolation and asked to project his mind to a room in another building.

His first attempt was amazingly successful. He not only correctly identified the four staff members present in the room, but accurately reported where each was seated. Harary would become the youngest remote viewer to participate in the SRI experiments.

Puthoff, meanwhile, was totally dedicated to understanding the phenomenon that Swann had so adequately demonstrated with the magnetometer. Before allowing Swann to return home to New York, he devised a short series of experiments in which Swann would try to identify objects placed inside a wooden case with thick walls and a snap lock.

The tests were so successful that Puthoff invited potential sponsors to participate and determine for themselves the reality of Swann's powers. Puthoff recalled:

> Two visitors, representing a potential sponsor, ran Ingo through a series of 10 hidden-object-in-a-box experiments. His descriptions were exceptionally good that day—motivation was high—but I was especially amazed in one of the series when Ingo said, "I see something small, brown and irregular, sort of like a leaf, or something that resembles it, except that it seems very much alive, like it's even moving." The target chosen by one of the visitors turned out to be a small live moth he had captured, which indeed did look like a leaf.[31]

Apparently, prospective sponsors were as impressed as Puthoff with the SRI experiments, for private funding was forthcoming from Texas chicken restaurant magnate George W. "Bill" Church, Jr. Swann soon returned to California for an intensive eight-month study.

Though utilizing some high-tech refinements, Swann and the SRI researchers continued to conduct the standard parapsychological tests (identifying hidden objects, describing things in envelopes or boxes, and so forth).

The statistical results were encouraging, but one day Swann grew bored. He longed for something more exciting.

He remembered the long-distance experiments he had done in New York with the ASPR, but also recalled the biggest problem: Critics could always claim that he somehow obtained the name of the target or that the experimenters in some way clued him as to the target. The problem was how to designate a target location without giving away the name of the target. Swann put it this way:

> We had to design experiments that were triple blind in order to get away from the idea that telepathy or whatever may have been involved. So, we put a target in an envelope and then in another envelope and they would keep it in a safe. Then they would draw a number and retrieve that number envelope, and nobody knew which envelope had what in it. That could be handed two or three times down the line to the experimenter, who would say, "Okay, here's the sealed envelope. What's in it?"

But this type of experiment didn't repeat itself enough and critics could always claim some sort of telepathy between the remote viewer and the experimenters. An additional problem was that by giving a viewer the name of a target—the Eiffel Tower, for example—the viewer automatically could draw on memory and his own imagination to produce a picture of the target.

Swann recalled that one day, while relaxing in the swimming pool of the apartments where he lived near SRI, he suddenly heard a small voice in his head say, "Why don't you try coordinates?"

"Coordinates!" Swann said, suddenly alert. "Why didn't I think of that?

"With only coordinates, we didn't even have to know what was at the target site. We could just generate those targets without knowing what they referred to. And there are billions of possibilities."

Swann hurried back to the SRI lab and approached Puthoff and Russell Targ with his new idea. He told them:

> I did some experiments at the ASPR in which I moved my viewpoint to some remote location and described what was there. That was fun to do and the studies were statistically significant. I think I could look anywhere in the world if you just gave me some coordinates like latitude and longitude. Let's design an experiment around that![32]

And with that suggestion, Coordinate Remote Viewing moved into the SRI laboratory.

Puthoff said he and Targ were not too keen on the idea because they both knew that latitude and longitude were "completely arbitrary man-made constructs, adding one impossibility on top of another."[33]

"Actually, they thought this was the silliest idea they had ever heard of," commented Swann in later years. "Until they started getting feedback."

Swann said the researchers did a series of 100 coordinate remote-viewing experiments. "The first 50 of which weren't very good," said Swann, "but the second 50 were dynamite." In the final run of 10 coordinate tests, Swann was given seven "hits" by independent judges and only one clear "miss."[34]

He said, just as, his experience at the ASPR, his ability improved as he went along.

Swann would simply be presented a set of coordinates and he would describe what he "saw" at those coordinates. A world atlas would be consulted and the researchers would get immediate feedback. The Australian desert, Madagascar, Hong Kong, Borneo, the Great Salt Lake, Mount Shasta, the Yukon, and the Indian Ocean were just a few of the sites given to Swann as only coordinates.

In a 1993 interview, Swann delighted in showing the list of coordinate targets and his correct responses. "I'm showing these because this is what brought us all our money," he said. "This is what eventually made our project possible." Swann said there was one particular remote viewing session that convinced him of the reality of the phenomenon:

> They were using a wall map to get their coordinates. Now this map had a picture of Lake Victoria in Africa, so they plunked a coordinate down right in the middle of the lake. I reported a land-water interface, a peninsula getting narrow here, etc. They said, "Well, that's not correct." and I said, "It has to be correct, I mean that's what I saw." I told them that the wall map ratio was pretty small and suggested that we consult a bigger map of Lake Victoria.
>
> So away we went and jumped in the car. We went over to a bookstore and Hal had to plunk down $110 for this huge atlas. We opened it right away, right there in the store, and there in Lake Victoria, on this larger scale map, was a land peninsula sticking out with a narrow point. Bingo! There was the coordinate right over it.
>
> They didn't know that—nobody knew that. I said, "Okay, Hal, this is what I'm going to offer the client as a repeatable experiment. Believe me, it is repeatable." So that is how it got started.

And started it was. The SRI team went on to produce bigger and better results—and their clients changed.

Their next big client was the U.S. government, in the form of the Central Intelligence Agency, and the creation of the Psi Spies was coming closer to reality.

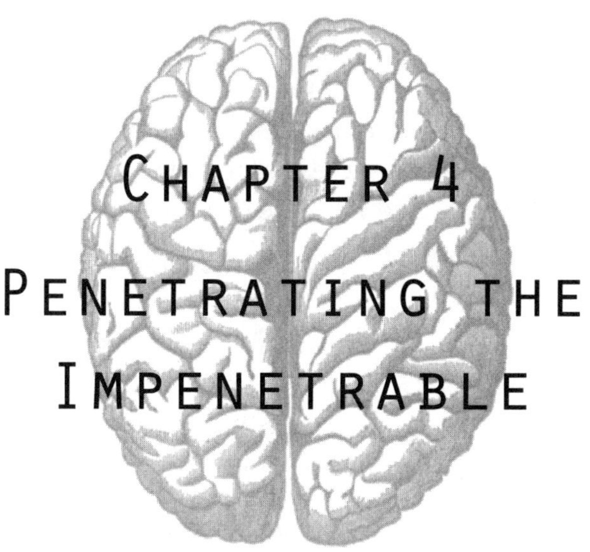

Chapter 4
Penetrating the Impenetrable

One of the greatest ironies of the Psi Spies story is that the entire affair began as a response to a perceived "psychic gap" between the United States and the Soviet Union—and this gap was generated by an apparent hoax.

The saga began in February 1960, when the French magazine *Science et Vie* published an article reporting that an American nuclear submarine, the USS *Nautilus,* had conducted successful telepathy experiments.

The magazine's headlines read: "US Navy Uses ESP on Atomic Sub!" "Is telepathy a new secret weapon? Will ESP be a deciding factor in future warfare?" and "Has the American military learned the secret of mind power?"[1]

The article described how a Navy lieutenant had received messages from a "sender" thousands of miles away while the *Nautilus* was submerged far below the Arctic ice cap. Years later the story, vehemently denied by the U.S. Navy at the time, was alleged to be a hoax perpetrated by a French writer who later sold a book on the subject. The writer had peddled the story to Gerald Messadie, an editor for *Science et Vie.* Messadie later expressed regrets for the story, which he too came to believe was false.[2]

Hoax or not, parapsychologists in the Soviet Union used the story to good advantage. Paranormal research in the Soviet Union had been discouraged during the years of Joseph Stalin because, under Communist theology, the spiritual side of man, including ESP, simply didn't exist. However, secret experiments were conducted in the belief that similar testing was being done in the West.

But following the accounts of the *Nautilus* tests, in April 1960, Dr. Leonid L. Vasiliev, an internationally recognized Soviet physiologist, spoke before a gathering of top Soviet scientists. "We carried out extensive and, until now, completely unreported investigations on ESP under the Stalin regime! Today, the American Navy is testing telepathy on their atomic submarines. Soviet science conducted a great many successful telepathy tests over a quarter of a century ago! It's urgent that we throw off our prejudices. We must again plunge into the exploration of this vital field," he told fellow researchers.[3]

Within a year of his speech, Vasiliev, a corresponding member of the Soviet Academy of Medicine and chairman of physiology at the University of Leningrad, was in charge of a special parapsychology lab at the university.

Although there also were skeptics in the Soviet Union, their research into the paranormal seemed to advance more rapidly than in America. The reason for this may have been stated by Edward Naumov, formerly Chief of Technical Parapsychology at a laboratory connected with The State Instrument Engineering College of Moscow, who said, "[T]hanks in part to Dr. Rhine's proof of ESP, researchers here aren't trying to prove again that ESP exists! We are trying to find out how and why psi works."[4]

Paranormal research blossomed throughout the Eastern Bloc during the 1960s and 1970s, prompting Czech workers in the field to coin the term *psychotronics* in 1968 as a replacement for the term *parapsychology.* They argued that the term *psychotronics* showed that "the issue in point is phenomena associated with the psychic aspect and nervous system of man," and "is general enough to include all pertinent phenomena..." and would not carry the "occult" connotations associated with parapsychology.[5]

Whether under the name "psychotronics" or "parapsychology," research into the paranormal increased within the Communist bloc nations.

In 1970, two Western authors, Sheila Ostrander and Lynn Schroeder, published *Psychic Discoveries Behind the Iron Curtain,* detailing what they had learned about such research after a lengthy visit through the Soviet Union and Eastern Europe. The book was a great success and proved to be an impetus to psychic research, particularly in the United States.

In their book, Ostrander and Schroeder stated:

> All research on ESP in the USSR is, of course, ultimately funded by the government. There is every indication from multiple sources that psi research with military potential is well financed by the Soviet Army,

> Secret Police, and other paramilitary agencies. Soviet scientists doing psi research in nonmilitary areas often have trouble getting money.[6]

Though admitting that the secrecy surrounding Soviet ESP research made an accurate assessment of their advances difficult, the authors nevertheless made it quite clear that America was definitely lagging behind the Soviets. This view brought unforeseen consequences within the halls of the CIA and the Pentagon.

After all, no one in 1970s Washington wanted to think that the Soviets might be ahead of the United States in anything, much less a human potential with such an application for Cold War spy craft.

CIA officers dreamed of contacting agents without using the normal detectable means. Military minds were agog at the notion that commanders might be able to anticipate enemy actions, read their plans, and break their communications codes. Both were astounded by the idea that leaders (enemy and our own) could be incapacitated by sickness, disorientation, or death induced by psychic means.

Leaders in the U.S. military, and even some members of Congress, demanded that whatever was necessary be done to prevent the Soviets from outstripping America in the psychic arms race. But interest in psychic phenomena within the ruling circles of Cold War leaders on both sides of the Atlantic remained very much a hidden agenda. Officially, the United States had no interest in nonexistent phenomena.

Even the Soviets began to backpedal. In a 1973 article entitled "Parapsychology—Fact or Fiction?" Soviet conservatives attacked the Ostrander and Schroeder book as a "low-standard work of sensational value."[7] They said that the authors were given stories of psychic experiments by Soviet scientists who were only seeking more research money. "In addition, parapsychology serves as publicity for anti-Sovietism, while the anti-Sovietism serves as publicity for the parapsychology," stated the report.[8]

Ron McRae, whose 1984 book *Mind Wars* detailed the psychic Cold War, wrote:

> When the Voice of America broadcast excerpts from *Psychic Discoveries Behind the Iron Curtain,* Soviet officials sharply curtailed foreign contact with parapsychology researchers. Naumov, who was one of the authors' primary sources, was arrested and sentenced to hard labor in Siberia. His laboratory was closed and his associates dismissed.[9]

Critics in the United States were also vocal and active.

Swann, who has been at the center of this collision of belief systems for many years, wrote:

> [A]n in-depth study concluded that the battlefield between parapsychologists and open science forums was not based on scientific merits, but on philosophical differences which would call for the complete philosophical restructuring of modern sciences' fundamental bases if any form of psi was to be accepted by modern

scientific mainstreams. The fight, therefore, was not and never had been a scientific one, but a philo-social one.[10]

So the debate goes on. Even the staid *New Encyclopedia Britannica* acknowledged the unresolved controversy about psychic functioning and left the door open for psychic reality by stating, "When such extreme and contradictory views are widely held, it is almost certain that the evidence is not conclusive either way and that confident conclusions are unlikely to be supported by a survey of all the known facts."[11]

By the mid-1970s, the public interest in psychic phenomena generated by the book on Soviet advances in the field had largely dissipated. But within certain CIA and military circles, officials had taken Dr. Truzzi's philosophy to heart, and interest was turning into action.

However, some interest may have been there all along. As far back as January 7, 1952, according to a CIA document released under the Freedom of Information Act in 1981, the agency was considering projects involving ESP. In part, the document read:

> If, as now appears to us as established beyond question, there is in some persons a certain amount of capacity for extrasensory perception (ESP), this fact, and consequent developments leading from it, should have significance for professional intelligence service.... [H]aving established certain basic facts, now, after long and patient efforts and more resistance than assistance, it now appears that we are ready to consider practical application as a research problem in itself....The two special projects of investigation that ought to be pushed in the

> interest of the project under discussion are, first, the search for and development of exceptionally gifted individuals who can approximate perfect success in ESP test performance, and, second, in the statistical concentration of scattered ESP performance, so as to enable an ultimately perfect reliability and application.[12]

The CIA continued its interest in the use of psychic phenomena when, in 1966, an agency-trained psychic told Ghanaian President Kwame Nkrumah that the stars were right for a proposed trip to China. While out of the country, Nkrumah was deposed by a military general more favorable to the United States.[13]

A 1972 CIA report released in later years showed that agency officials were most concerned about Soviet psychic research despite the skeptics. As quoted by the editors of *Time-Life*, the report stated:

> Soviet efforts in the field of psi research, sooner or later, might enable them to do some of the following: (a) Know the contents of top secret U.S. documents, the movements of our troops and ships and the location and nature of our military installations. (b) Mold the thoughts of key U.S. military and civilian leaders at a distance. (c) Cause the instant death of any U.S. official at a distance. (d) Disable, at a distance, U.S. military equipment of all types, including spacecraft."[14]

According to *Time-Life* and author McRae, the CIA had about six case officers whose job was to keep tabs on research within the parapsychology field and report any breakthroughs with a possible military or intelligence application. These officers, members of the Office of Strategic

Intelligence (OSI), met with Russell Targ in April 1972, and, after viewing films of Soviet experiments in moving inanimate objects through telekinesis, passed their evaluation to members of the Office of Research and Development (ORD).

An ORD project officer met with Targ and Puthoff at SRI and was impressed by their work as well as Ingo Swann's experience with Dr. Hebard's magnetometer. The officer made a favorable report to the CIA's Office of Technical Services, which contracted SRI for an experiment involving Swann in August 1972. Swann's description of hidden objects was so accurate that CIA personnel recommended further and expanded research. Puthoff and Targ, with CIA funding, began their "Project SCANATE" research at SRI.

Nationally syndicated columnist Jack Anderson in a 1985 column revealed Project SCANATE as a "series of tests sponsored by the CIA" and named Puthoff "as the Santa Claus for psychic research; funds are channeled through him to other research institutes."[15]

In the summer of 1993, long before the remote viewing program had been made public, Puthoff was asked about his role in the SCANATE program. Puthoff, who had signed secrecy oaths with the CIA, only smiled and said, "I cannot comment on that." But he then produced a copy of the Jack Anderson column and said simply, "We called it SCANATE for SCAnning by coordiNATE."

Editors at Time-Life Books were not so equivocal, writing in 1992: "Puthoff and Targ reached an agreement with the CIA—and possibly other government agencies—to further study remote viewing."[16]

Project SCANATE began on May 29, 1973, when Ingo Swann was utilized for the first of a series of remote viewing sessions that went on for two years. It produced some of the best remote viewing done up to that time.

It was "the most severely monitored scientific experiment in history," according to Jack Anderson's former investigator Ron McRae, who later authored *Mind Wars,* a study of government research into psychic weapons.[17]

McRae later wrote:

> CIA headquarters personnel would select a pool of potential targets all over the world, including secret sites within the United States, the Soviet Union, and the People's Republic of China. Another headquarters group would, without the knowledge of the first, randomly select the targets actually used from the pool. The National Security Agency would then encrypt the coordinates and transmit them, in code, to [SCANATE's CIA case officer] and other agency personnel assigned to monitor SCANATE at SRI. No one outside the headquarters, including [the case officer], knew which targets were selected.[18]

McRae added that the SRI researchers couldn't have cheated on these tests even if they had known the targets because the CIA would occasionally select sites scheduled for satellite surveillance two and three months after the SCANATE test.

Despite these precautions, Kenneth A. Kress, who had presented SRI with its first CIA contract, had reservations about remote viewing. In a 1977 classified report, Kress wrote:

> The expanded investigation included tests of several abilities of both the original subject [Swann] and a new one. Curious data began to appear; the paranormal abilities seemed individualistic. For example, one subject, by mental effort, apparently caused an increase in the temperature measured by a thermistor; the second subject could not duplicate the action. The second subject was able to reproduce, with impressive accuracy, information inside sealed envelopes. Under identical conditions, the first subject could reproduce nothing. Perhaps even more disturbing, repeating the same experiment with the same subject did not yield consistent results. I began to have serious feelings of being involved with a fraud.[19]

Targ and Puthoff, however, were increasingly impressed with the psychic experiments. They provided Swann with randomly produced coordinates and asked him to describe a site more than 3,000 miles away.

As detailed in that day's report, Swann closed his eyes and began reporting what he saw:

> This seems to be some sort of mounds or rolling hills. There is a city to the north; I can see taller buildings and some smog. This seems to be a strange place, somewhat like the lawns that one would find around a military base, but I get the impression that there [are] some old bunkers around, or maybe this is a covered reservoir. There must be a flagpole, some highways to the

> west, possibly a river over to the far east; to the south, more city. Cliffs to the east, fence to the north. There's a circular building, perhaps a tower, buildings to the south. Is this a former Nike [missile] base or something like that? This is about as far as I can get without feedback, and perhaps guidance as to what is wanted. There is something strange about this area, but since I don't know what to look for within the scope of the clouded ability, it is extremely difficult to make decisions on what is there and what is not. Imagination seems to get in the way. For example, I get the impression of something underground, but I'm not sure.[20] [Note: Swann sketched a map while giving this commentary.]

After getting feedback from the East Coast a few weeks later, Puthoff wrote, "Not only was Swann's description correct in every detail, but even the relative distances on his map were to scale!"[21]

Puthoff said this test also eliminated the possibility that the target information may have been available to Swann through a magazine article or TV documentary, as "the target site was small and characterized by controlled access"[22]—in other words, a government installation.

During SCANATE, and subsequent experiments involving the CIA and other government entities, feedback was a constant problem for the researchers. "We'd send the information in but we rarely got anything back," commented Swann. "Every once and awhile we'd get the word that we were right on target but not too often."[23]

Swann is quick to point out that remote viewing without feedback, or verification of what was remotely viewed, is little more than a dream, fiction in the head, or simply a good story.

"Feedback, then, is not trivial or incidental to the remote-viewing process and protocols," he has written. "It is *crucial* to them."[24] (Emphasis in original.)

Swann added:

> [R]emote viewing minus feedback actually equals whatever you do or do not want it to. For example, it can represent illusion to skeptics, who do not bother to study feedback even if it is available. It can represent wishful thinking to would-be psychics who do not bother to demonstrate feedback, especially if it cannot be available in the first place.[25]

He said feedback is more important than psi perceptions itself because, without feedback, the psi ability cannot be said to have occurred. At least one Swann-trained viewer has argued that feedback is only crucial in the training process, but for a veteran remote viewer feedback is merely "nice" to have.

From the massive files kept in his New York home, Swann can produce test after test that were demonstrated to be accurate thanks to adequate feedback.

It should be noted that, although the SRI researchers did not feel they were getting adequate feedback from their government sponsors, it is apparent that the sponsors felt they were getting adequate results from the remote viewing tests. One government agency after another continued to fund the Psi Spies for a period of almost 25 years.

Puthoff said the early SCANATE experiments were useful in establishing the existence of remote viewing, but lacked a true scientific methodology. He explained:

> What was needed was a protocol involving local targets that could be visited by many judges for independent documentation and evaluation. Furthermore, some procedures had to be devised to eliminate the possibility of target acquisition by ordinary means, such as the subject memorizing coordinates. Finally, a random target selection procedure and a blind judging (matching) of results would have to be handled independent of the researchers carrying out the experiments. Such procedures would have to be meticulously developed and rigorously followed to guard against charges of naiveté, in protocol which might permit cueing or, worse, charges of fraud and collusion which were bound to be raised should the experiments continue to be successful.[26]

One concern was that a subject, given a far northern latitude, could easily (and probably correctly) claim to see ice and snow.

Added to the concern for the strictest test protocols was the knowledge that their peers would be aghast at the mere mention of psychic research. "Scientists and nonscientists alike often find it difficult to confront data that appear to be greatly at odds with their world view," said Puthoff. "Entrenched belief structures die hard, even in the face of data."[27]

Swann said it was probably best that the government was involved at this point in the development of remote viewing because the CIA and others only wanted results.

"Since we did not need to explain how this could be done but only that it could be done, that was all we needed to do," he said. "They were looking for results, so it was easy to make this a classified project. They weren't interested in Ingo Swann presenting a paper in a scientific forum and arguing about the theory of this, which is what parapsychologists do endlessly."

He added that most of the government people who were interested in the remote viewing research had "an engineering mentality: Their attitude was 'we don't care how the bridge is built, as long as it gets built and it stands up.'"

It was with these concerns that the SRI researchers began a lengthy series of double-blind tests using local targets so that independent judges could visit the sites and confirm the remote viewing.

The tests went this way: The remote viewer remained closeted with an experimenter at SRI while a group of testers, called the target team, received a sealed envelope prepared randomly by the director of the Information Science and Engineering Division of SRI.

En route, target team members opened the envelope that contained detailed directions to a nearby location, all within 30 minutes drive time of SRI. After arriving at their destination, the target team spent 15 minutes looking about. It was during this time that the test subject back at SRI would make drawings of, or dictate into a tape recorder, his or her impressions of the location.

When the target team returned, the subject was taken to the test site for immediate feedback.

"Of course, no matter how we felt about the results of this informal comparison, the final determination of the success or failure of the experiment was made on the basis of independent blind matching by a research analyst not otherwise associated with the research," noted Puthoff. "As an added precaution, SRI management sometimes arranged for those who had been most skeptical to judge the results," he added, "and often, much to their chagrin, their target matching generated some of the best statistical results we obtained."[28]

One such skeptic was the CIA case officer for Project SCANATE. His experience was reported by author Ron McRae. According to McRae, he was able to interview the CIA official only on the condition that the official was not named. In both McRae's and Puthoff's accounts, the man was only identified as "V1" for Visitor One.

V1 arrived at SRI wanting "to see something psychic." According to McRae:

> V1 agreed to be the viewer in a remote-viewing test. While Targ and he [V1] waited in a comfortable lounge, Puthoff went to a target site selected at random by a neutral party. At the appointed time, V1 recorded his impressions on a cassette, describing a wooden walkway with a railing, and the ground falling away underneath. That description obviously matched the target, a footbridge over a stream in nearby Burgess Park.[29]

But V1 was not convinced; perhaps Targ had somehow cued him subconsciously. So on a second test, V1 huddled with the tape recorder in a corner by himself. He did even better that time, correctly describing a TV transmission tower and an adjacent movie theater.

Still skeptical, V1 asked for yet a third test. This time both V1 and the target team made recordings and sketches of the selected site. After the team's return to SRI, and before anyone said anything, the recordings and sketches were exchanged.

"This time, V1 had to concede, 'My God, it really works,'" reported McRae. "His taped impressions and drawings obviously depicted the target, a playground merry-go-round four miles from SRI."[30]

V1 was not the first, nor the last skeptical government official to be won over by the meticulous methods of the SRI researchers.

A typical remote viewing experiment during this time involved Ingo Swann, who was to remote view the Palo Alto City Hall (of course, he didn't know this at the time). He described and sketched a tall building with vertical columns and "set-in" windows. Swann also said there was a fountain at the site, though he added, "but I don't hear it."[31]

The city hall indeed was a tall building with many vertical columns and "set-in" windows. On the particular day in question, its fountain was not operating. "The judge had no difficulty matching Ingo's response to the target," commented Puthoff.[32]

In July 1973, Puthoff and Swann attended the First International Congress on Psychotronic Research in Prague, Czechoslovakia. In conversations with Eastern European researchers, they were continually asked about the psychological stress on test subjects. Puthoff later wrote, "We came to the conclusion that the emphasis on subject stability indicated that the Soviets were most certainly beyond any stage of trying to decide whether paranormal functioning was a real phenomenon."[33]

After returning from Europe, Puthoff and his associate, Russell Targ, were joined by another man with remarkable psychic ability: Patrick H. Price. Price, a scrappy Irishman, was a former police commissioner, detective, businessman, and vice-mayor of Burbank, California.

Puthoff had received a call at SRI from Price just days after the start of Project SCANATE. According to Puthoff, Price claimed to have psychic abilities. He was about to politely hang up on this unsolicited caller, when Price stated:

> In fact, as police commissioner I used my abilities to track down suspects, although at the time I couldn't confront the fact that I had these abilities, and laid my good fortune to intuition and luck. One day, though, I got a very clear picture in my mind of something that was going down that I couldn't possibly know about by ordinary means, and when I checked it out, it turned out to be true. After that incident, I began to wonder if all this psychic stuff I had put down for years might not have something to it.[34]

The subsequent conversation with Price intrigued Puthoff and, on impulse, he gave Price the coordinates of the East Coast site, which Swann had successfully viewed previously. He asked Price to view whatever was located at the coordinates. Price agreed, and within four days, Puthoff received a five-page "running commentary beginning with a description of the area from an altitude of 1,500 feet and ending with a tour through building interiors."[35] Puthoff said the tour included descriptions of office equipment, names on desks, even a list of labels on file folders in a locked cabinet. He recalled:

> I dutifully passed the information along to our East Coast challenger [V1, the CIA case officer], confident that there was no way that such detailed information could be true. I was stunned to hear some weeks later that Pat's description was essentially correct, and that the challenger was certain Pat could not have obtained the information by normal means.[36]

After a few weeks of further tests with positive feedback, Price was invited to leave his semi-retirement at Lake Tahoe and join the SRI researchers.

Price participated in remote viewing experiments and proved to be a talented, if erratic, psychic. Being a former policeman, Price apparently tended to strive for too much detail in his viewings. This brought his average number of "hits" down. On one of his first tests, which followed the same strict protocols as those of Swann, Price was given Hoover Tower, a landmark on the Stanford University campus, as a target. His taped description was played after the target team returned to SRI. After a general description of the target area, Price finally stated, "...seems like it would be Hoover Tower."[37]

Further testing through 1973 confirmed Price's remarkable abilities.

One afternoon in 1974, Puthoff's SRI division director, Bonnar Cox, apparently in an effort to determine for himself if the test protocols were flawed, accompanied the target team rather than give them the target in an envelope. "Cox deliberately drove in a random manner, turning left or right according to the flow of traffic," recalled Puthoff. "By this process, we ended up at the Redwood City Marina, a harbor for local boating enthusiasts."[38]

Upon arriving back at SRI, the group listened to Price describe what he saw on a tape recorder:

> We don't have to wait till then. I can tell you right now where they'll be. What I'm looking at is a little boat jetty or little boat dock along the bay....Yeah, I see the little boats, some motor launches, some little sailing ships, sails all furled, some of the masts are stepped and others are up. Little jetty or little dock there....Funny thing—this flashed in—kinda looks like a Chinese or Japanese pagoda effect. It's a definite feeling of Oriental architecture that seems to be fairly adjacent to where they are.[39]

Puthoff was astounded, as Price was accurately describing not only the marina but an Asian restaurant designed as a pagoda located on the dock.

Better yet, this particular experiment stood out from the preceding ones in one most important respect: Price apparently knew the destination of the target team 20 minutes before they arrived at the marina!

It seems that Russell Targ had turned on the tape recorder at 3:05 p.m. and was explaining to Price the protocols of the experiment when Price interrupted with the previous description given. By the time he finished, it was 3:10 p.m. Puthoff and Cox were still driving aimlessly at that moment. They did not arrive at the Redwood City Marina until 3:30 p.m.[40]

According to *Time-Life* editors, Price performed similar feats seven out of nine tests against odds calculated at 100,000 to one.[41] This experience with Price tipped off the SRI researchers that perhaps the remote viewing phenomenon was not limited by the constraints of time. They were already well aware that distance seemed to be no barrier to the experience.

Having been convinced of the remote viewing experience by their star subjects, Price and Swann, the SRI researchers decided to run tests on subjects with no previous psychic claims. "Eighteen months had gone by since the first experiment with Ingo," said Puthoff. "No longer doubting the existence of paranormal functioning, we had come to expect our experiments to be successful, and were beginning to look for some physical laws that might be governing the phenomenon we were observing."[42]

Puthoff said the researchers decided to work with only six subjects so that extensive medical, neuropsychological, and psychiatric tests could be performed on each person. This testing included complete medical and family history, protein electrophoresis, blood lipid profile, urinalysis, serology, electrocardiogram 12-Lead, electroencephalograms, audiometric exams, ophthalmology tests, special visual examinations, and an EMI brain scan. In addition, there were lengthy neuropsychological and psychological profiles worked up on each subject. "Our subjects had a degree of scrutiny probably second only to that endured by the astronauts," said Puthoff.[43]

Duane Elgin, an SRI research analyst with successful tests on an ESP teaching machine, joined Price and Swann as the third "experienced" remote viewer. The three SRI "learners" were Hella Hammid, a professional photographer, and two SRI staffers, Marshall Pease and Phyllis Cole. Hammid had once participated as a volunteer in an ESP brain-wave experiment, but otherwise had no previous experience with psychic phenomena.

On Hammid's first attempt at remote viewing, she described "a little house covered with red, overlapping boards. It has white trim and a very tall, pointed roof. But the whole thing feels fake, like a movie set." Her description was correct. The target had been a 15-foot-high model of a little red schoolhouse situated in a nearby miniature golf course.[44]

Puthoff said this was a classic example of the "first-time effect," when test subjects do best before becoming bored or too analytical. It is akin to "beginner's luck" in gambling.

Due to her artistic background, Hammid proved to be an exceptionally good remote viewer who offered sketches instantly recognizable to the independent judges. In one test, judges ruled she had correctly described five out of nine target sites, a feat beating odds of 500,000 to one. "In looking back on her past six months' work with us," said Targ, "we find that with only one or two exceptions, every experiment conducted under standard conditions showed good correlation between her descriptions and the actual target site."[45]

Elgin also proved a successful remote viewer. Once, when an evaluator monitored the testing, Elgin correctly located the outbound target group as playing tennis near a museum.

Pease and Cole, the other two "learners," were only marginally successful with two direct "hits" and two "second ranks" out of seven experiments. "The overall results in this case, taken as a group, were not statistically significant," concluded Puthoff.[46]

However, Puthoff said results of the RV tests were evaluated in a "conservative" manner that vastly underestimated the significance of the individual descriptions. The two "hits" demonstrated that the pair had some remote viewing ability no matter how immature or rudimentary. The idea that everyone has this ability to some degree was further substantiated after many other experiments involving visitors to SRI.

As Puthoff and Targ explained:

> We...carried out successful remote-viewing experiments with about 20 participants, almost all of whom came to us without any prior experience, and in some cases, with little interest in psychic functioning. So far, we cannot identify a single individual who has not succeeded in a remote-viewing task to his own satisfaction.[47]

During this time period, businessman Robert Monroe, who in 1971 published *Journeys Out of the Body,* founded the Monroe Institute for Applied Sciences in Virginia. Monroe, who had kept meticulous notes of his out-of-body experiences for a number of years, created audiotapes designed to synchronize the electrical impulses of the left and right hemispheres of the brain. His institute became heavily involved in parapsychological studies and provided psychological testing for prospective Psi Spies.[48]

One problem in RV was what the researches called "analytical overlay(AOL)," the mind's attempt to analyze its input. This impulse must be thoroughly suppressed for accurate remote viewing to take place. Analytical overlay was only one aspect of remote viewing the researchers were determined to understand. But the reality of RV was firmly established.

"To my way of thinking, there's no doubt that the phenomenon of remote viewing exists," said Puthoff.

In Targ and Puthoff's book, *Mind-Reach*, which details the SRI remote viewing experiments, the authors ask: "Where will you be standing when the paradigm [the popularly accepted view of the world which excludes ESP] shifts?"[49]

By the 1990s, Puthoff commented, "The paradigm has shifted, especially for those people close to the data, who have done experiments and seen the results. They've seen there is something to it and this has changed their world view.

"The public, by and large, rightly rejects what they see in the tabloids as probably being mostly nonsense, and this is probably true. Not having access to firsthand scientific or other kinds of data, for them the paradigm hasn't shifted."

Project SCANATE came to a close in 1975 on both a happy and a sad note. The project appeared to be an unqualified success. Remote viewing had proven to be an experience reproducible in the laboratory.

According to author McRae, the CIA commissioned intelligence consultant Joseph A. Ball of Santa Barbara, California, to evaluate SCANATE. Ball concluded the project "produced manifestations of extrasensory perception sufficiently sharp and clear-cut to justify serious considerations of possible applications." However, Ball cautioned that psychic spying should never replace traditional intelligence methods.[50]

Another consulting firm, AiResearch Manufacturing Company of Torrance, California, also was contracted by the CIA to evaluate SCANATE and, according to McRae, reached the same conclusion as Ball.[51]

By the mid-1970s, the CIA proved its satisfaction with the SRI results as demonstrated by the agency's continued financial support.[52]

In 1977, John Wilhelm, science correspondent for the *Washington Post,* hinted that the SRI research was somehow fraudulent. He said a trip to the East Coast coordinate site presented to Swann and Price revealed no government installation but rather "a sparse hillside, a few flocks of sheep, and a lot of droppings." However, a Navy liaison officer with Project SCANATE confirmed that the SRI test was "valid."

Furthermore, McRae, who stated in his book, "I personally might never accept the reality of remote viewing, no matter how overwhelming the evidence,"[53] investigated the allegations of impropriety at SRI. He concluded, "I found the allegations were simply not true. There is no evidence whatsoever that Puthoff and Targ or any of their subjects cheated on this contract; there is evidence some of the allegations against Puthoff and Targ were deliberately fabricated to discredit psychic research."[54]

Likewise, one of Targ and Puthoff's first papers on the subject was the object of much scorn and controversy. In 1975, the researchers submitted an article on their experiments with remote viewing to the publication of the Institute of Electronic and Electric Engineers (IEEE): *Proceedings of the IEEE.* The article was ponderously entitled "A Perceptual

Channel for Information Transfer over Kilometer Distances: Historical Perspective and Recent Research."

According to writer Alan Vaughan, the editor of *Proceedings of the IEEE,* he supervised successful remote viewing experiments before publishing Targ and Puthoff's paper.

But this didn't prevent controversy. Some 20 members of the IEEE's board demanded the editor's resignation for proposing to publish the paper, although the members all admitted they had not read it. It was finally published in *Proceedings of the IEEE* in March 1976 (Volume 64, Number 3).[55]

With the positive SCANATE review reports and the publication of SRI's research in a prestigious technical periodical, it appeared that continued government funding for the SRI research was assured, especially after Price began a successful operational test for the CIA.

CIA Project Officer Kress described how Price's descriptions of a missile and a guerrilla training site in Libya were confirmed by the CIA's Libyan Desk officer. But then, in July of 1975, as Pat Price was preparing to mentally gather further details on these sites, he died of a heart attack. "There have been no further CIA-sponsored intelligence collection tests," asserted Kress later.[56]

Researcher Targ commented:

> Pat Price...had psychic functioning totally integrated into his daily life. He would tell us each day about the course of world events—the day and hour of the Israeli-Arab cease-fire in the Yom Kippur War, the eventual outcome of a celebrated kidnapping,

the breakup of an OPEC conference by terrorists. Nearly every day it seemed that Pat would have some new piece of precognitive news for us to think about over lunch, days in advance of the event's actual occurrence.[57]

Adding to credibility problems of remote viewing were Price's unsolicited descriptions of UFOs and extraterrestrial bases.

Despite the success of SCANATE, there was foot-dragging within the CIA itself. Psychic research never became institutionalized, due to constant friction between believers and nonbelievers, as well as newly publicized revelations regarding agency improprieties including assassination plots against world leaders.

One potential boost came in late 1975 when President Gerald Ford named George H. W. Bush as director of the CIA. Bush, who was confirmed as CIA director in January 1976, was a longtime friend of astronaut Edgar Mitchell. Mitchell founded the Institute for Noetic (from the Greek for "new") Sciences in San Francisco.

Mitchell, who was dedicated to psychic research and had kept in close contact with SRI, convinced Bush to allow him to organized high-level seminars at the CIA to study the potential applications of parapsychology to intelligence gathering.[58]

But before anything profitable could come of these seminars, Jimmy Carter was elected president and, in 1977, Navy Admiral Stansfield Turner, a man with no particular interest in the paranormal, was appointed director of the CIA.

In an August 1977 interview, Turner referred to Pat Price, without using his name, as someone the CIA had tried to develop as a psychic agent. Turner said the project was discontinued in 1975. "He died and we haven't heard from him since," he flippantly remarked.[59]

But if interest in remote viewing waned within the CIA, such was not the case within the Pentagon.

Sponsorship of the SRI research shifted to the U.S. Army with an added component: the creation of an operational unit of soldiers to be trained in remote viewing.

America's Psi Spies had arrived.

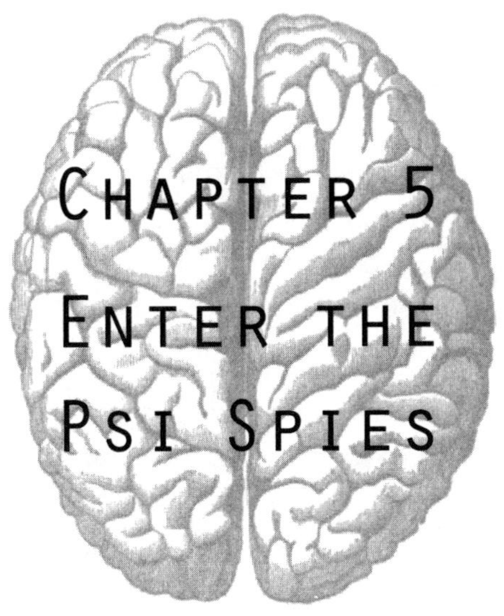

Chapter 5 Enter the Psi Spies

By 1976, the work done at SRI was being discussed in Washington, particularly in the top circles of the intelligence community. SRI funding had shifted from the CIA to the Department of Defense.

Pressure to produce intelligence during the Cold War was severe. Adding remote viewing to the U.S. intelligence arsenal was "a tactic of desperation," according to some within the Psi Spies.[1]

They said the officers who sought to create a unit of Psi Spies faced almost insurmountable obstacles. They were up against much more than simple conservatism. They were running counter to existing belief systems and facing narrow-mindedness, fear of the phenomenon, fear of embarrassment or ostracism, and political and professional suicide, not to mention professional jealousy.

But most insurmountable of all was the mindset voiced by a ubiquitous staff officer who commented, "Even if you can prove to me that this works, I will not believe it."

It was ironic that these obstacles were most prevalent behind the "green door" of top intelligence officials. Once briefed on the subject, many lower-level commanders had no problem accepting the existence and potential of psi functioning.

Project SCANATE had been caught up in the backlash of several CIA scandals in the mid-1970s. American news media were carrying stories of the CIA-Mafia assassination plots against foreign leaders, possible drug smuggling, and other horrors. "The 'Proxmire Effect' [named for the budget scrutiny of Sen. William Proxmire], the fear that certain government research contracts would be deemed ill-founded and held up for scorn, was another factor precluding the CIA from sensitive areas of research," noted Kenneth Kress.[2]

All operations that held any potential political liability to the Agency, or were even potentially embarrassing, were quickly and quietly given the ax, but not without a decrease of morale within Agency ranks.[3]

The operational Psi Spies unit came into being during the time of Lieutenant General Edmund "Mike" Thompson, then the U.S. Army's deputy chief of staff for Intelligence during the mid-1970s. While the CIA was shying away from "far-out" projects, Gen. Thompson was authorizing a handful of special unorthodox units to deal with the Army's "most intractable intelligence problems."

One of these "intractable" problems, according to the Psi Spies, was that of satisfying scientific and technical intelligence requirements. The military needed to know what the other side had, how it worked, and how it was used.

The units created by Thompson were secret, or "black," organizations, consisting of only a few people and generally off the regular Army books. Called "skunk works," each unit was commanded by a lieutenant colonel and composed of the best and brightest officers and enlisted men from both intelligence and Special Operations.[4]

Unlike the CIA, the Army was not as afraid of the political consequences of failure. Unlike their civilian government counterparts, military officers were not constantly looking over their shoulders to get feedback on whether or not their actions were politically correct.

According to Mel Riley, one of the original Psi Spies, these "skunk works" units were in place prior to the creation of the U.S. Army Intelligence and Security Command (INSCOM) in 1977.

Riley and the other Psi Spies declined to discuss the nature of other "skunk works" units, citing concern for national security and their secrecy oaths. "Also, we had no contact with them and so we couldn't speak with any authority," said Riley.

The original psi spy unit was one of these "skunk works" units designed to explore the use of psychic abilities for intelligence collection purposes.

"I became convinced that remote viewing was a real phenomenon, that it wasn't a hoax," recalled Gen. Thompson. "We didn't know how to explain it, but we weren't so much interested in explaining it as in determining whether there was any practical use to it."[5]

According to Riley, the CIA kept envious eyes on this fledgling Army program. He said the Agency even assigned their head psychologist to monitor the program in the event they took it back.

Melvin C. Riley, who goes by "Mel," was one of America's original Psi Spies. Riley bears no resemblance to how most people would probably picture a psychic spy. He is a quiet, unassuming man with a genuinely pleasant and open smile. At any given time he will have some sort of Indian trinket on him—a beaded hat band or a medicine bag hanging out of his pocket.

Following his service, Riley was curator for Native American Studies at the New London Public Museum in New London, Wisconsin. His home, complete with Indian teepee in the back yard, was in nearby Scandinavia, Wisconsin.

Riley said his interest in American Indians goes "back as far as anyone in my family can remember." This interest may tie in with a psychic experience he had as a boy.

As a young boy, about 12 or 13 years old, Riley recalled, he would explore the cliffs above the shore of Lake Michigan. One favorite place was a field that constantly yielded up Indian arrowheads and artifacts. In fact, in one area of this field there were so many arrowhead chips that Riley decided this is where an Indian craftsman sat while making arrowheads.

He recalled:

> One day I was in this open area, but facing the woods. Behind me I suddenly could smell smoke from a campfire and noises like people were there, children and dogs barking. It didn't make much sense because I knew there was nobody there. But I turned around and

> there was an Indian village, fully three-dimensional. There were round huts made out of bark and mats and things like that. And people, kids, and dogs. I saw it. I experienced it. I knew it wasn't really there but it was in the same location that I kept finding these artifacts. Then a most interesting thing happened, which, to me, took this whole thing out of the realm of imagination. I was wondering if my eyes were playing tricks on me when this individual standing next to his lodge or whatever, looked right at me and waved. He actually acknowledged me. Right after that occurred, the whole thing started dissolving or fading away until there was nothing left but the present day.

Riley said in recent years he learned that such an experience is called "bi-location," a situation of one's consciousness seeming to be in two separate places at the same time. He said he never had another experience to compare to that during his formative years.

After high school, Riley had a "great life," having worked his way up from an apprentice to a master machine repairman's position with a local union. "I was taking home about $300 a week clear—good money in the '60s—and I had a Corvette, a Dodge convertible, a Plymouth station wagon, plus my own place," he said.

Then in July of 1969, Riley was drafted into the Army. "I knew it was coming," he said, "so it was no big thing. I was willing to do my part, you know. I had lost some good friends over in 'Nam, so I figured I'd get even for my buddies, payback time and all that. But the strange thing is I never wound up in Vietnam."

Riley said in boot camp the Army "tweaked my interest" in imagery interpretation, the analysis of aerial photos and such. He recalled:

> That seemed pretty interesting to me, plus it was in the intelligence field and sounded kind of exotic to me. So I volunteered for that and it put me into a three-year enlistment. I was sent to military intelligence training school at Fort Holibird, Maryland, after basic training. I was in the last group to go through there. It's no longer there.
>
> After this course, they sent around the dream sheets, that's where you list where you want to go for your next assignment. This was 1969–70, the height of the Vietnam War, so I was quite realistic. I put down for my three choices—Vietnam, Vietnam, Vietnam. Everybody else put in for Hawaii, North Carolina, England, whatever. I was about the only one out of my entire graduating class that did not go to Vietnam. They sent me straight to Germany.

Riley said his unit in Germany was a "do-nothing tactical intelligence" group and he chafed under the inaction. "It took me about six months but I finagled my way through the back door to get up to a special detachment that was attached to the Air Force in Wiesbaden, Germany," Riley said. "And there we got into some genuine strategic-level imagery interpretation."

In 1977, he was transferred to Fort Meade, Maryland, to the newly formed Army Intelligence and Security Command. Here, Riley entered deeper into the intelligence community, working with one of the special units under INSCOM. "I wound up in a special group called the SAVE Team," he said.

"This was the Sensitive Activity Vulnerability Estimates Team. We were supposed to go out and evaluate the vulnerability of hostile agencies collecting intelligence on high-level stuff such as the development of the M1 tank or missile systems or such. It was counter-intelligence."

But Riley, who by this time was a staff sergeant, again felt his unit was greatly misused. "We were used as 'gofers,' furniture movers, you know, ash haulers. There were three imagery interpreters including myself, all enlisted men. We were sorely mis-utilized."

After complaining to his commander, Riley said he and his fellow imagery interpreters were sent to Washington, where they came under the command of Gen. Thompson. Riley recalled:

> They had just created the Systems Exploitation Detachment [SED]. It was more refined and more secret than the SAVE Team, if that was possible. Gen. Thompson set that up. They were kind of a unique, standoffish group. They went out and, to the best of my knowledge, researched Soviet technology. They looked into it, investigated it, whatever.
>
> Well, they had classified information that the Soviets were using "bio-energies," that the Soviets were using psychics and things like that. This is one of the things that Gen. Thompson wanted to take a look at. So they handed this over to the SED team. But this was not really within the belief structures of the SED team, so they only halfheartedly looked into it. Actually, they handed it over to the one and only enlisted man they had there, an E-8 master sergeant.

> Well, one day I was coming by and this sergeant had all these books on "Beyond the Body" and other psychic stuff, so I started a conversation. He told me he was researching psychic phenomena and such and I said, "Hey, I've got all kinds of books of that at home. I'll bring some for you to help you along."
>
> That established that I had an interest in these things, so word got back that Riley here seems to known something about this, maybe we ought to be talking to him.

The next thing Riley knew, he was approached by Capt. Fred Atwater, who was part of a "skunk works" unit called GONDOLA WISH. The unit was commanded by Maj. Scotty Watt, soon to make lieutenant colonel. Riley said:

> They made him program manager of a program they devised to create a team of people to see if they could reproduce the psychic phenomena being reported from behind the iron curtain.
>
> They went out into the intelligence community in the D.C. [District of Columbia] area with all these psychological profiles looking for people for their team. I guess they interviewed about 3,000 people. From that, they selected 12 people as a core group. These were the people they were going to get to try and reproduce psychic happenings. And I was one of the 12.

Riley said he was lucky to be selected for GONDOLA WISH because Watt did not want any enlisted men on the team. "So other than myself, everyone else was either an officer or civilian GS [Government Service]. Out of that core group of 12, there were two women. So they decided to create this unit and renamed it GRILL FLAME."

GRILL FLAME, according to Riley, was simply a computer-generated random code name and referred to the entire psychic program, the unit at Fort Meade, as was well as the work at SRI:

> So these 12 people were brought into a conference room, interviewed, and told what this unit was all about. They were asked if they wanted to become a part of this new unit that was being formed. And they all said, "Yeah, sure." And they all signed their name on the line and so forth. It was all voluntary. You could bail out any time you wanted to and, in fact, the attrition rate was bang, bang, bang. It wasn't very long before we were down to about six people.
>
> Some left because of job reasons, their workload was just too heavy. A lot of them were allowed to come to us on a weekly or twice-a-week basis to do their thing. Their parent unit, of course, was not told why or whatever. They were just told it was a special project at a higher level and so on. Sometimes their bosses made it tough on them and they just had to drop out.
>
> Others left because of their belief structures, what we were doing didn't go along with what they believed in. And some were discouraged because their belief structures were a little bit different. This one fellow, a Christian Scientist, had his Bible with him all the time. He was constantly reading it before he went into the sessions and he had a lot of questions about the morality of this and that.

> One of the biggest reasons I think Lt. Atwater wanted me in there on this program was that we wanted someone he could command. Being a young lieutenant, he was on the bottom of the totem pole compared to all those GSs and everybody else outranked him. I was someone he could boss around and feel important. But we worked together all right.

Out of the original six Psi Spies, three were part-timers. "It boiled down to three of us, outside Col. Watt and Capt. Atwater," said Riley. "We wore various hats, one day as viewers, one day as monitors, and so forth, but the core group was myself, Ken Bell, and Warrant Officer Joseph McMoneagle."[6]

McMoneagle, a soft-spoken intellectual who entered the Army after graduating from an all-male Catholic school in Miami, had experienced several spontaneous out-of-body episodes following a near-death experience outside an Austrian restaurant in 1970. "They interviewed some 3,000 people and winnowed it down to a final six," recalled McMoneagle. "We were sent out and tested at SRI International. As a result, I became Remote Viewer 001."[7]

Following his retirement from the Army in 1984, McMoneagle wrote a book about his remote viewing experiences entitled *Mind Trek: Exploring Consciousness, Time, and Space Through Remote Viewing.*

Riley recalled that the first Psi Spies used an old leather couch that once belonged to a general. "We just sort of requisitioned this because we couldn't get one through channels. There'd be too many questions," he said. He added that early on, the GRILL FLAME unit was linked with the SRI researchers in California. "We were supposed to go to SRI. Puthoff and Targ were there. Ingo Swann was out there at the time. This was all in preparation of using their techniques and sending people out there to work with them. But they didn't have any real training out there. They were just using our people to add to their data banks."

Through the late 1970s, the unit spent most of its time in training—and constant testing.

Riley said a typical training run during this time went this way:

> The project manager would dream up local targets in the area like McDonald's or a park or something and these would be sealed in envelopes. Only he had access to it or knew what the targets were, so it was like a double-blind test. Say Fred was going to interview me. He would go get a sealed envelope and give it to a target person. Then he and I would sit in a room. The target person got in a vehicle and started taking off. Once he was away from the place, he would open the envelope and be given instructions to go to a certain place, to be there at a certain time, and perhaps, to do certain things. Back in the room, me as the viewer would try to target that person and describe his surroundings, what he was doing, things like that. Some of the technical terms escape me.

He said that during this time, the remote viewers of GRILL FLAME were trying a variety of methods to induce an altered state of consciousness. "Everything except drugs," said Riley.

But as the viewers gained experience, they found they could do just as well without complicated attempts at meditation, biorhythm and so forth. "At least a half dozen methods (if not more) were adopted within the...program itself," recalled McMoneagle, "most of which have been used to one extent or another within the research side of the program as well. To date, there is no research or applications evidence to suggest that one method was better than another with regard to remote viewing."[8]

Riley said that every time someone new came along, the unit would be put through the same tests as before. "It was a constant thing, and we didn't like being played with after a while," he said. He gave this example:

> One of the things that happened was, early one morning we got a phone call that there was an A6-E aircraft that went down. They couldn't find it; they didn't know its location, only that it went down in the Smoky Mountains. They wanted to know if we could find it. Well, we busted our nuts trying to see it. One viewer, Ken Bell, really had an emotional experience. In fact, he bi-located, saw the charred remains of the pilot, and got real emotional about it. What was interesting was that when we called the position in, Ken Bell had been less than three kilometers from the crash site. How did we know that? It was one of the few times we got feedback. The dirtball on the other end of the line said, "Oh yeah, we know that, we were just testing you to see if you could find it."
>
> This is an example of Stage 4 overlay as it is known in Coordinate Remote Viewing. Nothing escapes you.

> If you begin to perceive that there is some hidden agenda, something they have not told you about, it comes out in Stage 4 overlay.
>
> My point is how remote viewing progressed. If this test had happened in later years, we would have detected the fact that they already knew where the plane was even while we were working. But in those days, we were so focused on the one specific aspect.

He said that at this time, the remote viewers were mostly working on "beaconing," a technique similar to the SRI experiments in which a viewer attempted to "see" the location of an outbound target subject or "beacon."

"The beaconing-type targets were designed to give you immediate feedback," explained Riley. "When you finished your session as a viewer, you took your notes. When the target or beacon came back, then you and the beacon and the monitor all went out to the site."

Riley said that one time Gen. Thompson himself asked to participate in a remote viewing session. Riley recalled:

> Col. Watt and I went to the Pentagon and went into Gen. Thompson's office. Gen. Thompson asked Col. Watt to leave. We shut the blinds and I let him cool down a bit and then had him do a session as a viewer. Now the target was selected by one of his aides, who would have liked nothing more than for the whole thing to fail because it was beyond his belief system, all hogwash. [The aide] selected a little railroad station in the D.C. area, which was within several blocks of the George Washington Masonic Temple. It's not a good thing to

locate small targets next to big targets because the viewer is naturally attracted to the more prominent feature.

Anyway, behind this train station were some pools of water that almost looked like rice paddies. So Gen. Thompson went through the whole thing and did his sketches and got his descriptions. Then we all jumped in this limo and went to see if we could find anything that related to the target. Nothing. Gen. Thompson said he was seeing bodies of water but all we could find was a little pail with some water in it. He had described various things which we just couldn't locate. So we all thought the session was a failure. But, amazingly enough, just a week or so later, Gen. Thompson was taking off from Washington National Airport and happened to fly over this area. From what I understand, his reaction was, "Oh my God, that's exactly what I saw!" He didn't realize it but he had been looking at his target area from an aerial viewpoint and we were trying to match it up from a ground view. I think that convinced him that there really was something to it because he experienced it himself even though at first it seemed like the session was a waste of his valuable time. But he knew better after flying over that area.

Riley said that the most disheartening thing about his experience with the Psi Spies was that no one in authority seemed to take them seriously, no matter what spectacular results were produced. "One case that sticks in my mind was the Iranian embassy hostage deal. We were in on this from day one. It was mostly pure drudgery and I think it drove some of our people off the deep end," Riley said.

On November 4, 1979, a mob of Iranian students stormed the U.S. Embassy in Tehran, taking the occupants hostage. Riley recalled:

> We were providing information and data constantly, day by day, repeating it time after time after time. We were supplying all this information to the intelligence community for months and months—and no feedback, zero feedback. We didn't get feedback until after the hostages were released 444 days later. Then some colonel shows up and said, "Oh yeah, this was good information," and so on. We busted our hearts trying to provide this information. We thought it would be utilized. We thought it would be important. But it was just run as a test.

Riley said that the lack of feedback on major targets was one of the Psi Spies' biggest problems. He added that, during the Iranian hostage situation, the remote viewers were picking up views of the ill-fated rescue attempt in April 1980:

> Again, there was no feedback. All we knew was that it had something to do with the hostage thing. I've got a viewer and after the session, he's drawing pictures of troops and stuff rappelling out of helicopters to the ground and conflict. We had no idea they were planning a rescue attempt, but he was picking up on it.

Riley also said that, during the hostage rescue attempt, the Psi Spies were sequestered in a local motel, apparently to prevent them from disclosing what they knew about the top-secret rescue attempt:

> I remember that we were locked in for the duration of the mission and we were remote viewing it as it was

> going on—up to and including the disaster. I'll never forget that experience. It was such a sleazy motel. Of course, it was the cheapest one they could get. It was riddled with mice. I was sitting in the dark and I've got a viewer who is under and I'm running him through his paces. And here's something crawling up my leg. So I had to shake this mouse off me before we could continue.

By the summer of 1981, Riley felt it was time to move on. He remembered:

> I could have stayed, but I just didn't see a lot of future in it. The colonel didn't like enlisted men and I was impatient because I felt we should have been used operationally and all we ever did was test, test, test....I just made up my mind that I would take the next set of orders that came along and, amazingly enough, it happened to be for Germany.

Riley returned to Germany, this time with the First Armored Division, and eventually worked his way back into his old imagery interpretation unit at Wiesbaden.

A few years later, Riley was flying in and out of Honduras as part of a mission to Central America in support of the Nicaraguan Contras. But he soon grew bored with this. "That was a nightmare," Riley said. "I really didn't like the tactical stuff, I mean it's gruntsville all the way compared to doing something worthwhile like remote viewing."

In 1986, Riley learned that the Psi Spies still existed and managed to get reassigned back into the unit. He recalled:

> The unit always seemed to survive under one name or another. It seems like the unit was always about to go under but then, like the Phoenix, it would rise again somewhere else with somebody else taking over.
>
> I finally received orders to go back up to Fort Meade in 1986, which I did. That's when I met the new crew up there. I was introduced to this entirely new process of remote viewing called Coordinate Remote Viewing, which is very highly structured. It was just the greatest thing, compared to what we were doing back in the stone age of remote viewing when we were flying by the seat of our pants.

One big boost to the Psi Spies unit had come in December 1980, with the publication of an article entitled "The New Mental Battlefield: Beam Me Up, Spock" in *Military Review.* The piece was written by then–Lt. Col. John B. Alexander with the Army's Inspector General Agency.[9]

Alexander, who earned a Ph.D. from Walden University and served with the Special Forces in Thailand and Vietnam, had been chief of the human resources division of the Organizational Effectiveness Staff Office at Fort McPherson, Georgia. He also had been interested in psychic phenomena since the 1960s.

It was largely this article, and its scientific citations, which brought the idea of psychic warfare or "psychotronics" into normal conversations between military officers.

He defined "psychotronics" as the interaction of mind and matter and specifically pointed to mind-altering procedures such as extremely low-frequency (ELF) energy bombardment and remote viewing as two areas where much scientific investigation had already been done.

He added that the "intelligence-gathering capability available through remote viewing...is obvious" and that the "strategic and tactical applications are unlimited."

In recent years, Alexander said he was aware of the remote viewing studies back in the 1970s, and that he knew some of the people who were doing it.

He said:

> It is certainly real and effective.
>
> The problem is knowing when the results were accurate versus when they were inaccurate and there wasn't a very good filtering mechanism.
>
> Then, of course, there was the issue of "how does this work?" So you got into the chicken and the egg problem if you didn't have a theory to support it. Whether it was real or not didn't matter because you didn't meet the scientific paradigm.[10]

Another boost to the Psi Spies came in 1981, when Maj. Gen. Albert N. Stubblebine assumed command of INSCOM. Stubblebine, a tall, imposing, white-haired figure, known for his firm handshake and his willingness to consider unorthodox ideas, was receptive to the idea of remote viewing.

His receptivity may have stemmed from a personal experience. As detailed in the book *The Warrior's Edge,* Stubblebine was at John Alexander's apartment in 1982 when a psychic named Ann Gehman attempted to bend a pair of forks without the customary stroking. Alexander wrote:

> Initially, she tried to stare down the forks, never a successful strategy, and had no success. Suddenly something distracted her and, in full view of the onlookers, one of her forks bent. The tines and neck of the fork drooped a full 90 degrees.

Both Alexander and Stubblebine, who saw the event and were certain that no physical force had bent the fork, agreed that the potential of this phenomenon warranted further research.[11]

In a 1993 interview, Alexander described another fork bending exercise as "one of the most spectacular ones that happened." He recalled:

> We were out at the Xerox Training Center in Leesburg, Virginia. It was a sequestered session—they are called "love-ins"—commanders from all over the world were there. At this particular one we had somewhere between 30 and 40 senior officers present, several "flags" [generals] but mostly colonels. We were plotting a course for INSCOM for the future. Gen. Stubblebine, who was my boss at the time, deserves a lot of credit because he gave me the latitude to go out and do these things. We used them as a mechanism to expand awareness that things might not always be the

way they seem....The point was that if you draw lines, you're pretty much going to find what you expect to find. And in the intelligence business, that can be very damaging.... So this was a hands-on demonstration that the world may be built a little differently than we once anticipated....

So this one particular night we got to the Advanced Session...and we had them holding two forks by the base and you were not to apply any physical force, just hold them by the base. What happened was that there was a scream and this guy yelled, "Look at that!" And we looked over to this individual who was holding a fork and it was bent a full 90 degrees. Now I didn't see this happen, but Ed Speakman, our science advisor who was a GS-18, that's equivalent to a three-star general, saw this happen. I didn't see it so I was frankly a little skeptical, especially since there were people there who wished I wouldn't do things like this in that environment. So I figured that somebody bent it and as soon as I acknowledged it, he would say, "Nah, fooled you. I bent it with my hand." I wouldn't have put something like that past some of those guys. So I just said, "Gee, that's really interesting." And then, with everybody watching, the fork straightened itself and came back down to a full 90 degrees, stopped, and came back up about 45 degrees. I can show you because I've still got the fork. The individual put down the forks and said, "I wished that had not happened." It turned out that it scared the shit out of the guy. Fortunately, we were sequestered and we had our psychologist with us. We spent a couple of days putting this guy back together. By the time he went home, he was in good shape and, in fact, replicated the event at his home station just to prove to himself he could do it.

Stubblebine's support of the unorthodox research earned him the epithet "Spoonbender" and he quickly became a target for his ambitious peers.

"Under the auspices of Major General Stubblebine, several advanced human technologies were extensively explored by the military. Unfortunately, there was a price to pay for venturing too far beyond the bunkers of conventional wisdom: Stubblebine retired from the service prematurely, after running headlong into the marshaled forces of the status quo," Alexander noted.[12]

Gen. Stubblebine has declined interviews regarding his remote viewing experiences, saying he had been "burned" too many times by members of the media.

Nevertheless, with approval from above, limited though it may have been, the Psi Spies moved ahead rapidly during the 1980s, training new remote viewers and developing new techniques.

One of the new remote viewers recruited during this time was a computer whiz named Leonard E. Buchanan. Lyn Buchanan had a background similar to the other Psi Spies. Born in 1939 in Waco, Texas, he moved around a lot, was a pretty independent young man, and even had a psychic experience as a youngster—but his was not as pleasant as the others.

Buchanan recalled:

> I had this experience when I was about 12 or 13 years old. Actually it was a very pleasant experience,

> it was what happened afterwards....I was playing around and found that I could put a rock on a metal plate and use my mind to push the rock through the plate. I thought that was pretty neat. So I showed this to a girl friend of mine. Well, it turned out that she was the daughter of a Seventh Day Adventist minister. That night there was a knock on the door and these people came in and grabbed me. They put their hands on my head and were screaming, saying I was "of the devil." It scared the water out of me.

Buchanan's father worked for a railroad and his family moved around quite a lot. "I attended 11 high schools," Buchanan recalled. Young Buchanan moved with his family from Texas to California and back. He graduated from San Jacinto High School in Houston.

After working at a variety of jobs, Buchanan joined the Army, where he was trained in computer technology. "During the 1960s I worked on computer systems for the Nike Ajax and Hercules missiles," he said.

After three years, Buchanan left the Army and earned an undergraduate degree from Lon Morris College in Jacksonville, Texas. He went on to earn a master's degree in psycho-linguistics from Stephen F. Austin University in Nacogdoches, Texas.

He recalled one incident that always reminds him of how far computer technology has come in recent years: "Once when I was looking for a job, I went to this little bitty company called CDC just south of Houston. This guy showed me a huge room full of big computers and told me that one day we'd have a computer as small as his desk. Of course, now we have computers you can hold in your hand."

Buchanan landed a job as a teacher in several secondary Texas schools, but soon tired of this and rejoined the Army. In typical military fashion, because Buchanan had majored in German and Spanish, he was sent to the Defense Language Institute in Monterrey, California, to learn Russian.

In the late 1970s, Buchanan made E-6, staff sergeant, and was stationed in Augsburg, Germany, where he did classified work dealing with computers. While in Augsburg, he made E-7 or sergeant first class.

It was here also that Buchanan said he had another "bad" psychic experience. "I can't really talk about that," he said, "but it drew the attention of the right people."

Soon afterward, he was transferred to the 902nd Military Intelligence Group at Fort Meade, home of the Psi Spies. Upon his arrival at Fort Meade, he was recruited as a remote viewer. He recalled:

> When I first came into the unit, I was there for the purpose of allowing Gen. Stubblebine to form a unit which would have the job of first learning how to destroy enemy computers and later, if possible, learning how to control the information within enemy computers. Anyway, Congress nixed that idea, since it smelled too much of "mind control."
>
> So, there I was in the unit, and they had just gotten the news that day that our funding wouldn't be renewed—the unit was out of a job. It did get funded at the last minute, but that was a recurring story for the unit. Anyway, they had basically nothing for me to do, so

> they decided to use me as a sort of guinea pig. They gave me a beacon exercise. The outbounders were given an envelope containing the directions to a site. They left the unit and opened it after they were out of sight of the building. Twenty minutes later, I sat down to do my session—no training, no protocols, no nothing. I kept seeing them driving around, looking out the car window and driving further. That's all I could get. I couldn't get any descriptors of a target location. I said, "I think they're lost," and Skip [Atwater] had me just end the session, thinking that I had failed. When the outbounder team returned, they said that they never found the target location—they had gotten lost.

Buchanan described himself as a computer "guru." "When all those kids with their computer degrees can't get the job done, they call me," he laughed. "I am absolutely convinced that remote viewing can be enhanced with computer technology," he said. Buchanan said he wants to link various remote viewers together using virtual reality in computers. "This way, they could all see what each other is seeing," he explained.

He also said he has been working on a book designing standards and formats for the use of psychic and remote viewers by police departments and intelligence agencies. "I think this could be very important," he said, "because they can be using techniques that I know work. I've worked with this for a long time."

Another of the new trainees was Morehouse. Morehouse said remote viewing training was particularly tough on him because "at that time I was not a real conceptual person." He recalled:

> It was tough to sit down and listen to some guy give me a lecture about a theory when they tell you up front that they don't understand. They say, "We don't understand what makes this work, so now let me give you the theory that we don't know how it works."
>
> And being just a dumb-ass old grunt like I am, I'd kind of just sit back and scratch my head sipping on my coffee and say, "Okay."

As the Reagan years came to a close, the Psi Spies were learning more and more. And their remote viewing techniques had advanced far beyond anything that Hal Puthoff, Russell Targ, and Ingo Swann could ever have imagined.

But there were dark clouds on the horizon: A congressional investigation, strange mental duels with psychic opponents from the Eastern Bloc, and "witches" were soon to cause big troubles for the Psi Spies.

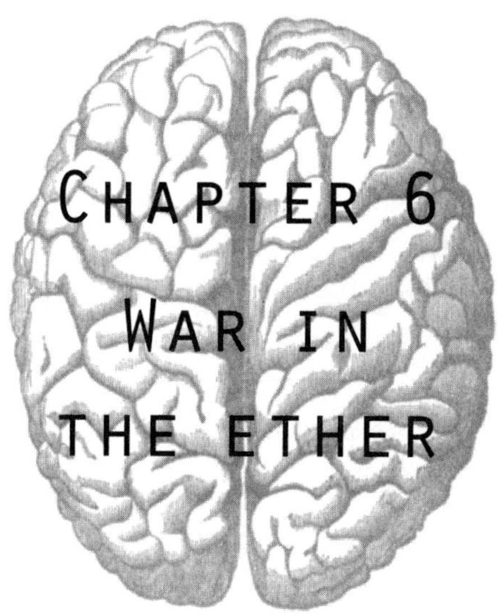

Chapter 6 War in the Ether

Throughout the Reagan years, fear and loathing of the Soviet Union's "evil empire" rose to new heights. Meanwhile, work both within the Psi Spies unit and at SRI continued at a rapid pace with new techniques being developed to increase both the efficiency and accuracy of remote viewing.

One of the biggest problems to overcome concerned separating the true psychic "signal" from extraneous mind clutter called "noise." Noise, quite simply, is the brain's normal conscious operation—fleeting thoughts touching on a wide range of topics. At any given time of day, the brain may be interrupted by thoughts of home and family, hunger or thirst, daydreams of faraway places, or longing for a date for Friday night.

"Basically, what you have is a signal to noise problem," explained Col. Alexander. "[Remote viewing] naturals and others could clearly produce results some of the time. But the problem was knowing when the results were accurate versus when they were inaccurate, and there wasn't a very good filtering mechanism."

The mental clutter problem is compounded in remote viewing by analytical overlay (AOL), the conscious subjective interpretation of the psychic signal. AOL is usually wrong, especially in the early stages of a person's remote viewing experience, although it often will possess valid insights of the target. For example, a lighthouse may produce an AOL of "factory chimney" because of its tall cylindrical shape.

AOL is relatively easy to identify in a RV session because there is usually a comparison involved. According to Riley, the viewer will say, "It looks like..." or "This reminds me of..." and so forth.

It is said that when a remote viewer gets a clear, sharp, and motionless image of a site—a mental photograph of sorts—this is always AOL.

Psi Spies monitors looked for little things to tip them off that AOL was involved in the remote viewing sessions. They watched for certain inflections in the voice or information being delivered in the form of a question. They particularly watched for deviations from the structure.

"The first few years I was in the unit, I was convinced that all the problems of CRV [Controlled Remote Viewing] would go away if only we could master the tendency to get AOL, " recalled Lyn Buchanan. "I worked on the problem all that time but nothing seemed to succeed."

He continued:

> But in an experiment [to use a Los Alamos mageto-electro encephalograph to register brain activity while viewing horizontal and vertical lines on a screen], instead of getting visuals of horizontal and vertical lines, I would get visuals of picket fences, stands of birch trees, railroad yards (horizontal lines), an old plantation home with the columns on the porch, etc. What I realized was that there is a kind of AOL which happens at the subconscious level, and is not analytical, at all. It happens when a perception comes bubbling up from the great unknown and gets a memory, fear, or desire attached to it before it ever reaches the conscious mind.
>
> After a year or so of study on this, I started calling this kind of AOL, the "Subconscious Transmission of Recollections, Anxieties and Yearnings to Consciously Accessible Thought" (STRAY CAT). It happens totally at the subconscious level, before you are ever aware of the perception, and can't be controlled or eliminated from the RV process. Getting to recognize the differences between AOLs and STRAY CATs was the only thing we could do, and we have since developed methods for identifying both, and for distinguishing between them."

Monitors were trained to call a break in the RV session whenever AOL was detected. Likewise, there were breaks for "confusion," when the viewer became confused by distractions in his environment or when the psychic signal became muddled.

Clearing or calming the mind is one of the first prerequisites of remote viewing. Mary Sinclair, the wife of author Upton Sinclair, who was well-known for her psychic gifts, said, "You first give yourself a 'suggestion' to the effect that you will relax your mind and body, making the body insensitive and the mind a blank."[1]

The idea is that if a person can quiet his or her mind—reduce or eliminate the noise, if you will—then the weaker psychic "signal" will be better able to reach the consciousness.

In an attempt to change remote viewing from an occasional burst of psychic thought to a repeatable and dependable tool, structure was introduced.

The Psi Spies learned that structure is the key to usable RV technology. It is through proper structure or discipline that mental noise is suppressed and signal line information allowed to emerge cleanly. As long as proper structure is maintained, information obtained may be relied upon. If the viewer starts speculating about content—wondering "what it is"—he will begin to depart from proper structure and AOL will inevitably result.

One prime duty of both the monitor and the viewer is to insure the viewer maintains proper structure, taking information in the correct sequence, at the correct stage, and in the proper manner. Col. Alexander said he found that another problem with remote viewing was that officials who evaluated the phenomenon wanted 100 percent accuracy 100 percent of the time.

"Unlike any other system that you might use, this one had to be 100 percent accurate," said Alexander. "They wanted all or nothing. There is nothing that is 100 percent accurate."

Ingo Swann, who continued to develop remote viewing techniques at SRI through the 1980s, said:

> The average accuracy of a spontaneous [or natural psychic] remote viewing is about 20 percent at most. Sometimes Pat Price would every once in a while get something on the order of 95 percent correct. But it would be 100 targets later to get that good again, so, on the average it was about 20 percent.
>
> And 20 percent accuracy is not competitive with other intelligence-gathering methods. I mean, if you only got 20 percent accuracy investing in the stock market, you'd go broke.
>
> So it has to be 51 percent at minimum. And I said, "Well, if we're going to head for 51 percent, we might as well head for 100 percent." It's the same problem, you see. So I got money to increase the efficiency of remote viewing. In order to do that, I had to find out how it worked.
>
> I isolated seven general stages of the different kinds of information, which came psychically in exact order.

Swann described the seven remote viewing stages as follows:

Stage 1 = The formation of an ideogram, a spontaneous mark with a pen or pencil representing the target site.

Stage 2 = Sensory impressions the viewer might experience if he were at the target site, such as smells, sounds, feelings, colors, and so on.

Stage 3 = Dimensional references, the height and length of the site, most often represented in sketches.

Stage 4 = Refinement of the dimensional references, gaining tangible details of the target site, such as surroundings (trees, buildings, tables, chairs, and such). Also, the recognition of intangibles such as the use of the site (governmental, medical, religious, museum, and so on).

Stage 5 = Integrating the preceding four stages into the understanding of the remote viewer. It is here that the viewer interrogates his own memory, drawing out further details of the target site.

Stage 6 = Making accurate renderings or drawing of the target site. This may also include modeling. It was learned that often viewers could use modeling clay to make three-dimensional models of the site that were superior to line sketches.

Stage 7 = This seldom-used stage involves the use of verbal sounds to approximate the precise names of individuals, streets, towns, and so on. For example, if a certain street name in Arabic is desired, the viewer would continue to approximate the sound until a linguist could interpret the name.

Swann explained:

I spent a great deal of time trying to understand how it worked. I wanted to understand how the data

> debriefed itself. You see, when these guys make an ideogram, there's a chain of unraveling that takes place. The signal line is being incorporated into the viewer's mind or something like that. And they are trained to discriminate between noise and signal. But the signal line does its own thing in these stages and in the way that it does that, you come up with practically a noiseless session. That's if they adhere to the format, the structure. But it's very hard to get people to do that because people like to contribute themselves, you know.
>
> This is not a contributive process. The viewer has to be passive, not active, and just receive what's coming in.

"Many psychic methodologies try to send the conscious mind on vacation. That is, they try to put the conscious mind into a trance or 'altered state,' explained Buchanan. He continued:

> These are the people who insist that psychic work can only be done "once you have achieved theta," etc. In actual fact, the conscious mind sits in that altered state and keeps checking back every few seconds to see how the process is going. The person isn't usually aware of it, but a part of them is constantly monitoring the session and either giving its approval or stopping the subconscious from doing its job by giving disapproval.
>
> You have heard, of course, that a person who is hypnotized cannot be made to do something he/she doesn't want to. This is the reason why. The conscious

mind, although apparently in a trance, is ever vigilant. A well-trained CRV monitor can watch a psychic who is doing "trance-channeling" work, and can see, like a neon sign, each time the psychic's conscious mind "checks back in" to the process. It happens constantly in all trance-state work.

Seeing that this is the case, Controlled Remote Viewing takes another tack. It gives the conscious mind a ton of other work to do. The rules and protocols of CRV are very complex, actually, for two reasons: First, to get as deeply into the subconscious as possible, but second, to also simply keep the conscious mind so busy that it can't get in the subconscious mind's way.

When someone claims to have improved on the Ingo Swann method, you will generally find that what they have done is to simplify it and make it easier and faster for the public to learn. They think that they are doing the public a service—and making money in the process—but in actual fact, the simplified methods give the conscious mind more free time to interfere, and the accuracy of the viewing process drops drastically. The sad part is that these "for the masses" types of methodologies not only fail accuracy-wise, but also actually train the student to never let the subconscious mind do its work cleanly. As such, they are actually harmful to the student's progress—sometimes permanently wrecking their chances for ever achieving their highest personal potential.

As though a proud father, Swann produced a number of testing files from the mid-1980s. He gleefully pointed to the impressive results recorded utilizing his techniques. Swann spoke of one student named "Tom" who continues to hold a very sensitive government job.

"In May, 1984, Tom was among the last of my students. He became the first to finish all seven stages. He was better than me," recalled Swann. Tom correctly identified, then created a model of, the two nuclear reactors in Russellville, Arkansas, said Swann. Then he went on to correctly identify the racetrack at Churchill Downs, Kentucky, as a "horse track." Next Tom correctly described the Bunker Hill Monument, even writing down the word *bunker* as one of its names.

Tom's correct identifications of target sites went on for 17 tests.

It was at the conclusion of the remote viewing course and he had to view 19 sites. Every one had to be flawless. He had to call exactly what was at the site. As Swann recalled:

> Well, he got to number 17 and the target was Oral Roberts University, which is a collection of many different styles of buildings. I thought sure he would flop on this one.
>
> Tom began to write down his impressions. He wrote, "tall, smooth, gray, angular, curving." Then he got to Stage Six, the intangibles, and he wrote "buildings, school, complex, church school." Then as a final statement, Tom said, "Oral Roberts University." I was amazed.

> I let him off the hook at test 17. He did 17 so perfectly, there was no need to go on and do the other two.

By 1986, Swann had trained a whole new generation of remote viewers. "People that are trained thoroughly in this can train somebody else, so I was no longer needed to be a trainer," he said.

Swann said he trained 28 remote viewers by the end of 1986. They were in two groups, neither of which knew about the other. Morehouse was a second-generation viewer, having been taught by others who had been taught by Swann.

Both groups went through SRI but at difference times. Swann said:

> I can't really talk about this second group. They were kept completely separate from [the Psi Spies]. I don't even know where they went. They were much more "black" and much more covert. I don't think I ever had their right names. But they were smart as hell.
>
> That group that Dave Morehouse was a part of didn't really work as a group. They were just together, you know.
>
> This other group really worked as a group. They were much meaner and tougher than the first group. They might have been engineers because they knew what a three-dimensional model was supposed to be and they came out there with these little tools, modeling tools, and everything. If they didn't have what they wanted to make their models, they sort of slipped through SRI and went down to the engineers' section and came back with pipes, cuttings, whatever they

> could find. They raided the storage bins. They built three-dimensional models that were incredible. They made the superstructures of high-tension wire from toothpicks and things like that. When I passed their projects, they demolished it, took it apart right away. When they left, not one thing remained of that group.

It is not unusual for the military to duplicate a covert program, and the Psi Spies were not surprised to learn of this second group. Where they are today is anybody's guess.

Some viewers speculated that members of the second group may have returned to top-level combat groups such as the Navy SEALS or Delta Force. Swann reasoned:

> Any group which might be given a hostage-rescue-type mission would greatly benefit from a remote viewer because the success of such missions depends greatly on the intelligence you have beforehand. You need to know where the hostages are located, where the guards are, alternative entrances and exits, things like that. This is where a remote viewer might give them the edge they need.

Swann said that at the height of the Psi Spies training in the mid-1980s, there were as many as 600 people aware of the unit and its achievements. He recalled:

> We had oversight committees of sometimes more than 50 people on them, some composed of really imminent scientists. We had committees everywhere and also inspection teams.
>
> The clients were protecting their investments, believe me. Early on, the clients [initially the CIA and later

the DIA (Defense Intelligence Agency)] had a big effort to find out if there was any way I could be getting information other than how we claimed. So I underwent batteries of psychological testing and the complete physical thing. I even had a CAT scan of my brain to find out if perhaps a tumor could account for all this. It went on forever. There were psychologists, psychiatrists, testers, consultants, oversight committees, and security people. There was a lot of people involved.

McMoneagle supported Swann's statement, writing:

Contrary to popular belief, and like nearly all experimental projects, [military remote viewing] was never 100 percent successful. However, during its full operational period, I know that we did provide information of critical intelligence value in hundreds of very specific cases. On scores of occasions, this information was also described within government documents as being unavailable from any other source(s).

Also contrary to popular belief, the program operated throughout its history under the very watchful eyes of numerous oversight committees, which were both scientific and governmental. During the seventeen and a half years it ran, it provided support to nearly all of the United States intelligence agencies. Its very existence was approved on a year-to-year basis by these committees and agencies, and it was judged and funded not only by its successes, but according to how well it operated within the rules and scientific boundaries set by those agencies and oversight committees.

> Any suggestion that the program operated loosely, or with a lack of control, is pure bunk.[2]

According to the Psi Spies, there are more than 120 boxes containing the unit's operational files, most of which is still kept secret from the public.

Asked why the Psi Spies story had not been told earlier, Morehouse explained: "Most people take very seriously the fact they have been read onto a program, particularly in the [intelligence] community that we are talking about. It's very seldom that somebody breaks rank and steps forward to say, 'Let me tell you a story.' Most of them will go to the grave knowing what they know or they might just tell a story in small circles."

The secrecy involved created a serious problem in trying to reconstruct the Psi Spies story. Public statements and published pieces from former members appear sketchy and even contradictory. It has proven very difficult to separate the truth from cover stories, faulty memories, and the unwillingness to divulge what many still consider military secrets. This situation is compounded by the spin and disinformation made public by the government in an effort to discredit remote viewing technology in the public mind.

Swann was quick to point out that he has no classified material in his files. He too said that anything that might have impinged on national security was quickly taken away by the remote viewing sponsors. "When the clients came for their meetings, they walked off with every piece of paper, and even the pencils and pens we used. So, I don't have a shred of classified materials," he said.

But Swann did hold on to his remote viewing techniques. "These techniques are proprietary to me—I own them," he said. "It's in my contracts, and there were a lot of them. I insisted on that. That's why I did not become an employee of SRI because then SRI would have owned what I developed. So I acted only as a consultant and I maintained control of this for whatever it was worth."

By 1988, Hal Puthoff had left SRI, and Swann was becoming engrossed in the finer points of remote viewing and tired of the constant testing, which had changed little from the 1970s. "In 1988, I decided to take a year off, so I resigned," said Swann. "Then I took the next year off and it all vanished." Swann was never again to work with the Psi Spies as a military unit.

Signed secrecy agreements are also a part of Swann's background. "I signed agreements that said I would not break open the programs I worked on and I have to be a man of my word," he said. "But I can certainly talk about what I have in my possession."

Another technique that proved successful in increasing the accuracy of remote viewing was the use of multiple viewers against a single target. An example of this can be found in the witnesses to an automobile wreck. If there are 10 witnesses, investigators usually get 10 different versions of the accident. But a synthesis, or combining, of the witnesses accounts will provide a version of the accident that nears 100 percent accuracy.

Hence in remote viewing, if six or eight viewers are given the same target and their accounts are combined, the accuracy rate is greatly enhanced.

Morehouse said that the remote viewers in any given group were not told their target, so as to act as a control group. The control group is kept in the dark because once you become aware of something, you may lose many other subtle things, he explained. "For example, let's say you were looking for a camouflaged sniper. You notice the trees, the birds, the grass, but you don't see the sniper. But if the sniper is called to your attention, you focus on that and might miss other things—like a second sniper."

During the early 1980s, the Psi Spies conducted their operations using altered states of consciousness to facilitate the remote viewing. It required about six years to go from hit-and-miss remote viewing operations to a calibrated team approach, utilizing soldiers who had demonstrated some natural psychic ability.

A typical early operation went similar to this: At first, a monitor—often another unit member—sat at a desk next to the viewer, who was lying on a bed in a small, dark room. A dim red lamp allowed the monitor to take notes after the viewer had reached an altered state. Later, electrodes, hooked up to a remote voltmeter, were affixed to the viewer. The unit commander and operations officer often would monitor this operation. Both the viewer and the facilitator were equipped with earphones and a microphone. The facilitator watched the voltmeter specifically looking for a whole body polarity shift. When a 180-degree voltage polarity shift from head to toe occurred, this almost always indicated that the viewer was in the desired altered state. At that point, the facilitator simply instructed the viewer to "Move to the target area" or "There is a person you need to locate," or something to that effect. As a control measure, the viewer was never provided with specific information about the target.

Various other consciousness-altering techniques were tried, such as Transcendental Meditation. Morehouse said they even tried out-of-body travel, but couldn't duplicate it on demand. McMoneagle said he gave up on trying to control his out-of-body experiences and concentrated on the more controllable remote viewing.

One of the major problems with the use of altered states was that the viewer was never aware of his dimensional orientation to the target. For example, a viewer would refer to "the room next door." But satellite imagery would indicate that the "room next door" was really in a building down the street. Worse yet, a viewer might not even be aware of his own orientation—sometimes reporting information from what would be an upside-down position if one's body were actually present at the site.

And there was another factor: Remote viewing became an experience rather than work. Riley said the military was not paying for soldiers to have an experience. They paid them to collect information, to produce intelligence. They wanted results.

"When you go out of body, it is such an awe-inspiring experience that the viewers would forget about their mission," he said. "I mean when you are able to move out among the stars or see other dimensions, that Soviet rocket launcher seems pretty tame. You lose interest in it real quick."

By the mid-1980s, another unanticipated side of remote viewing was discovered: Someone was looking back at the Psi Spies as they worked.

The Psi Spies unit first became aware of this situation from Robert Monroe, a former advertising executive whose studies of the out-of-body experience led to the creation of the Monroe Institute for Applied Sciences in Faber, Virginia. The Monroe Institute, according to the Psi Spies, was used to screen potential remote viewers and to acquaint them with psychic experiences.

Monroe was experimenting with out-of-body and other altered states of consciousness when he realized that three people were with him. He was afraid because he didn't know who they were. One of these three was a woman who seemed particularly powerful. They were trying to probe his mind. Having never had this experience before, Monroe felt very vulnerable. So, he called upon the Psi Spies for help.[3]

Having been alerted to the existence of foreign remote viewers, the Psi Spies joined in a game of psychic cat and mouse with the other side. "We would go looking for them and they would come looking for us," Morehouse said. "Gradually, a sense of camaraderie grew. They were experimenting and learning just like us. We thought of them more as an opposing team than an enemy."

The Psi Spies had trouble locating the others at first. But once contact had been made, the Soviet remote viewers—called "extrasensors"—began looking for the Psi Spies.

In this time of Psi Spies vs. Psi Spies, America's remote viewers learned much about the Soviet team.

They too had started by using altered states of consciousness to achieve success in remote viewing. But to attain this mental state, the GRU (Soviet Military Intelligence) used a variety of techniques including drugs, electric shock, and even sensory deprivation. Such harsh methods produced ruthless, but less effective, remote viewers for the Soviets.

"This was their downfall," said Riley. "We heard they killed several young people trying this, and it also reduced their remote viewing capability because remote viewing requires alert concentration. When a person is on drugs, their remote viewing capability is diminished."

Unlike the GRU, the Soviet KGB laboriously screened more than a million people in an effort to locate "super naturals," persons with the greatest amount of psychic power. These super psychics became the Soviet Union's Psi Spies, sometimes assigned to seek out their Western counterparts.

Riley said that the situation became bizarre, even for the Psi Spies unit. So they didn't speak about it outside the unit. "Our commander knew but not the oversight committees," recalled Riley. He added:

> And in the Soviet Union, they were scared to tell their bosses that they have been uncovered. They were afraid that their program would be closed down. I guess we were afraid of the same thing. So we had a sort of gentleman's agreement with our opposite numbers—we'd both drop in and look around on occasion, but neither of us would tell the bosses.

On one occasion, Morehouse personally remote viewed Soviet extrasensors and discovered that the Soviets had developed a countermeasure to psychic spying. He described his experience this way:

I went to one of the remote viewing rooms and listened to the Eagles' "Desperado" through headphones for my cool down session. Then I was read the mission coordinates, closed my eyes, and within seconds, I landed crouched on a rooftop. It was freezing cold with snow covering everything as far as I could see. The wind was blowing in waves, piercing right through me. I was on top of a three-story building which was part of a compound somewhere deep inside Russia. It was surrounded by forests and farmland. Huge drifts of white snow were piled high against everything standing upright. I closed my eyes and tried to sense anything which triggered my psychic interest. Presently I was drawn to a small outbuilding near the edge of the compound. I was getting numb from the cold. I was told later that, back at Fort Meade, I actually had goose bumps on my body.

I willed myself to move through the building's wall and instantly was relieved by the warmth of the interior. After a few moments basking in the warmth, I began exploring the building and found it had six rooms surrounded by a main room in the center. There was a large, barren entranceway and a stone fireplace. The center room obviously was a lounge or meeting room of sorts. The building was deserted but I definitely felt it was an important place. I told my monitor that there was nobody home and he suggested that I move backward in time a day or two. "I haven't learned how to do that," I objected. He said, "Dave, its as easy as moving room to room. Do it the same way—just concentrate on it, think yourself into yesterday."

So I concentrated and, at first, nothing happened except I started to feel foolish. But then I saw a man sitting at a desk in the hallway near the front entrance. He was reading a worn and raggedy paper under a small light. When I placed my phantom hand on the man's back, I sensed a lonely and forgotten spirit, a life nearly over, and remembrances of times past clouded with age and vodka. I left the man in peace and moved on down the hallway. The man hadn't been there before so I knew that I had shifted in time. I concentrated again, thinking about moving in time. The world started to move in reverse, slowly at first but gaining speed. Faster and faster it moved until everything became a kaleidoscope of colors and speed. I became dizzy and dropped to my knees. "Slow it down and you'll be all right," I heard the monitor say. I did and the dizziness passed.

I saw people working at their desks. Some talked on the telephone, some simply were doing paperwork, and still others were conferring with each other. The offices seemed to be for administration, not remote viewing. But there was a strong sense of heat apparent to me. The heat interested me and I began making sketches of what I was seeing. But I also began experiencing trouble bending my legs and moving my head. The sensation became stronger as I drew closer to a small, flat, box-like device mounted high up on a wall. There was a bright light coming from it. It was like staring into a car's headlight. It felt like all my cells were tingling. The closer I came, the weaker I felt. It was like being Superman around Kryptonite.

I became uneasy and returned to my physical body. Later that day, I compared my sketches with some Mel Riley made during his session and they were identical. He too had seen the box on the wall, as had others. After I left, they had really looked into the box. It turned out to be some type of energy shield or screen, which the Soviets had been working on for years. This device recognized all of the familiar forms of energy—extra low frequency, radio, television and the like. But when it encountered a form it didn't recognize, it sounded an alarm and emitted a low-frequency wave designed to disrupt and confuse the psychic signal. The Soviets had mounted some of these shields in rooms where highly-sensitive meetings took place or where their extrasensors were operating.

Following unsuccessful early searches for their opposite numbers, the Psi Spies realized that the extrasensors were not only operating in Russia, but moving about in the United States. They became concerned that the Soviets might not be content with simply remote viewing their foreign opponents—that they might have a much darker agenda.

Riley said unit members became convinced that the Soviets were experimenting with psychotronics, particularly the ability to kill or disable at a distance. He recalled that sometime in 1984, a representative of the U.S. Secret Service came to the Psi Spies unit and expressed the concern that the Soviets might make a psychotronic attack on then-President Ronald Reagan, causing a heart attack or worse.

Based on this concern, the unit began their series of remote-viewing sessions, but could not substantiate any part of the psychic heart attack story. The Secret Service was told that the Soviet extrasensors could watch President Reagan all the time. They knew where he was and what he was doing, but they couldn't do anything to him physically. Secret Service agents were relieved at this information and were not heard from again.

But the Psi Spies mounted an offensive against their opponents.

According to several unit members, the Psi Spies ran a series of remote viewing sessions against the interlopers. They first remote viewed Robert Monroe's out-of-body event to see what was happening. Sure enough, they quickly realized that three people were present observing. One of them was a woman.

The psychic spies mentally followed the trio back to their physical bodies. This was not truly following them, it was more akin to shifting their attention to the location of their bodies. The Psi Spies found that the trio's physical bodies were near Moscow. Each one was in a separate 5-foot-by-5-foot room at a remote compound.

Riley recalled:

> We decided that they might be vulnerable to a concentrated force. It was just a hunch, but after a while we noticed that they always seemed to operate independently. They didn't even use a monitor. They were natural psychics and I guess they felt they didn't need any supervision out there. We figured that if we could put four or five of us in their face all at once, it should scare the shit out of them. And it worked.

The unit members concentrated on the woman, who seemed to be their opponent's most powerful viewer. Monroe had gotten the impression that her name was Inga Arnyet. This was confirmed by the Psi Spies.

An entire six-man Psi Spies team concentrated on the female Soviet psychic. The unit commander acted as monitor. The military-trained viewers were excited—this resembled the tactics of an infantry rifle squad moving into battle. They each made their own last-minute preparations: Some drank coffee, some rested to music, but all tried to clear their minds.

At a given time, they took their positions in the remote viewing rooms and the commander began a countdown over the speaker system. One by one, the Psi Spies psychically slipped away into the ether.

Using the same coordinates, they assembled in the Soviet compound. First one, then another, until all six members were there, aware of each other only as nearby translucent figures. Even though they appeared as ghosts to each other, the numbers were comforting.

Moving down a large hallway, the group found two men in an office. One man sat at a large desk writing on sheets of paper. As he finished each sheet, the second man would collect it and place it neatly on a nearby stack of papers. There was no sign of the extrasensors.

The Psi Spies then split up, inspecting nearby offices. Suddenly the female extrasensor was located. According to Riley, the woman became very upset when confronted by the team because she had never expected anything such as this. With the team collectively viewing her, she lost all concentration. She was rendered ineffective as a remote viewer.

Following the operation, the Psi Spies team looked at each other. It was time to return home. As though they were helium balloons released, the group shot into the air one by one and faded from sight. It was a spectacle that none had seen before because, until then, all sessions had been conducted individually.

Back home, the unit members were filled with a sense of pride and accomplishment. Thinking back over the mission, Morehouse said, "That was a brave bunch of folks. I know grown men—Rangers—who would have wet their pants doing that. They all did it as though it was just another cup of coffee."

Lyn Buchanan described his confrontation with a psychic spy from China:

> I was doing a practice target once. The target was a museum, somewhere—don't even remember much about it anymore. But in that session, I was looking around, describing what was in the cases, who was there, etc. In a normal CRV session, you reach the target at a static moment, and everything is frozen in time. You have to give a command to get the viewer moving in real time. But we hadn't done that. I was just looking at and describing everything and everyone. One of the people I described was looking directly at me. She was a young Chinese girl. She wasn't moving, but there was something different about her. I looked away, but got the feeling that she actually was looking directly at me. I looked back, and she realized that I had seen her, so she quickly turned and disappeared. That wasn't supposed to happen. The shock of it took me

out of session and I told my monitor what had just happened. He said, "Go back into session and follow her to see where she went." I did, and the session then took us to an isolated place in the mountains, where there were a bunch of very young children, all working some kind of sessions (not CRV or any RV that I recognized), and reporting back what they were finding. They were China's "Psi Spies."

Having found the place, I "pegged the location" so I could return. Over the next few months, I got to know the girl who had been spying on me, and we started up a strange, mental friendship. She was 13 years old, and was about to be retired from the spying unit because of her age. I didn't understand that, because she was very good at what she did. It was only years later that I learned that the Chinese retire their psychic spies when they reach puberty.

I kept up with her after she left her unit, and one day, found her going to work from her home, riding an extremely crowded streetcar in a very large city. She acknowledged my presence, but let me know that this was not a part of her life anymore and was, in fact, a part of her life she would like to forget. I never bothered her again.

She had never told her unit about me, and after the original session, I never told my unit about her. It was a simple friendship which didn't include spying on each other's country or revealing secrets of any kind. In our session-based meetings, we had talked about childhood in China, and everyday life in the U.S. She had been mainly interested in Hollywood stars, New York City, and American boys. I had learned early on that she didn't want to talk to me about her work, and I had honored that. As for the rest of our unit, I think that they did some sessions on the Chinese psi-spy effort overall.

After such incidents, the Psi Spies talked a lot about how to block or confuse the foreign remote viewers. There was talk about building their own energy shields, similar to a Faraday (copper) Cage, and things along those lines. But unit members knew that such things, though disruptive, could not truly prevent remote viewing, so they soon moved on to other things. Buchanan explained:

> One of the reasons that CRV was so good is because there is virtually no protection against it. You can put up "attractors" and "distractors" in your work place, but that only helps against inexperienced CRVers. The Soviets were not ignorant of this fact, and sometimes held their most top secret meetings in whorehouses and/or near such things as carnivals or more exciting but less classified targets, etc.
>
> One day, I was monitoring a viewer who suddenly looked up at me and said, "There is protection at this target. I can't get through the protection to get the information we need." I don't know where the idea came from, but I asked, "Well, if the protection weren't there, what would you find?" The viewer looked back his paper and said, "Uh, I'd find..." and started viewing the target, in spite of the protection. Believe it or not, that

simple dodge got us through many a time when "protection against Psi Spies" had been applied to some target.

In fact, we found that a person who has gotten someone to protect him or her psychically wouldn't do so unless they believe in psychic protection. That very belief makes them lower their own natural defenses, and in the process, actually makes them easier to view. We loved it when some foreign political or military leader would get psychic protection. In effect, it made them sitting ducks for the unit's CRVers. Instead of getting the information we needed in a couple of hour-long sessions, 20 minutes later, we were done, kicking back and drinking coffee.

Riley recalled that someone even came up with the idea of remote viewing while wearing a Ronald Reagan mask. "We figured the Russians would freak out, thinking, 'My God! The American president himself is remote viewing us!'" Riley laughed.

Despite the advances made in remote viewing during the 1980s, it remained difficult to sell Pentagon officials on this novel means of intelligence gathering, although Ingo Swann claimed that almost every intelligence agency contributed funds to the Psi Spies unit at one time or another:

In fact, I don't know exactly where the money came from because I think two or three agencies kicked in their share. And they all shared the data eventually anyway, provided that no one told them where it came from.

> The only group I don't think kicked in was the Navy, and that could only have been because they had their own thing going.

Swann recalled one of the many presentations he made during this period:

> I was supposed to give a 10-minute presentation in this windowless room deep in the Pentagon. It was very structured. The actual presentation was going to be six minutes with four minutes for questions and answers. The staff people gave us only 10 minutes because they didn't want us "wasting" the time of these generals. So, I hurried my presentation and finished in five minutes. The room was filled with brass and their aides along with some congressional observers and, of course, all these security men with guns.
>
> Well, after I finished everyone looked to this head honcho, some general. And he said very quietly, "What's your schedule, Mr. Swann?" and I told him, "I'm at your disposal." He turned to an aide and said, "Clear my calendar." Everyone else took the cue and we spent another two hours in discussion. And, as you know, our funding came through.

In late 1984, Gen. Stubblebine retired and Maj. Gen. Harry E. Soyster took command of the Army's INSCOM. Soyster apparently did not have the same interest in the Psi Spies unit as Stubblebine.

According to the Psi Spies, in 1985 the unit came under the control of Dr. Jack Verona, then head of the Defense Intelligence Agency's (DIA) Scientific and Technical

Intelligence Directorate. From that time onward, the Psi Spies were part of the DIA organization. The unit code name underwent several changes: GRILL FLAME became CENTER LANE, another computer-generated name, then SUN STREAK, and finally STAR GATE.

Officially, the Psi Spies were never supposed to be operational, despite the active missions they undertook. On the books, it was only a research program. This meant the Psi Spies were considered human guinea pigs, and thus came under the scrutiny of human use protocols. After revelations of past wrongdoing, particularly the use of LSD on unsuspecting military personnel, the Pentagon has been very concerned about the use of humans for research purposes.

The Psi Spies unit thus became one of only two programs within the military that was perceived as using humans for experimental purposes.

One member of the Human Use Committee, which acted as an oversight group for the Psi Spies program, was Navy Capt. Paul Tyler, who was also a medical doctor. Dr. Tyler was the former director of the Armed Forces Radiobiology Research Laboratory at Bethesda, Maryland.

"I had been at briefings at the Agency [CIA] regarding GRILL FLAME," recalled Dr. Tyler.[4]

Dr. Tyler mentioned the covert use of LSD as one of the reasons for the creation of the committee. Another he mentioned was the infamous Tuskegee Study, in which a large number of poor, southern, black men were studied to examine the long-term effects of syphilis, long after penicillin became known as a cure. He said, "Those people were not treated and this program was run by the Public Health Service with good intent. They didn't know what happens with long-term effects, so they decided to find out. But that was a real stink."

The Tuskegee Study and the revelations of drug testing, produced a demand that programs be designed to ensure ethics in the use of human subjects.

"They passed a group of laws," said Dr. Tyler, "and all of the federal agencies developed their own set of laws and regulations for using human subjects."

Dr. Tyler explained that, if humans were being used in experimentation, the law required a Human Use Committee, usually composed of a minimum of five members representing the local community, the scientific community, the legal community, and a person unconnected with whichever program is being scrutinized.

Upon learning of the Psi Spies, Dr. Tyler said he was drawn to the subject of remote viewing.

"It was fascinating. It works," he stated flatly, and continued:

> It was very interesting. I've always wanted to sit down and analyze myself to find why I have such an open mind. I basically had the traditional scientific background, training, but I have always been interested in, well, weird things. I have always been more interested in why people don't get sick than in why they do get sick. Medicine studies sick people all the time, but they never study well people. They never

study why people stay well or get well and that is where my interest lies and, in many respects, that's weird.... I think the most important aspect of any disease is the patient's mental and belief system. If you don't think you're going to get sick, you probably won't, even though you are exposed to the tuberculosis bacteria. The combination of your genetics and your belief systems will have a major influence. Therefore, when somebody tells me they can go to some far distant point with their mind, I'm at least open to that.

Of course, in general, there are no bigger bigots than the scientists. They're afraid. I don't know why. To me, the scientific approach is "Show me." If I say I can fly, you should not call me a liar, you should say, "Prove it." And if the person can fly, then you change your belief system. If they can't, then you know you were right in your belief system. I don't think people can fly, but to say that is a dumb idea is totally unscientific. Yet, you find most scientists are very opinionated about what they think.

Asked, based on his knowledge of the Psi Spies unit, if he was satisfied that remote viewing really works, Dr. Tyler replied confidently, "Absolutely!"

Asked how it works, he turned pensive. He mused:

That's the $64,000 question. There may be several things involved. Take one classic physics test. If you send two photons, a pair, one goes this way and the other goes that way, there's good experimental evidence that no matter how far distant these photons go, the spin of the photons are always opposite. You can guarantee the spin by sending the photon through a magnet. Let's say I send one through a magnet and make sure I have a left spin on it. You go over and measure the other and it's a right spin. Every time.

This is a well-known experiment, but it's not well accepted, even by physicists, because it counters locality. And everybody thinks cause and effect is a local effect, not one for distance.

What we have here is communication between the photons, an instantaneous communication at distance. They can be miles apart, but the minute you measure the spin on one, the other becomes known. And if you change the spin on one, the other changes also. So, how does this photon instantaneously know what its partner is doing? We don't know, but it does. Now that is pure known physics although a lot of physicists ignore it.

Dr. Tyler said that something akin to Einstein's unified field theory might explain remote viewing: "If we are on a single plane of existence and we can rise to a higher plane, now we can look down and know what happened behind us and you can see a little bit ahead."

He gave the analogy of a phonograph needle as the point where we are in our reality. If you raise the needle up a bit, you can see beyond your single groove. You can see the entire record, both forward and backwards. He noted, "You might have a universal consciousness that a lot of people talk about, not only New Age folks, but the mystics. They all talk about a universal consciousness that has all the information, and at times, we can tap into this universal knowledge."

Dr. Tyler said humans are constantly learning more about themselves and their environment. "There is no reason to suppose that we know all there is to know at this point," he said. He went on to explain:

> We are still thinking of the brain as a computer. We're looking at the structure. We're looking into the structure. We're looking at the physiology, we're studying the electron flows. We're looking at the circuitry. We stimulate here and see a signal come out there. And we think we are learning something about the brain. But this tells us nothing about the brain's content.
>
> We used to think that the brain had cells continuously dying its entire life and that when you lost a function, you lost it. Now we've learned that the brain has plasticity, that areas can pick up functions that have been lost in another area which was damaged.
>
> You can take a computer and study all you want about the structure and the wiring, the setup and the boards inside, but that will never tell you what the program is. I feel it is the same with the human brain. I think we haven't begun to tap the minimum capabilities of the mind, which can do tremendous things both with the body and out of the body.

Dr. Tyler said very few persons, even within the military, knew about the Psi Spies. He said:

I certainly didn't discuss it with very many people because I was new and things were classified at that time. Most of the people I worked with didn't even have the clearances to know about it, even if they wanted to. And most of the people I worked with in the Navy were pretty conservative. There were even fewer open-minded people elsewhere. I think the Air Force had even less. I think the Army had the most open-minded people. They had a somewhat pragmatic approach. They said, "Well, I don't know if that works, but if it works, then we need to be studying it."

We got every view across the spectrum, from "It's all hogwash," to "It's the end-all." But actually there were very few at the "end-all" end. The majority were at the skeptical level.

And I'd like to say that I'm a skeptic about a lot of things, but most people who claim to be skeptics are really biased against something. They're not real skeptics. Skeptics say "I don't know, but I'll look at it."

Ingo Swann also was at a loss to explain the mechanics of remote viewing. "I never did dwell on that because my mandate was to provide a useful tool, not to explain it," Swann said. Pressed for his theory, he said, "It's obvious that at some subconscious level we are all connected to the universe and everything in it. But since we did not need to explain how this could be done, only that it could be done and that people could do it for some profitable purpose, that's all we needed to know."

Despite the "plausibility" of the remote viewing phenomenon, credibility remained elusive for the Psi Spies. Not that the other intelligence services weren't quick to make use of their information—it was just that no one wanted to acknowledge how this information was obtained.

The Psi Spies unit became a military mistress: Everyone wanted to court them for their information, but no one wanted to be associated with them. It became apparent that, no matter what information was obtained through remote viewing for the military, they would never be taken seriously. At this point, Riley and Morehouse each said, several of the Psi Spies agreed to go under the table.

The Psi Spies commanders wanted to keep all information close to their chest, because they thought it was a political hot potato. They were afraid of being censured or ostracized. Therefore, much of the information gained through remote viewing was not being disseminated to other agencies.

To bypass this roadblock, some unit members simply called up people they knew in other agencies and passed along information in the form of conversation. Morehouse said that these recipients knew about the Psi Spies unit and would consider the information accordingly, sometimes even utilizing it for their own missions.

The year 1988 proved to be a watershed for the Psi Spies unit: That year, as the Psi Spies continued to run operations against their Soviet extrasensor counterparts, remote viewing came under scathing attack in a National Academy of Sciences report, and the unit came under the scrutiny of Secretary of Defense Frank Carlucci.

In 1984, the Army Research Institute (ARI) asked the National Academy of Sciences (NAS) to form a committee through the National Research Council (NRC) to investigate various techniques that were claimed to enhance human performance. These techniques spanned a wide range of topics including sleep-assisted instruction, biofeedback, stress management, neurolinguistic programming, and parapsychology.

The committee took nearly three years for its study at a reported cost of $500,000, an amount, according to Col. Alexander, comparable to that spent each year from all sources on psi research.

In June 1985, the first meeting of the NRC's Committee on Techniques for Enhancement of Human Performance adjourned. The committee was chaired by John A. Swets of Bolt, Beranek, and Newman Inc. of Cambridge, Massachusetts, best known as the firm that produced the controversial acoustical study for the House Select Committee on Assassinations that indicated a second gunman in the John F. Kennedy assassination.

In regards to parapsychology, their report, published in 1988, concluded the following:

> The committee finds no scientific justification from research conducted over a period of 130 years for the existence of parapsychological phenomena. It therefore concludes that there is no reason for direct involvement by the Army at this time. We do recommend, however, that research in certain areas be

monitored, including work by the Soviets and the best work in the United States.[5]

Ray Hyman, of the department of psychology at the University of Oregon, an ardent debunker of parapsychology and editorial board member of the Committee for the Scientific Investigation of Claims of the Paranormal (CSICOP), managed to secure the position of chairman of the group's Subcommittee on Parapsychology. Hyman was particularly pointed in his criticisms of the remote viewing studies at SRI.

In an introduction to the committee's section on "paranormal phenomena," the report's tone was dismissive and contemptuous, focusing on the most far-out psi possibilities:

> The claimed phenomena and applications range from the incredible to the outrageously incredible. The "antimissile time warp," for example, is supposed to somehow deflect attack by nuclear warheads so that they will transcend time and explode among the ancient dinosaurs, thereby leaving us unharmed but destroying many dinosaurs (and, presumably, some of our evolutionary ancestors). Other psychotronic weapons, such as the "hyperspatial nuclear howitzer," are claimed to have equally bizarre capabilities. Many of the sources cite the claim that Soviet psychotronic weapons were responsible for the 1976 outbreak of Legionnaires' disease, as well as the 1963 sinking of the nuclear submarine Thresher.[6]

The report attempted to indicate the "fairness" of its restricted investigation by stating: "The phenomena are real and important in the minds of the proponents, so we attempt to evaluate them fairly."[7]

The report did address the long-standing controversy concerning the existence of paranormal phenomena, admitting that proponents, including some scientists, firmly believe that psychic functioning has been demonstrated "several times over." "At the same time, most scientists do not believe that psi exists," the report continued.[8]

Harking back to the "chicken or the egg" argument, the report cited a 1985 paper by J. Palmer entitled "An Evaluative Report on the Current Status of Parapsychology," which stated, "[W]e cannot argue that a given effect has a paranormal cause until we have an adequate theory of paranormality."[9]

However, Palmer admitted that certain anomalies—defined as "a statistically significant deviation from chance expectation that cannot be readily be explained by existing scientific theories"[10]—have been demonstrated.

Palmer, therefore, preferred to consider demonstrated psi functioning as a scientific anomaly rather than proof of paranormal phenomena. "We tend to agree with Palmer on this matter..." stated the research council's report.[11]

But other credible people familiar with the committee's work have raised objections to this conclusion.

Dr. Paul Tyler said:

> From my experience with the National Academy of Sciences, you tell me the answer you want and I will find a committee that will give it to you. I can sandbag

> a committee any way you want, it just depends on the group of people you want.
>
> The majority of the people there had their minds made up before they even went there. They thought, "This stuff doesn't work, so I will just listen to them but I already know that the answer is."

Dr. Tyler compared the NAS report to the 1969 Condon Report on UFOs. Dr. Edward Condon, at the behest of the U.S. Air Force, published the results of his study of the UFO phenomenon. In later years it was established that Condon conveyed an image of impartial investigation while systematically debunking the entire issue.

Dr. Tyler said that the NRC report went through a similar series of "filters" that prevented them from a full and truthful assessment of psychic functioning. He explained:

> These filters have to do with our perceptions and language. We often don't communicate in the same language. A good example of this would be if you asked me, "What do you do to relax?" and I answered, "Well, I go home and sit in my chair." If all you had experienced in the past had been straight-backed wooden chairs, you'd think I was crazy; that is, if you had never sat in an overstuffed, reclining chair.
>
> And the irony of this is that the most solid filters are among people who claim to be scientific.

Dr. Richard S. Broughton, a former president of the international Parapsychological Association, agreed that the committee was highly subjective and condemned the use of Ray Hyman as chairman of the Subcommittee on Parapsychology. Broughton wrote, "The [National Research Council] declined any assistance from parapsychologists and instead appointed Hyman to head the parapsychology subcommittee. No one with parapsychology research experience sat on the committee....Hyman is a founding member of ...[CSICOP] the advocacy group widely known for its crusade against parapsychology."[12]

"Did the Army get what it paid for—an objective and unbiased assessment?" asked Broughton. "Certainly not where parapsychology was concerned."[13]

Col. Alexander, then-manager of the Technology Integration Office of the Army's Material Command, along with Maj. Gen. Stubblebine, made presentations to the committee:

> I was a briefer to the NRC committee members as they researched the EHP [Enhancing Human Performance] Report. I have served as chief of Advanced Human Technology for the Army Intelligence and Security Command [1982–84] and, during the preparation of the EHP Report, was director of the Advanced Systems Concepts Office at the U.S. Army Laboratory Command. I believe I am personally well qualified to review the committee's findings.[14]

Alexander took the committee to task in an article entitled "A Challenge to the Report," published in the March/April 1989 issue of *New Realities* magazine.

He, too, compared the NRC's report to that of Condon's, stating, "Predictably, the National Academy of Sciences convened a panel immediately after the [Condon] report appeared that endorsed the report's findings and its methodology....During the two decades since its publication, the findings of the Condon Report have been conveniently cited by anyone wishing to stop UFO research...."[15]

Alexander noted that the NRC report seemed internally inconsistent:

> On the one hand, they had disclaimed, in one broad stroke, over a century's worth of psychic investigation; on the other, they were concluding that the best of that discredited research should be monitored. Did they, or did they not, support further parapsychological research?
>
> Obviously, the findings and final report of the NRC's committee are not very comforting or acceptable to those of us who have worked in the field of enhancing human performance.[16]

And he was not alone in this assessment. He noted:

> The...committee's conclusions have been denounced by no less than the board of directors of the Parapsychological Association (PA), Inc.... The PA is an affiliate of the American Association for the Advancement of Science, and membership is attained only by formal approval of its council. The members of the PA were so outraged by what they considered to be distortions and outright errors in the...report that they took the unusual step of commissioning a team to analyze the parts of the...report referring to the work of PA members and to prepare a rebuttal.[17]

The parapsychologists' rebuttal stated:

> The...committee's primary conclusion regarding parapsychology is not merely unjustified by their report, it is directly contradicted by the committee's admission that it can offer no plausible alternatives. This concession, coming as it does from a committee whose principal evaluators of parapsychology were publicly committed to a negative verdict at the outset of their investigation, actually constitutes a strong source of support for the conclusion that parapsychology has identified genuine scientific anomalies.[18]

Alexander echoed Broughton and others in criticizing the committee for placing Ray Hyman, a public critic of psi research, in charge of the parapsychological subcommittee. He pointed out that it was Hyman, along with another acknowledged skeptic, psychologist Dr. George Lawrence of the Army Research Institute, who in 1972 had effectively killed government research funding for the Stanford Research Institute at the time they were beginning their work on remote viewing. Fortunately, the CIA picked up the research.[19]

Alexander concluded: "[I]t seems clear that Lawrence [who also briefed the committee] and then Hyman and James Alcock...proceeded on an intentional path to discredit the work in parapsychology. The background of the authors, as well as their "findings" speak for themselves in this regard."[20]

To further support his contention that the NRC committee was weighted against parapsychology from the beginning, Alexander pointed to the fact that committee chairman Swets had asked that a committee-requested report, which turned out to be favorable to parapsychology, be withdrawn because it was not of "high quality." Alexander argued, "...I see no basis for such a questionable request."[21]

To further illustrate that the committee took no notice of anything outside their preconceived worldview, Alexander told the following anecdote:

> I had Cleve Backster under contract at the time, so when it came time for the NRC to do their thing...we said "Why don't we do a demonstration for them?" It turned out very interesting. I got there ahead of time to make sure the system was working. It was a test where we put white blood cells in a little test tube and had electrodes connected to an EEG [electroencephalograph] machine with a signal amplifier. With this you would get a chart recording of the cells. What we were finding was that there was a high degree of correlation between the emotional state of the individual who donated the cells and the chart recording, even if the individual was in another room.
>
> So on this particular day, I had donated some white cells and we hooked them up to the EEG, just to make sure that everything was working correctly. The building we were in has two wings, there's Backster's laboratory in one wing and classrooms in the other. We took the majority of the visitors to the classrooms to give them backgrounding, while two others went to the lab to donate cells. I was with Cleve and he was giving a talk that became much longer than we had planned. I said, "Cleve, you've really got to get on with this because these guys want to get moving." I must have

become somewhat agitated because when I got up and started to talk, Cleve's lab assistant ran into the classroom and said, "What happened about a minute ago?" And I replied that that was when I had begun to speak. He said, "Well the graph just went crazy. You're not going to believe this signal!"

So we all went in and you could see on the chart when I started to speak and then, when I came into the lab, the signal dropped off. Again, this is an example of one's cells registering the emotional state of the donor even at a distance. Now this body of scientists, led by Ray Hyman, ran into the lab and pulled the chart recording and looked at it. It didn't take a signals analyst to see there were differences. Here it was.

You can always state positively there is no such thing as a white crow. My point is that it only takes one white crow to prove that all crows aren't black. And here was the white crow. The white crow flew right in front of them and you'll find no mention of it anywhere in their report.

We should worry about the fact that the highest scientific court in the land operated in such a biased and heavy-handed manner, and that there seems to be no channel for appeal or review of their work. What, we may ask, are they afraid of? Is protecting scientific orthodoxy so vital that they must deny evidence and suppress contrary opinion?

> It now appears that the EHP Report, with all of its flaws, will be likewise considered impervious to criticism and [will] be enshrined in the scientific consciousness in a position all too similar to that of the Condon Report.

Another briefer to the NRC's Enhancing Human Performance committee was Dale E. Graff of the Defense Intelligence Agency. Although several Psi Spies said Graff was well aware of the unit's work, he apparently made no mention of the Psi Spies to the committee. Just a year after the remote viewing studies were made public, Graff, identified as a former head of the remote viewing unit, was a guest lecturer on a "psychic cruise."[22]

In 1988, Dr. Jack Verona, the DIA's scientific and technical chief, named Graff to head the Psi Spies unit, according to Riley, Morehouse, and others. According to several unit members, Graff was a civilian who disliked military types because they would not yield quietly to political expediencies.

Also in 1988, Secretary of Defense Carlucci responded to the ongoing Iran-Contra scandal by launching full-scale investigations into any other fringe programs being conducted by the defense department. He found only two—and one of those, Morehouse and Riley noted, was the Psi Spies.

An inspector general's team from the Department of Defense was sent to find out about the unit. Because the unit was supposed to be research only, Morehouse and others said Fern Gauvin proceeded to shred all documents that did not look to be pure research.

Lyn Buchanan explained:

> He was shredding our history. I ran to my desk and phoned the DIA and finally found someone connected to us....I told them what was going on and had them call to talk to Fern. When the phone rang a minute or so later, I went in and got Fern from the shredder. He told me to keep on shredding and when he went into his office to talk on the phone, I shredded a bunch of blank pages, then stuck a screwdriver down into the shredder slot, breaking the machine.

Morehouse said most of what was shredded was "operational stuff," and explained:

> Luckily, several of us held onto copies of our work, particularly the "Enigma Files," which we were just getting into. I would have to say that there was even some "research data," which was fabricated for the IG team. Anyway, they seemed satisfied that we were just a research project and they went away. It was about this time that the unit was placed under civilian control.

After this time, according to the veteran Psi Spies, the unit went downhill. Morehouse said, "You see, in the military, the mission comes first," explained Morehouse. "But once the civilians were in there, politics was everything. Nobody wanted to stick their neck out and the leaders all wanted to curry favor with their superiors, which more and more became selected members of Congress."

He recalled that before the unit was turned over to civilian control, morale was high. The last military commander was Lt. Col. Bill Xenakis, who had once been named "Army Father of the Year."

Morehouse and others said Xenakis insulated the unit from all the turmoil that surrounded its existence. This allowed unit members to concentrate on their work. It was during his tenure that the Psi Spies took on one of their most difficult tasks: helping the CIA to identify a "mole," a counterintelligence agent inside the agency. "We could not have successfully accomplished this mission without absolute military teamwork," recalled Morehouse. "We were a military team, like a regular Army unit. There were no prima donnas." Once the unit was taken from INSCOM and placed under the DIA, things went awry, according to veteran Psi Spies.

The DIA's primary responsibility was for intelligence analysis and reporting, not intelligence collection or operations. No charter existed allowing DIA to conduct intelligence operations; the Psi Spies could not be placed legitimately on DIA books. Because they were connected with the DIA funding of psi research, the unit became the illegitimate child of the Scientific and Technical Intelligence Directorate under Dr. Jack Verona.

Verona, unlike Gen. Odum, reportedly saw the unit as a valuable asset and was very covetous of his new acquisition. Morehouse and others said Verona walked a fine line, maintaining the story that the Psi Spies unit was strictly for research, while allowing psychic operations to continue.

In Washington, a town where information and knowledge equates with power, Verona carefully cultivated connections who could help both him and the unit, said members. "Verona selectively read on all those who could help him, including politicians," said Morehouse. "He did not read on those people who could really have used our intelligence. He had become a politician."

The Psi Spies said Verona took a number of steps to ensure his total control over the unit, including replacing military members of the unit with civilians and appointing a civilian administrator who was acquiescent to Verona. In the military, the mission is paramount, unit members explained—whereas, to civilian government employees, pleasing the boss and getting promotions are paramount. Verona, who continues to work with the government, declined to be interviewed.

In at least one instance, it was clear that certain individuals did not want the effectiveness of the Psi Spies to become known. The unit was told to prepare a report for Congress on the status of its work and its accuracy. Buchanan recalled:

> We did a two-month study of practice sessions, pulling out every single perception in every viewer's summaries and checking them against feedback for accuracy. The results showed conclusively that we had an average accuracy rating of 72.8 percent. Fern saw the data and made me start changing "Ys" to "Ns" in the database until we showed an accuracy rating of 24 percent. I made a copy of the database and changed its name, in order to have a backup copy of the original before changes. What happened to the renamed database I don't know, but I'm sure it is in a box in some warehouse, still undiscovered.

By the end of the 1980s, morale within the Psi Spies unit was at a low ebb. Then came the witches.

Morehouse and others said that shortly after the unit came under civilian control, two women showed up as trainees: Angela and Robin.

Robin had been an entry-level clerk at the DIA, whose mother was a "channeler." Angela's mother, on the other hand, was a regular one-man band. She not only was a "channeler," but also a Tarot card reader, a practitioner of "automatic writing," and a master of the Ouija board. Angela brought all these "skills" to the unit. According to several Psi Spies, Angela worked for some sort of "institute" in Washington on the weekends, giving psychic "readings" for $50 each. Half of the money went back to the institute.

Soon, Dr. Verona was showing up at the Psi Spies unit and obtaining a "reading" from the two women, who the veteran Psi Spies had begun to call "the witches."

According to several of the Psi Spies, the "witches" were never trained in remote viewing structure. Morehouse explained:

> They had never been exposed to any form of discipline. Angela would revert to "automatic writing," saying she could get much better information that way.
>
> As civilians, the two women could not be ordered to perform the job that the taxpayers were paying them to do. So they just did their own little thing—all the civilians. Even the civilian secretary suddenly became a "viewer." We couldn't believe what was happening.

"They just had their own agenda," Mel Riley recalled. "It was their thing. Angela was into channeling and Robin was into Tarot cards. They tried remote viewing. In fact, as I recall, Angela was particularly good when she was willing to put her nose to the grindstone. But I think it was too much work for her."

Morehouse and others said that the "witches" were careful not to leave behind any paperwork from their channeling or Tarot cards sessions. They said the women quickly shredded all paperwork after a session. "It was very convenient," said Morehouse. "If you wanted to go back and question them about a session, there was no record to go back to." Riley said that, if there was any feedback from their work, "we were never told about it."

Morehouse said the DIA most likely would have killed the Psi Spies program about this time except for the Congressmen who were being brought in for psychic "readings." "It was congressional oversight which wouldn't allow it to be killed," he said.

Morehouse, Riley, and others said it is vitally important to understand that Coordinate Remote Viewing, as developed scientifically through a number of years with a structure that had proved operationally successful, was a totally different thing from the channeling and psychic "readings. of the civilians that ended up in control of the unit.

Although the Psi Spies unit existed into the mid-1990s, it was never what it had been throughout the 1980s. "The unit just went downhill," said Riley. "There was only one problem with this: We were still performing operations."

A study of the psi spy operations proved both fascinating and impressive.

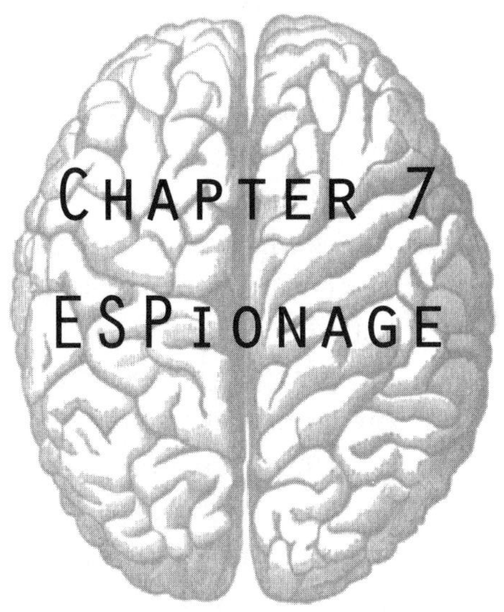

Chapter 7
ESPionage

A perusal of the Psi Spies' remote viewing targets indicated a wide variety of targets—from a simple look at both well-known and not-so-well-known buildings, to viewing a hostile nation's chemical warfare plant.

The following sessions were gleaned from the Psi Spies files, which have been retained by several of the unit's members.

Although targets within the Soviet Union remained the mainstay of the spies' early operational activities, they were not exclusive. The vast majority of missions were highly classified, with little or no feedback being passed back to the unit, as they had to do with military targets within hostile nations.

Before the Psi Spies were used on serious operations, there were the unremitting tests.[1]

One practice session in 1989 produced this report, according to Morehouse:

> Site is a structure. This structure is moderate in size and is rurally located. The site is frequented by people who spend time observing its contents. The site has many boxes and crates which are aligned uniformly for the purpose of display of their contents. The interior of the structure is both modern and old. There are suspended lights and spotlights throughout the interior. There are wooden floors and carpeted floors. Other aspects to the site are that there is a large central room, which is supported in purpose by other smaller rooms. Each of the rooms has cases inside of it. There is a "turnstile" at the site and concepts associated with the word "turnstile" are: tickets, people, theatre, passages, admittance, historic, pay, enjoyment, looking, history, war, music, blades, swords, combat, smoke, and war. Throughout the interior of the site are long objects in large numbers, uniformly positioned. The objects are made of metal and wood—many have brass or gold-colored metals on them.

Briefly stated, this is obviously a description of a museum dedicated to guns and weapons of war. The site was the J.M. Davis Arms & Historical Museum in Claremore, Oklahoma. A promotional piece for the museum stated, "Visitors can walk for a mile through the collection, viewing some relics that date far back, such as a 14th-century, hand-held cannon from the Orient. Along with the guns, the museum also has large collections of antique German steins, Indian artifacts, World War I posters, and a John Rogers statuary, popular during the Victorian period." Many of the guns displayed are decorated with "natural and stained ivory, brass and gold inlays."[2]

In another practice session, Morehouse (the viewer) gave the following description of the Bunker Hill Monument:

> Site is a structure. The structure is made of stone or concrete. The dimensions of the structure are that it rises sharply from relatively flat sides or base supports....The structure is somewhat central to its surroundings. It is used as a rallying point of sorts (AOL/S like a library, city hall, theater), it is something used or seen regularly....The purpose of the site seems to [be] related to art or remembrance of some past event or person in history. The site is meant to preserve the memory of the event or person. There were perceptions of war, opposing forces in facing lines or ranks. There were trees, ramparts, embattlements, smoke, and haze. I think the structure is some kind of war memorial.

The Bunker Hill Monument and the Davis Gun Museum were only two of several hundred target sites within the files of the Psi Spies unit that were used for training purposes.

An early remote viewing operation is described in a "GRILL FLAME Program Session Report" marked "Top Secret" and dated August 1, 1980. It stated: "This report documents a remote viewing session conducted in compliance with a request for information on a target of interest. The mission was to describe a tent at a designated intersection at Teheran, Iran."[3]

The report stated that the remote viewers' impressions of the target were only provided as raw intelligence data and "as such have not been subjected to any intermediate analysis, evaluation or collation." It further warned that the "interpretation and use of the information provided is the responsibility of the requester."[4]

Also, in this particular session, the remote viewer was cued by the use of a street map of Teheran. During the remote viewing session, the viewer got these impressions:

> I have an impression of a...it's a sidewalk...food concession...on the curb...there was a display next to the building...metal objects, artifacts, brass...I see...a kiosk...there's something green after that...I think it was some kind of vegetation, to the west of the structure...[the monitor said "Let's try positioning over the target. Move up in the air and look down obliquely at the target...Tell me what, the things you've told me about, tell me what they look like from this angle."] The food concession looks like it has a...canvas cover...parasol, cover, sun cover...cover from adjacent building sticks out over sidewalk.... But I see an entryway.[5]

In this particular report were handwritten notes, marked "user comments," which were apparently feedback from whomever requested the RV session. From the comments, it appeared that the viewer did a very good job: "Viewer appeared to have independently identified the tent known to exist on the SW corner of intersection," was the first comment. The next comment indicated the viewer's measurements were close to correct. "Size of the tent: Viewer speaks of the 'concession place' being 4–5 feet wide and 8–9 feet long—our data is that the tent is approximately 2 meters wide (6 feet) and 4 meters (12 feet) long." The third comment read, "Viewer's observation of something to the west being green is supported by the trees to the NW of the intersection in the embassy compound. This, however, may have been discernible from the cueing photograph."[6]

The final remark in the "user comments" stated, "The viewer commented on the 'bolt heads' that were 'cast into the pavement'—note the bolt heads appearing on the manhole cover on the slide."[7] Because no one contradicted the remote viewing session, it would seem that final comment indicated that the viewer's description of the bolt heads matched those seen in a slide of the target site, which was not shown to the viewer.

Viewer McMoneagle gained a reputation for accuracy after a series of RV sessions in 1979 during which he correctly described a new type of Soviet submarine then under construction in a secret facility at Severodvinsk.

Following these tests, the Psi Spies inquired about the disposition of the information gleaned through remote viewing. They were told that the Air Force colonel in the DIA to whom they were reporting had locked all of the reports in his safe, with no intention of acting on the information or even distributing the reports to other agencies. "What am I supposed to tell department heads when they ask about the source?" he reportedly told unit members, according to Morehouse.

Once again, instead of being used as an operational tool, the Psi Spies unit was considered just a novelty used to satisfy the curiosity of intelligence officials.

Some time later a remote viewing operation almost blew the cover off one of the United States' most top-secret weapons. And, again, it was supposed to be just a test.

As reported by unit members, officials in charge of the Psi Spies unit were courting the U.S. Air Force as a prospective client for their intelligence. So Air Force officials agreed to a test. The Psi Spies were given a sealed envelope containing a photo of their target and told the photo was possibly of a new generation of Soviet aircraft. The envelope remained sealed throughout the week that the viewers worked the project. The work moved ahead, but the viewers smelled a rat. Again, it was Stage 4 overlay, where the tasker's hidden agenda overlays the nature of the target.

The Psi Spies not only described and sketched the aircraft, along with its hangar facilities, but also described an existing variation. It turned out that this so-called Soviet aircraft actually was a U.S. Stealth fighter prototype, and the variation, of course, was the Stealth bomber.

The Air Force officers had given the Psi Spies unit one of our country's most classified programs as a test. This was a program to which none of the unit members had been given access, until now. Morehouse recalled:

> Well, the Air Force went nuts. They didn't know what to do. Normally, if someone accidentally finds out about a highly classified project like this, they have to sign an inadvertent disclosure statement, stating they will never reveal what they learned inadvertently. But in this case, the Air Force guys just ate crow and went away. You see, if they had required us to sign this statement, it would have meant two things—one, it would have been an admission that what we saw was accurate and correct, and two; they would have had to admit that they showed us top-secret, classified material.

> It just terrified them. I mean, if we could get into their most secret program, we could get into anything.

The Psi Spies said that many of the operational missions of their unit involved groups other than the U.S. Army. There were missions for the CIA, the National Security Agency (NSA), and even FBI and DEA counterintelligence operations.

"We would like to talk about some of these missions," explained Morehouse, "but since they were operational missions for others, we really can't get into these. Just understand that they existed."

One of the most difficult missions given to the Psi Spies involved Soviet nuclear warheads. During the Cold War, secrecy and subterfuge were used by all sides to keep their enemies from knowing the true strength and disposition of weapons systems. To this end, the Soviets deployed a vast array of nuclear warheads, many of them harmless duds. The team was tasked with determining which Soviet missile warheads were real and which were decoys for countermeasures—a particularly difficult assignment, because both real and bogus warheads looked identical. This mission required an indirect approach and a measure of creativity.

The methodology used went this way: First, they had to distinguish between the radioactive substances U-235 and U-238. Both radioisotopes have similar qualities and were impossible to tell apart. So, a backdoor approach was required. It turned out that, in at least one case, the ore used for the production of U-238 existed in a separate region of the USSR than that for U-235. So the unit members simply tracked the particular metal back in time, through all the production phases, until they arrived at the mine where the ore originated. Then sketches of the mine site were compared with known intelligence to deduce which isotope was produced from that ore, and so on. Once they perceived the difference in the ore, then they could deduce which warheads were real and which were dummies.

This backtracking method may have been pioneered years earlier by psi spy McMoneagle, who was given a wallet as a remote viewing target. "He was given no direction or cues," said Mel Riley, "so he soon began to describe fields and grass. It seems he had remote viewed back to when the wallet was the hide of a cow."

Unit members stressed that information produced by the Psi Spies, such as the warhead probe, was never used by itself but only to double-check other intelligence sources or to point to an avenue of investigation by other sources.

One of the stranger mission requests occurred when a viewer was instructed to place himself in front of a foreign energy weapon, such as a particle beam or laser, to determine the weapon's operating perimeters, such as polarization, temperature, impact energy, and so forth.

Lyn Buchanan described this incredible experience:

> One of our customers needed some intelligence about a Russian particle beam weapon at Semipolitinsk. A particle beam weapon is basically the ultimate ray gun. It destroys everything in its path. Even small ones can blow large holes through solid steel blocks a foot thick within a matter of microseconds....Our scientific customer even referred to it as "a death ray." They needed a single bit of intelligence which could evidently

not be obtained through any of the other spy options available to the U.S. In order to obtain that information, they had to know what was happening inside the beam itself. There is, of course, no way to place a piece of test equipment inside a particle beam, since the beam will destroy anything in its path. Even if there had been a way, the fact that it was a Russian classified project prevented access to the weapon or any information about it.

Someone came up with the brilliant idea of placing a remote viewer mentally inside the beam and having him describe what was going on in there. The targeting was effectively rejected by our director at the time, because of possible unknown dangers to the viewers. But the information was of vital importance, so it was explained to our group, and the tasker asked for volunteers....I thought it would be a really unusual target and an interesting experience, so I raised my hand. Mine was the only hand up....

In Controlled Remote Viewing, you use your body as an interpreter between your conscious and subconscious minds. The subconscious sends its impressions to the body, and you experience them. In effect, you begin to set up a sort of mini-virtual reality. The problem with virtual realities, of course, is that at some point, you buy into them and they become more real to you than the room around you....That can become dangerous....It still posed an extremely interesting opportunity for me, and I couldn't resist taking it. The lure of the experience and the information to be gained from it was just too great to pass up....

I had just entered Phase 4 when I felt I had sufficient site contact to proceed to the weapon....There was a sudden visual impression of some large, round, tubular thing about 50 yards in front of me. The impression was not just a vague impression, but was very real. I was "buying into" the virtual reality. When you buy into it completely, you reach what is called "bi-location," or Perfect Site Integration (PSI). At that time, you can only sense the information coming from your subconscious, and cannot sense anything from the room around you. You can no longer tell that you are not at the target site....

As I studied the beam closely, my full interest in it enveloped me....I was now standing in front of a sparkling, dancing, horizontal flow of energy, looking into it as a child would look into a toy store window at Christmas. It was totally captivating. The beam seemed like a constant flow of light brown liquid streaming by at supersonic speeds. It was a perfectly round, horizontal, tubular flow of this energy/liquid, but without any physical tube to contain it. As I put my face nearer to it, I could see that it was different down in the middle than it was on the outside edge.

I put my fingers into the flow, to see what would happen. As my fingers entered the liquid streaking by, the flow parted for only a split second, then resumed coherence as my finger melted and streaked off towards the right, leaving a discoloration within the flow. My finger appeared to have become part of the flow, but was still, even in its melted state, somehow a part of me, as well. There was a feeling of searing heat and bitter cold, both at the same time. I stood watching my fingers melt and flow outward along the beam, totally fascinated by the process. It then dawned on me anew that this might be dangerous. I pulled my hand back, and the beam resumed its former shape and color. My fingers were intact. I realized that my hand had not melted, at all. It had been placed into an area where time was proceeding at a different speed. I had been seeing the hand in that time-space locale from the vantage point of normal time and space.

I shoved my whole hand into the beam and watched as the same thing happened again. This time, the searing heat and bitter cold did not seem quite as intense. I thrust my arm in up to the middle of the forearm. Then, my wrist became icy and painfully cold and I instinctively jerked my hand back. The beam resumed its former shape and color. My arm was as it should be.

I looked to my left and saw the machine from which the beam originated. There were some men standing around it with goggles. They were checking dials and gadgets. I wanted to go down and see what they were doing, but vaguely remembered that my tasked purpose for being here did not include side trips. "Oh, yes!" I remembered. "I'm supposed to step into it and describe it from the inside." Without any further thought for personal safety and without even remembering what I was to look for, I stepped into the beam.

I experienced something at that moment that I have never been adequately able to explain to anyone.

It was something so totally strange and unique that nothing in my life had prepared me for it. I suddenly realized that my body was spread along the beam for what seemed to be endless miles of distance. My back was against the melting metallic plate, but was also a part of the metal, itself. I could look forward and backward along the beam and see myself standing at thousands of places within it. Thousands of images of myself were spread along the tube, yet blurred somehow into one image. I was aware that I could see each of the other images from the vantage point of each and every one, all at the same time. It was like something out of a high-budget science fiction movie, but this was real.

Each of the thousands of awarenesses began to converse with one another, somehow showing different personalities and thought patterns within each, but somehow all unified into a single mind. As the many awarenesses conversed, they quickly came to the same conclusion: I had a job to do.

With a difficulty almost like that of walking into a strong, gale-force wind, I saw all the many images struggling to join together into one, back at the point where I had entered the beam. They did not all make it, but enough of them did that I was able to turn and face into the oncoming beam of energy, to study it from the inside.

At first, I began analyzing the beam. The very center of the beam was swirling rapidly in a counterclockwise direction. The outside edges of the beam were coming directionally straight, with no swirl at all. Between the exact middle and the outside edge, the swirl dwindled from the rapidity of a central hurricane to the directional straightness of the edge.

But the analysis ended there. I could no longer keep an analytical mind as I looked into the beam. Each particle within the beam was every color of the rainbow, all at once, but never blending into white. The colors were more vivid than I have ever seen, even in the most vivid nighttime dream. I found myself facing an oncoming rush of beauty like I have never seen before. Repeatedly, the beauty of the scene made me lose coherence, and I would see the oncoming beam from a thousand places along it. I would regain physical coherence, only to become totally awe-stricken and lose it again.

To this day, I do not remember the end of that session. I suppose that I must have come out of the Perfect Site Integration experience and finished the session, written a final summary, and gone back to my desk to do other work. I must have closed up for the evening, locked my papers away in the safe, and gone to the car to drive home. I honestly do not remember. The next memory I have of that day was driving into Waldorf, Maryland, almost 60 miles from the office, almost home for the evening. The awe of the beauty I saw at that target did not wear off for weeks to come. I'm not certain it has completely worn off, still.

Amazing as this experience sounds, it was nothing new to the Psi Spies. It only required bi-location, in which the viewer's body is in one place while his mind is totally absorbed with the experiences of another place. Mel Riley explained:

> I guess the most fun part of remote viewing is bilocating, because then you are actually there. Sometimes there comes a time when you're not reporting information back anymore, you are in a survival situation. It would depend on where your monitor would send you. One of our monitors must have thought we were masochists because during testing he would send us to places like sewer treatment plants so we could get in there and really smell and taste.

Riley said he remote viewed historic battles, even ones fought during the Middle Ages. "The thing is, you don't always bi-locate," he said. "But when you do make that separation and you are there, trust me, you are ducking axes and swords. You are choking on the dust. I mean you are there. It's hard for anybody to fathom this unless you have experienced it."

Asked what would happen if he were struck by a weapon during one of these bi-location experiences, Riley laughed and said, "We don't know. At the time, I was too obsessed with ducking these things. It's instinctual. So, I don't know if it could hit you or not. As far as I know, it has never happened."

One of the last Psi Spies operations to be directed against the Soviet Union came in 1989 as the "evil empire" was breaking up. Morehouse participated in a remote viewing session against a suspected Soviet biochemical warfare plant. Morehouse gave the following description of his experience:

After receiving coordinates from Mel Riley, who was acting as monitor...I felt myself falling through a tunnel of light, but I managed to maintain control throughout the descent. I found myself doubled over, but on my feet somewhere in time and space. I could feel the sun warm against my back. I could see some buildings in the distance. I floated toward the buildings....

I moved forward and passed through the wall of a large building feeling only a small bit of pressure. I was in a large hallway with polished floors. It was very clean and bright, a hospital-like atmosphere. My phantom body flowed down the hallway and into a large room. I chuckled to myself because I felt like a ghost. In the room, I saw several people in lab coats. There was glassware all over the place and I don't mean dishes. There were test tubes, beakers, hoses, you name it. This place obviously was some sort of laboratory. Moving along, I passed through four or five more walls, looking at the contents of each passing room.

I finally came to a large room where a pungent odor caught my attention. It smelled septic, or actually more like a chemical, like acid or burning metal. My mouth tasted of chemicals and copper and my nose burned from the fumes. I was becoming dizzy and wanted to leave, but I continued my search. The sting in my eyes made it difficult to focus. It seemed the people there were packaging something vaporous or perhaps liquid. It was getting harder to breathe, so I turned my consciousness homeward. When I recovered myself, I was still sitting at the table in the room at Fort Meade. But I was gasping, sweaty, and my nose was bleeding. Blood had dripped onto the paper where I had made notes.

Morehouse's official session report read:

> Site is a structure. The structure is made up of a central building which is large and hollow (AOL like a hanger or warehouse). This central structure—several stories high—is surrounded by other smaller structures—one or two stories high—some of which are attached to the larger one while others are spread out away from the main structure. The main structure is constructed of thin metal over a metal frame—some of the roof is corrugated and there are large openings at both ends of this structure....The activity in the main structure is associated with assembly, production, putting together, building, development, study and the creation of something. The end result of this product is something dangerous, hazardous (AOL chemical or biological). Much of the activity centers around the packaging for delivery of the product....There is somewhat of a laboratory atmosphere....Personnel at the main structure often wear masks with filters and protective suits. The key event associated with the structure seems to be in the future—and appears to be related to the destruction in some kind of "attack" on a governmental target of national value."[8]

Riley and others in the unit concluded that this site appeared to be a new-generation Soviet biochemical warfare agent production facility, in existence due to loopholes in the

1972 biological warfare treaty. Information regarding this facility was passed along to the Biological Threat Analysis Center and the State Department.

Although most of the missions undertaken by the Psi Spies dealt with serious national security issues, there were moments of levity.

Riley recalled one Christmas when several members of the unit, including the commander, pressed one of the remote viewers into service to locate a suspected terrorist. The viewer was told that this terrorist was a foreigner who was well known and bent upon making mischief during the holiday season. Riley recalled:

> This guy really busted his ass on that one. But nothing seemed to make sense. He saw this person dressed in red and that he had several small helpers and that he traveled very unconventionally. This guy worked for several days and finally decided to closely remote view this person's means of transportation for a clue to his identity. He saw what appeared to be a sleigh and that it would travel over the North Pole and, wham, it hit him—he had been remote viewing Santa Claus! He was really mad for a moment, but then laughed at this joke along with everyone else.

The interesting point here is that, although Santa is not a real person, there is enough human involvement with his myth and his image that the remote viewer was able to pick up sensations relating to Santa. This phenomenon undoubtedly deserves more study. It also serves as a warning not to rely unduly on raw remote viewed data.

One main reason the Psi Spies continued the RV missions, despite low morale and orders to "do nothing" while under official scrutiny, was their "Enigma File"—records of sessions that touched on some of Earth's strangest mysteries. They were gaining knowledge in areas that for centuries had been solely the province of guesswork and speculation. They felt compelled to continue their work.

The whole issue of the Psi Spies unit was causing great consternation in the halls of government. By 1990, all of the original military remote viewers were gone, either resigned or transferred. The "witches" were left in charge.

Unlike the proverbial old soldier, though, the Psi Spies didn't just fade away. They took their remote viewing experience to the public.

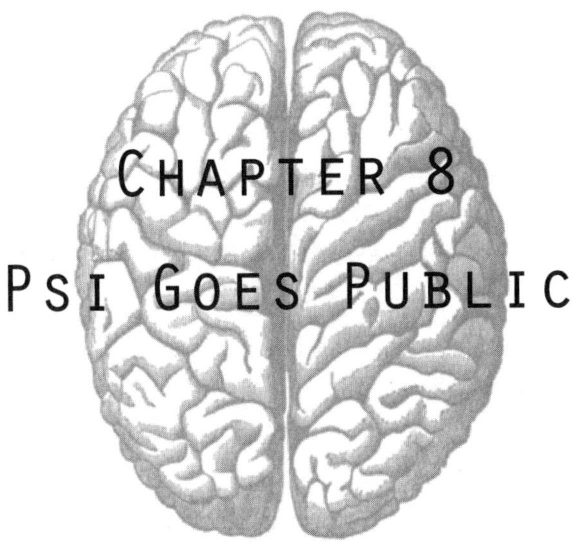

Chapter 8

Psi Goes Public

By mid-1989, all but one of the military-trained remote viewers had left the Psi Spies unit. Some, including Morehouse, transferred back to other units within the Army, whereas others simply retired. But all of them were determined not to let their remote viewing experience go to waste. McMoneagle had retired in 1984 and already was working on his book about remote viewing, *Mind Trek*. Several veteran unit members vowed to pursue SRI's discoveries and techniques, even though the government apparently had discarded them.

Morehouse, along with Ed Dames and others, decided to form a private company. In November 1989, PSI TECH, Inc. was founded. The company's initial home base was in a private home near Fort Meade, Maryland. Morehouse became vice president of PSI TECH.

Quickly, the members of PSI TECH discovered the problems of capitalizing a new company. They realized that one of the reasons that soldiers were able to develop their remote viewing was that, as government employees, they always knew there was a paycheck coming. "We were very lucky in that we had the opportunity to develop our skills before we had to compete in the business world," Morehouse later commented.

By 1993, PSI TECH comprised seven remote viewers, most of them veterans of the Psi Spies unit, with Ingo Swann as mentor and consultant.

PSI TECH brought in a collection of outside directors from the scientific, industrial, and business communities to act as consultants. Additionally, a group of scientists, engineers, and medical doctors from various national laboratories, major corporations, and universities provided analytical support to PSI TECH projects as required. Many of these people needed no convincing of the reality of remote viewing as they had served as consultants to the Psi Spies unit.

The credibility of the remote viewing capabilities was enhanced in June 1990, when Gen. Stubblebine, the former supervising officer for the Psi Spies unit, was named chairman of PSI TECH's board of directors.

By 2007, Dames, Morehouse, and virtually all its original members had left the company in the hands of Jonina Dourif. The company, which sells tapes, DVDs, and training, proclaimed itself the "Founders of the Remote Viewing Industry."[1]

Later in 1990, the existence of the Psi Spies came to the attention of a major news outlet.

KIRO News in Seattle, Washington, conducted a five-month investigation that essentially confirmed the existence of the super-secret psychic spy unit. Then-Secretary of the Navy Lawrence Garrett, when cornered by a KIRO reporter, said, "I know about the project, but I can't answer your questions."[2]

However, Representative Norm Dicks of Washington State's 6th District and a member of the House Intelligence Committee was not at all hesitant to speak on the record. He told KIRO, "There are some [remote viewers] that have a record of being relatively accurate, in having some ability to, in essence, see what's going to happen. Obviously, in the world of intelligence that could be very important."[3]

Another government official, speaking only on the promise of anonymity, confirmed to KIRO that the program was used to give intelligence leads during the whole Desert Storm period.

Once word of PSI TECH's existence began to circulate, queries began to flood the office. They ranged from the scientifically sophisticated to the lowbrow blunt. ("Can you give me the winning lottery number?" was a frequent request.) One letter-writer put it this way:

> Gentlemen: Since, as your leaflet describes, a remote viewer is able to describe things and events distant in time, one is allowed to assume that future values of [the] stock market could be accurately described by your disciplined experts. If this is so, then I would like to avail myself of your services and shall be looking forward to your detailed offer.

The writer's hopes for a stock market killing were dashed when a PSI TECH officer replied:

> Whereas a technical remote viewer can lock onto a target and follow it backward and/or forward in time, our capabilities do not extend to fixing the target's position in time...nor can a remote viewer easily discern alphanumerical data, only its related analog states and associated ideas. These things are highly left-brain—linear analytical—in nature, while technical remote viewing depends strictly upon right-brain—gestalt pattern recognition—functioning....I cannot place a high enough confidence level upon the success of such a prospective remote viewing project to guarantee that its results would be useful to you.[4]

As the Psi Spies attempted to explain many times, remote viewing cannot produce the winning lottery number or the best-selling stock. Numbers are abstract ideas, an artificial creation of humans, and are primarily connected to left-brain structure, with little or no relation to physical reality. Therefore it is almost impossible for remote viewers to determine numbers with any precision.

It is most interesting that, although it is possible for trained remote viewers to predetermine a lottery winner—whether it will be a male or female, what he or she looks like, where he or she lives, and so on—they cannot determine the winning numbers. It appears that the psychic "signal" is very weak and that it does not produce a clear enough image long enough to determine precise numbers, names, or dates.

Lyn Buchanan said he still gets a kick out of people who call him and offer to split the winnings if he will give them the winning lottery numbers. "If I had the lottery numbers, I'd keep all the money," he laughed. "They just don't seem to think about this."

However, there could still be real-world advantages to remote viewing. One business world application of remote viewing had to do with the field of publishing. Viewers could look into the near future and describe to a publisher what the topics and themes of upcoming best-selling books would be, although they could not give the titles or the authors of those books. Publishers then could use this information to take special notice when material such as that described crossed their desk.

Also, no one should be overly concerned that some remote viewer might peek in on his or her private life. For example, should some unscrupulous male viewer decide to spy on his girlfriend in the shower, he would not have the experience he desires. The viewer could only focus on one aspect of the scene at a time. Though an experienced viewer might determine that the person under psychic observation is female and that water is running, he would not get the grand aesthetic appreciation that one would standing there in person viewing the scene through normal eyesight. There is no erotic sensation to remote viewing; it is merely a source of information.

Several Psi Spies stated that to use remote viewing in such a manner would "trivialize" the experience. "It is such a powerful tool that it changes your life," said Morehouse.

Mel Riley agreed. "When you can go out and see the universe, who wants to go look at a Russian submarine?" he asked with a laugh.

Another aspect of accurate remote viewing seems to be the necessity of using the team approach. Although there are differences of opinion, according to most veteran viewers, on any given mission, multiple viewers should be utilized to assure the highest accuracy ratings. It is the team effort that produces the best results.

McMoneagle, on the other hand, argued, "Over two decades of research fails to support multiple viewer accuracy.... In fact, the results of such research tend to flow in the opposite direction. If you are using multiple viewers, the one or two viewers who differ from the majority view are just as likely to be the ones that are providing the correct information."[5]

Buchanan agreed, saying:

> The idea is that multiple viewers on the same site increase accuracy. On the surface, that seems like a simple thing, but it actually isn't. If you put a group of viewers onto a single site and have them all view everything, then you will get some viewers who will get different parts of the site and others who will get other parts, and the whole thing winds up being almost wholly dependant on the analyst to sort it all out. In that situation, the increase or decrease [of accuracy] is not a matter of having more viewers, but one of having a really talented analyst.

As with language, the ability to remote view is innate in everyone. However, also like language, it must be learned to be used effectively. Training is highly structured and regimented. It does not allow for creativity on the part of the student.

Can everyone be a successful remote viewer?

The Psi Spies offered the following tips on how to test oneself for remote viewing ability.

1. Try to clear your mind of any preconceived ideas and beliefs. Start by asking yourself, "Is it okay with me if psychic functioning is really a natural part of the world?" Next ask yourself, "Is it okay with me if I have psychic ability?"
2. Take a positive tone. Say to yourself, "I can remote view a location." If you sense any resistance to the idea that you can remote view, then take some time to work this out and become comfortable with the idea that you can function psychically, even if it is only temporary.
3. Sit comfortably in a quiet, undisturbed location. Try to find a place that is neutral in color and atmosphere. Avoid places with many distractions. Dim the lights, but darkness is not necessary.
4. Sit upright and remain alert. Have some clean sheets of paper and pen or pencils at hand.
5. Begin to quiet your mind. Relax and take deep breaths. With each exhalation, relax both your body's muscles and your mind. Let your mind go blank but do not try and stop thoughts that come. Simply let them go without focusing on them. No special meditation is required, although one useful technique is to imagine yourself in an empty theater staring at a blank screen. Relax until images appear on the screen.
6. When images come, describe what you see, not what you think. View the images

as if you were an unaffected observer. Observe them carefully, because the images often flash through the mind rapidly. The more basic the impressions, the more likelihood of an accurate viewing.

7. Try to draw what you see, even if you don't know what the drawing represents. Don't attempt to connect images. Simply draw or describe them. Try for an initial ideogram, which is a simple line drawing representing the whole idea of the target. Concentrate on the idea of the target and let your pencil hand move automatically.
8. Next, concentrate on shapes, forms, colors, and textures. Don't be concerned if something doesn't seem to make sense—just record it.
9. Try to get a feel for your target, then interrogate yourself about it. Is it a person, place, or thing? Is it natural or man-made? What is it used for? Who goes there?
10. Limit your remote viewing session to 15 or 20 minutes.

Whenever possible, a novice remote viewer should visit the target site as soon as possible after the RV session. Look about carefully and compare what you see with the images you received. If feedback is done while the images are still fresh in your mind, the comparisons made will benefit you during subsequent RV sessions.

The following is an account of the author's first attempt at remote viewing.

In October 1992, I was preparing to travel from my home in Texas to Albuquerque to meet members of PSI TECH for the first time. I had no idea what I was getting into, but I already knew it concerned remote viewing. I decided that I would try remote viewing before I left. I had been told that PSI TECH was planning to build an office, so I thought I would attempt to view their office.

Already having some knowledge of meditative techniques, especially Transcendental Meditation, I just sat quietly in a comfortable chair and closed my eyes, wondering in my mind what the PSI TECH office would look like. I immediately got the image of an office in what appeared to be a strip shopping center or plaza. The corners were higher than the rest of the building and there was something sticking out near the roof. Not knowing then about the danger of analytical overlay, I thought that these jutting objects must be the wood beams so prevalent in New Mexico architecture. I then saw the floor plan of this office from an overhead, or bird's eye, perspective.

After arriving in Albuquerque, I learned that PSI TECH was temporarily operating out of a private home, which bore no resemblance to what I had seen. On October 30, 1992, I sketched what I had seen, but was told it did not resemble anything that PSI TECH had planned. I figured my career as a remote viewer was over and promptly forgot the incident. Then on August 16, 1993, I returned to Albuquerque. There I was informed that because training had become a priority at PSI TECH, the company had postponed its building plans and had rented office space to conduct training. I was reminded of my earlier description of PSI TECH's office and handed back my drawing, which carried a stick-on note reading "Good job, Jim! Spontaneous AOL sketch." I was then driven to the new office and it indeed resembled what I had seen and described almost a year earlier. The office was in a complex that resembled a strip shopping center. It was a dark earth tone, and the corners were higher than the remainder of the building. But instead of wooden beams near the roof, there were lion heads jutting from each corner. My drawing of the office building's floor plan matched the building's printed floor plan 100 percent, hallway for hallway, office for office. I was told this was a case of my looking forward into time rather than viewing the present. It was also suggested that the "first-time effect," or beginner's luck, may have explained my seeming success. It was certainly an eye-opening—and mind-opening—experience for me.

There is one simple remote viewing test is one that requires only some time and at least three persons. One person is the remote viewer, the second acts as monitor, and the third is the target contact.

While the viewer and the monitor go through the previous list for conducting a successful RV session, the target contact should journey to a predetermined target site. Do not let the viewer or the monitor know the location of the site. Choose a site with distinguishing features that can be readily identified.

At a predetermined time, the target contact should be at the target site. He or she should simply be alert and paying close attention to the site and its environment. There is no need to try to send pictures or messages to the viewer.

At the same time, the monitor should encourage the viewer to describe the location of the target contact. Again, do not attempt to analyze the incoming data. Simply describe or draw the basic shapes, forms, or colors that are seen.

According to several of the Psi Spies, this test should not last more than 15 or 20 minutes. At its completion, both the viewer and the monitor should be taken immediately to the target site for feedback.

Morehouse said most people will be surprised at the success of their remote viewing. However, he added that not everyone produces the same results. Some viewers start off strong and then weaken in their ability. Others are consistently reliable. Some start weak, but grow stronger with experience.

PSI TECH's remote viewers continued to work on a variety of projects.

Though they said they could not elaborate on some of their contracts, as they involved secrecy agreements with the company's clients, three recent projects were described.

These projects included a "crisis profile of Saddam Hussein" and "projected key technologies for lunar in-situ [at the site] resource processing."[6]

One customer, a large company with strategic oil interests in the Mid-East, was concerned about a potential conflict's effects upon the near-and far-term price of oil just prior to the Gulf War. A statement of work directed PSI TECH in mid-1990 to provide data and analysis on Saddam himself (that is, his mind—intent, motivation, emotional, and behavioral states) to penetrate his war room for information concerning battle plans, operations, force strengths, and possible deception schemes, and to provide a six-month general outlook for the Gulf region.

While fulfilling this contract, the PSI TECH remote viewers actually foresaw the Persian Gulf War. Viewers described a "monstrous" and "fearful" event. They foresaw enormous devastation, particularly along a coastline. And they saw "dark, roiling, apocalyptic clouds over the ocean with volatile, aromatic petroleum compounds in the air."

But one of the most interesting aspects of this project was that more than six months prior to Desert Storm, with the Allied troops poised to move into Kuwait and the Israelis declaring, "If you don't get Saddam Hussein, we will," PSI TECHs remote viewers perceived that Saddam was alive in December 1991, despite at least two assassination attempts—one by poisoning and one by pistol.

Their former colleagues in the intelligence community laughed at their report, declaring that Saddam didn't have a chance of living out the year. Even the client said this information was going to be a hard sell. But, until well after the Iraq invasion of 2003, Saddam Hussein was still alive.[7]

Another contract came from a major automobile company that was curious about the future of hydrogen-fueled cars. The remote viewers performed a worldwide search for current research and applied engineering work related to hydrogen-powered automobiles. They located and described engineering projects in North America, Japan, France, China, Germany, and Russia.

Their final report placed emphasis upon the most potentially successful of these projects and included sketches of prototype designs and descriptions of associated engineering features such as turbines, flywheels, hydraulic and electric components, and so forth. Significantly, they determined that the most successful design would not come from their client.

Another contract for PSI TECH was with a large engineering firm. The research and development section wanted help in studying the most economical technologies with which to extract elements, such as oxygen, as an energy source for a future moon base. They were looking for both life-support energy and propulsion energy for expeditions to both the moon and Mars.

PSI TECH furnished the company descriptions and sketches of actual future lunar mining and resource processing operations along with recommendations for power generation devices.

Following the Gulf War in 1991, one contract for PSI TECH was picked up by the Associated Press and made headlines in several major newspapers. In an article entitled "U.N. enlists psychic firm to find Iraqis' weapon sites," the *Washington Times* reported that PSI TECH had been contacted by U.S. Army Maj. Karen Jansen, a special United Nations envoy assigned to locate and destroy Iraq's hidden stocks of chemical, biological, and nuclear weapons.[8] Maj. Jansen sought help in finding hidden weapons sites. PSI TECH proceeded to locate two such sites.

Four PSI TECH remote viewers volunteered to work on this project. The work was accomplished between November 5 and 8, 1991. A letter accompanying the RV results addressed to Maj. Jansen stated: "I am confident that the added degree of insight resulting from these few technical remote viewing 'sorties' will be useful to you—as well as nonplusing to your Iraqi hosts."[9]

A summary report of this project stated:

> The primary target is associated with a long, underground, labyrinthine layout that is self-contained and very much like a submarine in many respects. The entrance is down a set of cement stairs, in or near a large, open-bay building...where uniformed soldiers are present. When examined superficially, the target gives the impression that it is a bomb shelter in the basement of a building. However, the furthermost end is complex and there are concealed (buried) power conduits attached to that end. Associated with that end, also, is the sensory impression of violent, powerful, painful, wrenching stomach contractions, along with the idea of something like a medical clinic. What appear to be glove boxes are present or will be installed.[10]

The report added that the viewers had the impression that the access to this underground facility was covered with sand and rubble "as part of a deception," a decoy.[11]

Some of the above-ground structures were designed to be decoys, to be bombed; the actual facilities were underground. Some had purposely been covered with rubble to simulate bomb damage. Just as in the military-trained Psi Spies, Maj. Jansen had gone outside of her civilian chain of command to get the job done.

Derek Boothby, an official with the UN commission assigned to find the hidden biological weapons, confirmed that germ warfare research facilities were found, but said no actual weapons were recovered.

Boothby said he was unaware of PSI TECH's involvement, but told the Associated Press, "We welcome all information, if it is practical and can be substantiated."[12]

Unfortunately, due to the sensitive nature of this mission coupled with the chagrin of UN officials once the use of psychic investigators was revealed, there was no feedback. Morehouse said PSI TECH was never told if their information was correct or not. "But then they didn't say we were wrong either," he added.

As 1993 drew to a close, PSI TECH was drawn more and more into the training of remote viewers. More than a dozen persons were trained in Technical Remote Viewing in PSI TECH's Albuquerque offices. These included academics, people from the business community, and even a few scientists.

Some of those who received training declined to talk about their experience, apparently fearful of public reaction. One who did agree to speak on the record was George G. Byers, vice president of Government Affairs for Santa Fe Pacific Gold Corporation, the third-largest U.S.–based gold mining company. Byers earned both a B.A. and a masters degree from the University of Mississippi and rose to the rank of captain as an Army Ranger and infantry officer in Vietnam.

Byers said he took the PSI TECH remote viewing course between October and December 1993. He recalled his experience this way:

> It didn't cause me any problem. I felt okay. I did it mostly on weekends, Saturdays and Sundays.
>
> At first, I'd sit there and think, *Why am I doing this? I'm wasting my time. I could be out raking leaves.* You

see, I was a total skeptic. I had heard about PSI TECH from a TV producer. I met with my monitor several times and found him to be a sharp individual. So, I thought why not give it a try. After all, wouldn't it be great to remote view where our next big gold strike would be made?

I signed up and began my training. At first, the most difficult part was analytical overlay. I kept wanting to interpret what I saw. I didn't differentiate AOL from the signal line. I was constantly declaring AOL breaks.

I took a long time because I was slow and deliberate about it. I tried to think too much, you know, trying to force it. It's like Yogi Berra said: "You can't think and hit at the same time." Well, you can't think and remote view. It's something that you have to allow to happen. But I finally got it. I found it's like riding a bicycle—once you ever do it, you never really lose the ability.

Once I got it, then I was really amazed. My monitor had told me about remote viewing into space, but I had taken that with a large grain of salt. But then he put me on Titan, the largest moon of Saturn.

Of course, I didn't know where I was at first. I was just given some coordinates. But I saw a harsh terrain. I ended up focusing on this one site—a deep chasm on the surface of this moon. It was deep-walled, very inaccessible. I recall a rushing sound and there seemed to be objects in motion at the bottom of this chasm. At first, I kept thinking I might be in some big city because of the sheer walls on either side.

> And there seemed to be kind of a chocolate odor prevalent there. My monitor immediately told me I had been to Titan and that others who remote viewed that site also had picked up the chocolate odor. It has something to do with the chemical makeup of the atmosphere.
>
> Well, I was astonished. I found it very hard to believe. The belief came later as I developed more and more confidence in my ability to remote view.
>
> When I finally began to believe was a session in early November of 1993, when I saw a white cloud in swirling motion over land. My target was a photo of a white tornado swirling over some flat, Midwestern countryside. This tornado was where I truly became a believer in Coordinate Remote Viewing....
>
> Once you have experienced these things, your confidence increases and you are more open to the far-out things like viewing into space or encountering the surviving Martians.
>
> There is no longer any doubt in my mind that the remote viewing experience is real and valid. It's hard for me to sell others on this, but I'm sold on it myself.[13]

As can be seen from Byers's experiences, PSI TECH members continued to work on their Engima Files, sessions relating to some of Earth's most implacable mysteries.

Another PSI TECH trainee was Dr. Courtney Brown, an associate professor of political science at Emory University. Based on his RV experiences, Dr. Brown produced a 1996 book entitled *Cosmic Voyage: A Scientific Discovery of Extraterrestrials Visiting Earth.*

America's first psi spy, Mel Riley, agreed to conduct a demonstration of an actual remote viewing session, which I was able to witness on August 18, 1993. Unexpectedly, Riley was sent to view a recent mystery.

At my last-minute request, Riley was given a coordinate representing the time and place of the assassination of President John F. Kennedy. He was sent to Dealey Plaza in Dallas, Texas, on November 22, 1963.

What was supposed to be only a demonstration of an RV session turned into an emotional experience for Riley and his monitor. The session was conducted in the training office of PSI TECH in Albuquerque. Riley was the remote viewer; I was merely an observer. The following recollection was culled from my notes from that session as well as Riley's original drawings and audiotapes of the session.

Riley, as per normal procedure, was not given any clue as to the RV target. Having been in constant contact with me since his arrival in Albuquerque and with the target of the session decided upon only minutes before it began, it seemed certain that he had no prior knowledge of his target.

Riley got coffee and sat quietly at one end of conference table in PSI TECH office. [The monitor] sat opposite. It was cool and quiet, with low light in the small room. There were free-flowing ink pens and paper in front of Riley.

Two four-digit coordinate numbers—in this instance 8976-4130—were given to Riley. The coordinates represent Dealey Plaza, Dallas, Texas, November 22, 1963.

At the top of the first sheet, Riley wrote "P.I.'s [Personal Inclemencies, or personal considerations that might interfere with the psychic functioning]—it's been a long time." This meant it had been a while since Riley had last remote viewed with a monitor.

Under A.I.'s (Aesthetic Impact or any advance response to the target) Riley wrote "none." Riley took a deep breath and, with eyes open, began marking on his first sheet of paper. He drew an S-shaped curving line and said, "across, curving, curving around, an incline." Then he stopped and closed his eyes as if in concentration. He said, "hard, dark, gray...like asphalt, a surface, a road."

He seemed to have trouble focusing his attention on the target. [The monitor] asked if he wanted the coordinate again. Riley nodded and sipped coffee. He closed his eyes. "Any sounds?" asked the monitor. Riley replied, "A breezy sound, like leaves rustling in the wind."

"Textures?"

Riley said, "Rough, gritty."

Then Riley said there was motion. "Wavy motion, flowing, rocking...a feeling of vertigo with this motion."

Riley looked up with his eyes closed as if he was looking at something internally, then opened his eyes, lowered his head, and made more marks on the paper. The impression is that, like an art student, he looks up to see his subject and then looks down to record his impression on paper.

More images were coming. "There is confusion, chaos." Riley draws a small cloud-like image with a jagged lightening bolt coming out of it. "It's puffy, cloud-like. Something is coming out of this," he said. "It's fast. Trajectory. A shooting out, shot like.... Don't ask me how I'm going to explain this one, but something shoots out from this circle."

Asked to mark precisely where the event is taking place, Riley again sketched an elongated S-shaped curing line and drew a dot past the middle of the S figure. Riley appeared to become agitated with what he was seeing. "There is something about this...." His voice trailed off. "There are things around me." Riley made a long, slow exhale as he tilted his head up, eyes closed. Then returned to his paper with eyes open. He began to sketch.

There was no question what he was drawing. It was a curving street lined with trees with tall buildings in the background. In front of the trees, lining the street, was a crowd of people. As if his sketch needs further interpretation, Riley wrote, "Tall structures in background. Green, tree-like, curving over, tall, hard, crowds, crowded, people."

At this point, Riley asked for an "analytical overlay" break, meaning that he was beginning to analyze the information he was receiving. He got up and left the room for several minutes.

Upon his return, Riley was asked by his monitor, "You know what the target is, don't you?" He nodded somberly. "It's the Kennedy assassination. That's why I had to leave for a while."

Riley later said that up until the break he had no idea of what he was viewing. But as it became clear to him, it was necessary to take a break. "I already felt that this was the Kennedy assassination. It was coming to my mind so strongly. But I had no feedback and I wanted to make sure that I had no preconceived ideas about what I was seeing."

Riley was asked to sketch what he saw, especially bullet strikes.

He sat back down and began sketching, commenting as he worked. "I get two hits, the first came from the back and hit in the shoulder area. The second hit was almost instantaneous. It was from the front. His head was thrown back when he was hit from behind, but the instantaneous one hit head-on and threw his head backwards, boom-boom like.

"I'm going into ERV [Extended Remote Viewing or bi-location] as long as I'm already there," Riley said. This meant he attempted bi-location, to pick up on the deeper feelings, sounds, impressions of the event.

"The number-one shot that came from behind appears to be a normal, high-powered projectile, a bullet. But number two is small and long and skinny, very hard. It came from the front and there is a word associated with it. I'm not sure how to spell it, but the word is 'flechette,'" Riley said. "And the point of origin of this thing does not seem to be much outside the vehicle."

Later, Riley commented, "I thought it was really strange because I was in the same position as the president. It was like I was him. This little projectile came at me from the direction of the car's rearview mirror."

Both Riley and his monitor were quick to point out that this session was strictly for demonstration purposes and that they could not guarantee their conclusions unless a full-blown remote-viewing study involving other viewers took place.

"This was only a cursory look for demonstration purposes," explained Riley's monitor, who added that his own remote viewing of the assassination agreed with Riley's assessment.

Riley said under tight RV protocols involving a number of viewers, it would be possible to determine precisely how many shots were fired, and these shots could be tracked back to their points of origin.

However, both men were visibly moved by the experience, especially the PSI TECH monitor, who commented, "Hey, I always believed what my government told me. This really shakes me up because now I have direct knowledge that President Kennedy was hit from the back and the front. They've lied to me. They've lied to all of us."

Riley said that "like the majority of the public" he long suspected a conspiracy in the JFK assassination, but that he had not read assassination literature or even seen films about it.

Interestingly enough, psi spy McMoneagle had done his own viewing of the Kennedy assassination. He too perceived that the act was the result of a conspiracy and that JFK was shot at from three or even four different positions. He wrote:

> I do believe the originators/initiators of the plan came from at least the cabinet level of government, and they probably used less than a handful of resources within their offices (DOD) [Department of Defense] to effect coordination between them and the Cuban/organized crime organizations involved.[14]

During the years the Psi Spies were honing their RV techniques and running operational RV missions, they found an "enigma" factor creeping into their work. This factor was sights and events that could not be explained by man's traditional science or by normal experiences.

The Psi Spies moved beyond the fabulous to the fantastic—and the creation of their Enigma Files.

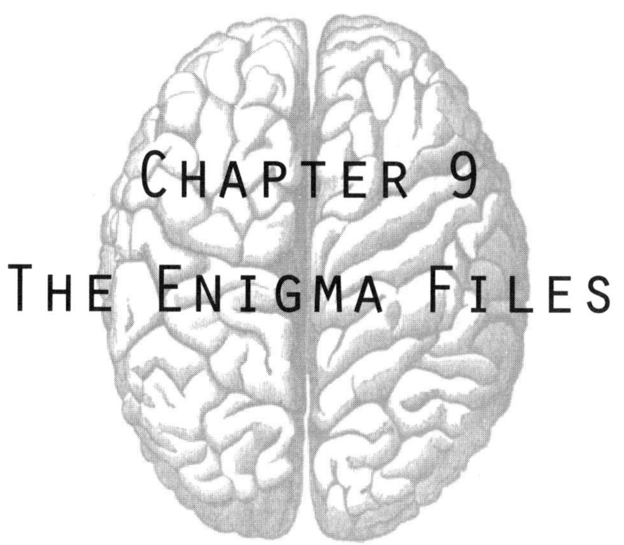

Chapter 9
The Enigma Files

One day in the fall of 1985, according to author and Pulitzer Prize nominee Howard Blum, a collection of ranking military officers met in a lead-lined conference hall on the third floor of the Old Executive Office Building across from the White House. Though details of this meeting have been contested by some of the persons involved, the essence of the experience is acknowledged as true.

Seated in front of the officers and the President's science adviser were two SRI scientists, most probably Puthoff and Targ, and a remote viewer, reportedly Ingo Swann.

The occasion was yet another demonstration of the remote viewing phenomenon, but on this day the extraordinary moved into the fantastic.

The viewer was asked to sketch his view of a Soviet submarine. He rapidly began drawing circles. One was elongated—apparently the submarine—but above this was a circle with no wings. Asked if he saw a rocket, the remote viewer could only shrug.

Finally, expressing the hopes or fears of many in the room, the scientist said, "Well, what else could it be? I mean, you're not going to tell me it's a flying saucer."

"Yes," replied the viewer. "That's it exactly."[1]

Despite this brush with the fantastic, the DIA, along with Naval Intelligence, accepted the legitimacy of the demonstration and within six months launched a classified operation using remote viewers against Soviet submarines.

This demonstration and its acceptance by high-ranking military and scientific officials was just one more episode in a long history of Washington duplicity. While officially scoffing at any publicized report on unidentified flying objects, various government agencies quietly continue to give serious attention to such matters. The Psi Spies unit was no exception.

The laboratory studies of remote viewing had indicated the phenomenon is limited by neither time nor space.

The space aspect of RV was confirmed in the early 1970s, when Ingo Swann recorded his impressions of various bodies in our solar system using remote viewing. His visions were taken lightly at the time, but later confirmed by feedback from various NASA deep space missions.

While undergoing endless tests with the SRI scientists, Swann grew eager for excitement, some diversion from the structured testing:

> In the midst of this desperation during March, 1973, I noted with growing interest the approaching

> bypass of NASA's *Pioneer 10* spacecraft with the distant planet Jupiter. *Pioneer 10* would begin to send back data about Jupiter approximately December 3, nine months away. Wouldn't it be interesting if a psychic probe of Jupiter could be compared to the eventual feedback from Pioneer 10?[2]

Swann, in conjunction with another psychic, Harold Sherman, conducted a remote viewing of Jupiter on April 27, 1973. The recorded impressions of both Swann and Sherman were virtually identical. Swann gave this description of Jupiter:

> There's a planet with stripes. I hope it's Jupiter. I think that it must have an extremely large hydrogen mantle. If a space probe made contact with that, it would be maybe 80,000–120,000 miles out from the planet's surface....Very high in the atmosphere there are crystals, they glitter, maybe the stripes are like bands of crystals, maybe like the rings of Saturn, though not far out like that, very close to the atmosphere....Now, I'll go down through....Inside those cloud layers, those crystal layers, they look beautiful from the outside. From the inside they look like rolling gas clouds—eerie yellow light, rainbows.
>
> I get the impression, though I don't see, that it's liquid. Then I came though the cloud cover, the surface looks like sand dunes. They're made of very large grade crystals so they slide. Tremendous winds, sort of like maybe the prevailing winds of Earth, but very close to the surface of Jupiter. From that view the horizon looks orangeish or rosecolored but overhead it's kind

> of greenish-yellow. If I look to the right, there is an enormous mountain range....Those mountains are huge but they still don't poke up through the crystal cloud cover....I see something that looks like a tornado. Is there a thermal inversion here? I bet there is.... I'll move more towards the equator. I get the impression that there must be a band of crystals similar to the outer ones, kind of bluish. They seem to be sort of in orbit, permanent orbit down through another layer farther down which are like our clouds but moving fast....Tremendous wind. It's colder here. Maybe it's because there's not a thermal inversion there....The atmosphere of Jupiter is very thick.[3]

Crystal rings? An atmosphere? These were ridiculous concepts at the time. Even after the passage of *Pioneer 10* in December 1973, there was not enough data to substantiate Swann's descriptions.

SRI scientist Hal Puthoff said, "In post-experiment discussions with astronomers, the consensus was that the results of our experiment were not at odds with either what was already known or what additional data were radioed back by the flyby, but no definite evaluation could be made either."[4]

Full confirmation of Swann's descriptions did not come until the *Voyager 1* and *2* space probes in 1979. *Time* magazine reported:

> The most unexpected phenomenon, however, occurred when Voyager began detecting a stream of matter inside the orbit of Amalthea [one of Jupiter's satellites]. Fortunately, mission controllers had programmed the camera shutter to remain open for 11.2 minutes on the

remote chance—no one took the possibility very seriously—that Jupiter had some kind of ring.

To everyone's amazement, Voyager's time exposure produced a streaky image that the scientists could explain only as a ring of boulder-sized debris. The findings seemed so unlikely that the NASA team delayed making the information public for several days while the data were checked and rechecked. Saturn was long the only planet known to have rings and was considered to be the only one that could have them. In 1977, that theory was shattered with the discovery of rings around the planet Uranus. Jupiter itself was surveyed earlier by the Pioneer 10 and 11 spacecraft, but it is easy to see why no Jovian ring was found. Jupiter's ring is almost paper thin, perhaps 1 km (0.6 miles) high and impossible to view from Earth.[5]

But not impossible for Ingo Swann to remote view six years earlier.

Many other Jovian features described by Swann were confirmed by the later NASA missions: the high winds, towering mountain ranges, and thick cloud cover.

Scientist Hal Puthoff said he believes that space exploration may be one of the most important and cost-effective applications of remote viewing.

On March 11, 1974, Swann made a mental trip to the planet Mercury in anticipation of the upcoming *Mariner 10* flyby. This remote viewing session was monitored by Dr. Janet Mitchell. Swann's comments were recorded, transcribed, notarized, and deposited by noon March 13 with various parties, including the Central Premonitions Registry in New York.

His recorded impressions included these:

> I guess I have to go in the direction of the sun, so I can see the moon in back of me. There we go. Do you suppose Mercury has—what shall we call it?—a magnetosphere? Like a circular sphere of magnetism, except with Mercury, they are not a sphere, but on the sun side of Mercury, it is set closer to the planet's surface and on the far side of the planet, it is sort of pushed out into space....Everything seems very clear. Oh, I don't know why!
>
> There seems to be a thin atmosphere, but it is not enough to—it doesn't make a blue sky like on Earth, so you see blackness except where the sun is, maybe it is purple, I guess. There is not much haze. I get the impression of humidity—water. And tides, huge tides; liquid tides....[A]s the planet turns, the sun creates waves of earth tides, so that the surface has lots of cracks and fissures. The gravity must be uneven, pulling more towards the sun at all times. I see clouds—electrical storms now. These clouds come and go very fast and they form sort of on the day side of the planet, on the two peripheries of the day side. I see rainbows that seem to leap up. They arch—they are more like auroras, I guess. On the surface there is both a liquid—it seems heavier than water—but liquid. It's water of some sort, and land tides, both water tides and land tides and a fast condensation cycle. I guess that is what you would call it. This creates the leaping rainbows in

> all directions sometimes. It must have different gravities, depending upon which side you are on. It's beautiful—God, it's beautiful....I see land masses, but they look waterwashed, as if the water just twirls around the planet all the time....It seems a lovely little planet. There are differences in land masses, in a way mountainous, but not too mountainous. Everything looks chewed down, I guess because of the land tides. I'd say that the planet is characterized by sort of a low-keyed electric magnetic splendor. That's all.[6]

Swann's detailed description of Mercury was thought to be a novel oddity by those few astronomers who read the report. After all, it was established dogma in scientific circles that Mercury had no atmosphere, no magnetic field, and no ionosphere.

The established view of the planet was overturned less than a month later when the *Mariner 10* flyby began producing man's first close-up photographic view of Mercury.

Science News reported:

> Until last week, the majority of planetologists felt, with good reason, that Mercury was a pretty nothing planet. No atmosphere (the solar wind would blow it away), no magnetic field (the planet's slow rotation would not create the dynamo effect necessary to sustain one), no ionosphere (no magnetic field to trap the ionized particles), no moons. All in all, a dull world. Now it is "strange," "startling," "spooky," and "fascinating," all thanks to a few days of observations by Mariner 10. The first spacecraft ever to fly by Mercury has taken close-up photos which reveal a heavily

cratered surface and transmitted reams of surprising data that invalidates many of the theories about the sun's nearest and smallest planet.[7]

One by one, Swann's remote viewing observations about Mercury were proven correct as the data from *Mariner 10* continued to come in.

Swann had correctly identified Mercury's thin atmosphere, magnetic field, and the helium trail streaming out from the planet away from the sun. These observations were in direct contradiction to the scientific thinking of the time. Swann certainly didn't read about such planetary attributes beforehand.

Because the credibility of remote viewing in space appeared established by the Swann experiments coupled with scientific feedback, serious consideration must be given to other experiences reported by the Psi Spies.

During the Inspector General's 1988 investigation, the Psi Spies unit kept a low profile. They were ordered, "Don't do anything!" Only ongoing training was allowed. Under the guise of "advanced training sessions," unit remote viewers were sent against unusual targets. This led to the production of information and intelligence that went far beyond the ordinary.

The extraordinary became commonplace around the Psi Spies unit. The Psi Spies created what they called their "Enigma Files," in which they accumulated their most extraordinary cases. These cases involved remote viewing sorties that went far beyond Earth. What sounds as though it's the wildest fantasy to most of the public became the norm for the Psi Spies.

Morehouse recalled his first experience with the unknown:

> I remember hearing voices after I had cooled down...And I kept hearing these voices. Now one of the RV protocols is not to disturb someone when they're locking on a signal....I remember footsteps and laughter and I couldn't concentrate....
>
> I got up and opened the door and it was still dark in the office, dark in the hallway, dark everywhere. It was broad daylight and we were in this old World War II building where there was plenty of light, I mean it comes through the damn holes in the walls if it doesn't come from somewhere else. And it was dark. There was nobody around and as I began to walk down the hallway, I remember feeling strange. Then it dawned on me that I wasn't really there. I was somewhere else but I'm here. Then I thought to myself, *I'm having an out-of-body experience.* And I said, "I know that if I'm having one than I can walk through this door." So I go back up and I hit the door and I remember the cold steel of that door smacking me right in the side of the face. I just went "Ka-foom!" and struck my right eye on the side of this door. I pulled my face back off and said, "God, that was stupid!"
>
> So I went to the front door and opened it and looked outside. It was like there was an eclipse of the sun because everything was dark gray, everything. Nobody

> was around. There were no cars moving. Everything was hot but black. I walked down the steps and I had this sensation come over me that this is not normal. I couldn't understand what was happening. But I decided to try one more thing. I bent my knees and put my hands up on my sides. I did like I was going to come off a diving board. And I jumped up into the air. I went soaring like a goddamned rocket straight up into the sky. Then I remember being completely frightened. Because when I looked down, the earth was spread out beneath me and I knew that I would die from a fall like that. The next thing I knew, I came to with Mel Riley standing over me. He took me out and walked me around for awhile until I got grounded. We walked around hugging trees and picking up rocks.

Morehouse went on to have a wide variety of experiences beyond Earth. He describes other dimensions close to ours, filled with beings both strange and wonderful.

Mel Riley, the first psi spy, also claims to have visited other worlds and dimensions via remote viewing. To him, it's no big deal. "It's interesting that a bunch of soldiers, GIs, started out with the skills to look inside of things and ended up doing these kinds of things," said Riley. "But all this has been such a part of my life for so long that it's just part of my life."

Lyn Buchanan also viewed incredible scenes far from Earth. He even described the experience of being offered a job piloting a UFO by a nonhuman. (See my book *Alien Agenda* for details.) In fact, every single one of the Psi Spies experienced firsthand knowledge of UFOs and unearthly vistas, although even today some of them decline to talk about it.

McMoneagle recalled:

> I was targeted against a UFO sighting that was witnessed by nearly 2,000 people in Tacoma, Washington, in the 1950s. The witnesses reported "dancing lights in the sky." ...My first statement in the remote viewing room was "I see lights dancing on the horizon." This was followed by a spontaneous out-of-body experience, wherein I saw and interacted with an apparition of my father, who had died three years earlier, and a multi-light, humanoid-shaped entity.[8]

Dr. Brown wrote that, as he remote viewed UFOs and their occupants, he began to realize that "the ET situation was much more complex than I had previously thought. It was no longer a simple situation of ETs flying around Earth. There was real purpose behind their activities...."[9]

The Psi Spies said it is difficult to concentrate on the mundane problems of earth, once a person has traveled to other realms.

Riley said he found a lot of pleasure in psychically dropping down through the cloud layers of Neptune, approaching the surface. "It's so beautiful. It makes you want to be there. I plan to do this a lot when I have the time," he said.

"We, as remote viewers, went to places that were so beautiful. And that's about where your ability to describe it ends," Morehouse said. "There were people there. It was a place. Ours is a world with other worlds on top of it. We just don't have the ability to come back and describe to people what we've seen."

One of the sights most fascinating to remote viewers who have soared through space is not the vehicles flying around with living beings inside, but towers located on airless worlds throughout the galaxy. They seem to be sort of relay towers. They claim these towers appear to zing vehicles beyond light speed from one part of the galaxy to another, bypassing time and space. "There are technologies far ahead of us out there," commented Riley.

All of the Psi Spies said such wondrous visions only strengthened their religious beliefs. According to Morehouse:

> Once you know, really know, that death is not the end of your existence, then you are truly liberated, truly free. The only thing I can imagine it being like is going into the presence of God and standing there in a four-dimensional world where you can go forward in time and backwards in time—everything at any given distance. Omniscient, omnipotent, that's how you become. That is the realm of God.
>
> We hear people stand in a pulpit and read words, saying God is omniscient, omnipotent and all knowing. And we sit back and say how the hell can you be that? But if you've been to a fourth dimensional world than you see how that can be. I've seen it. Mel and the others have seen it....
>
> People have asked me if remote viewing has allowed me to go beyond a belief in God. On the contrary, what I have seen has just confirmed the existence of

God. It has confirmed the existence of all the things which have been laid out for us—the other worlds.

Morehouse said the remote viewing experience has strengthened his religion, helping him to put things in a broader and clearer context:

> You can't have the experience of remote training without having your life changed drastically because you become so aware of so much more than you knew before.
>
> I guess that one of the hardest things to fathom is that we on Earth are so insignificant. We're such a small part of one dimension among countless worlds. Our universe is countless worlds. Our planet is like one page in a huge encyclopedia.

He added that the Psi Spies have learned that other dimensions apparently intersect with our own, so it is often unnecessary to "go out there" to experience these worlds.

Unfortunately, all of the remote viewing experiences have not been as uplifting as those just described. Within the Enigma Files are reports laden with foreboding. One of these has to do with the continuing problem with our ozone layer.

In March 1992, five PSI TECH remote viewers were commissioned to explore the ramifications of the ozone problem. This contract came from the Institute for Human Potential, a think tank formed in honor of Senator Claiborne Pell, chairman of the Senate Foreign Relations Committee. Funding for the institute comes primarily from grants by Laurance Rockefeller.

"The outlook is grim," succinctly stated a cover letter with the final project report.[10]

The report contains this sobering assessment:

> Atmospheric ozone depletion/replenishment was perceived to be driven by a natural ebb and flow process—a geophysical cycle. But this process has become overwhelmed by manmade activity....A critical point is reached, circa 2005–2012, where the destruction will begin a runaway course, in a fashion analogous to metastasis [the transfer of malignant cells from one location to another]. During this period, the problem—and its potential consequences—will no longer be subject to question....The ozone decay will not necessarily be slowed down, but its effects temporarily ameliorated by coincidental volcanic activity. One such related event will be the explosion of an "extinct" volcano in the North American Cascade chain.... The volcanic activity will literally and figuratively eclipse the ozone problem, but decreased sunlight will wreak havoc with crop production in many places. Chaotic weather patterns in combination with decreased sunlight will necessitate the construction of huge environmentally-controlled greenhouses, so that food production can carry on without being subject to vicissitudes of climate/weather. Unwittingly, these structures form the templates for technologies that will become increasingly critical to sustaining human life. They will begin to be seen as sanctuaries—then habitats, as society begins to "migrate" into them.... A point is reached where very little life is seen outside of the

> artificial structures. The atmosphere outside these "biospheres" is almost antiseptic. The sky is striated and multi-hued. Earth's remaining (surviving) inhabitants have either been driven underground or into these very large, climate-controlled domes, which now house complete medium-sized cities. Our children's children are residents there. There is no perceivable violence. Most creative energy is directed to questions of survival.[11]

But the report moved farther into the future, indicating that humankind is not doomed. According to the report, the human race will adapt to the new conditions and to living in domed cities. Although our bodies will become less attractive by current standards, they will be more durable.

Furthermore, the viewers foresee another race, not from Earth, joining us in the future. According to the report:

> They were once endangered also and suffered similarly, but now serve as "consultants": friends, brothers from another place....Eventually, the inhabitants jointly build very large generators which will produce molecules, not oxygen, that rise to "seal" and form a protective layer, artificially restoring the Earth's atmosphere.[12]

The truth of these dire predictions probably won't be known for several years, but the negativity of their view of the future did not deter the viewers from continuing to probe "Enigma" targets.

The quest for more knowledge led the Psi Spies into some of the Earth's greatest mysteries. They have remote viewed the Loch Ness monster, the infamous crop circles, the disappearance of Amelia Earhart, Noah's Ark, and the mysterious 1909 Tunguska explosion in Siberia, among others.

Claiming to have answers where other researchers have only offered theories or raised questions, the Psi Spies said that their remote viewing brings direct knowledge. They also stated that they hope to learn some long-sought answers regarding life beyond Earth. They base this hope on continuing studies of aerospace anomalies.

The Psi Spies explained that their quest began with NORAD (the North American Aerospace Defense) Command, which has a number of satellites called DSPs (Deep Space Platforms) more than 500 miles out in space that monitor missile launches on Earth. Utilizing "over-the-horizon" radar technology, these deep space satellites can pick up the launch signal of any missile fired on the planet.

What the DSPs were not prepared for were high-performance craft coming in from over their shoulder, coming toward the Earth from deep space. These fast-moving objects became known as "fast walkers." Morehouse said NASA claimed they were small meteors called "boloids."

But some of these boloids possessed characteristics that suggested that they were of artificial origin, so the Psi Spies began taking a special interest in these high-flying, high-performance craft.

Late in 1988, Riley recalled that their superiors brought them a satellite photograph to study. The photograph showed simply a glowing object, but remote viewing sessions indicated the object had humanoid people in it and that it was hovering above a nuclear storage facility. Their impression was that these visitors were "bean counting," taking inventory of the number of armed warheads at this depot.

It didn't take long for the Psi Spies to realize that these "fast walkers" contained technology that was neither American nor Soviet. "We found that they were 'man made,' but not by anyone from around here," Morehouse quipped.

When the Psi Spies remote viewed and tracked these objects back to their point of origin, they found that they came from subsurface locations on our moon and from Mars, and that they would come to rest in subsurface locations on Earth.

The locations of such bases were first noted by Pat Price back in the 1970s and later confirmed by Psi Spies during the late 1980s.

Capt. Frederick "Skip" Atwater, former operations and training officer for the Psi Spies unit, declined to talk about the then-secret Army unit in 1994. But in February 1998, after the government acknowledged the unit's existence, Atwater spoke at the 7th Annual International UFO Congress in Nevada.

Atwater, who was awarded the Meritorious Service Medal for his work within the psychic unit and went on to become research director for the Monroe Institute, stunned his audience by announcing that a Psi Spies study had confirmed previous reports of four separate alien "bases" on the Earth.

He said that the initial reports of the bases came from Price, the policeman and psychic who proved so accurate during testing at SRI. In the late 1970s, while working at SRI,

Price had remote viewed the bases, which he claimed were located underground across the world.

According to Price, a main base involving flying units is located under Mount Perdido in the Pyrenees Mountains between France and Spain; a maintenance and repair base is under Mount Inyangani in the African nation of Zimbabwe; a weather and geological study center is located under Mount Hayes in Alaska; and the fourth base, located under Mount Ziel in Australia, was described as a rest and recreation center for personnel from the other bases.

Atwater said he became a training officer for the Psi Spies in the mid-1980s and was ordered to test the government-trained remote viewers by presenting them challenging targets. So during one formal but unofficial session, as with the Enigma probes described by Morehouse and Riley, Atwater sent unit members to look at the four bases described by Price.

To his amazement, this remote viewing session, which utilized strict RV protocols, confirmed Price's accounts and even added more details on the bases and their operations. What was even more amazing to the attendees of the UFO Congress was that this incredible confirmation of alien bases on Earth by a decorated military intelligence officer was neither covered nor reported by any news media.[13]

The Psi Spies did not tell their own superiors about their Enigma sessions because "everyone would think we had gone nuts, and second, none of the intelligence services, particularly DIA, had any charter to study such things," said Morehouse.

He said that initially the Psi Spies applied remote viewing to almost everything they could look at, one target to the next—an abduction here, a sighting there, a photograph of a moving object here. He added that, due to that lack of systematic work, they were not able to form a definite opinion as to what was really happening. "We only now have some inklings into the agenda, but this is largely personal opinion, based on individual interpretation," he said.

The Psi Spies worked hard to systematically study these visiting vehicles. Remote viewers had to learn how to distinguish man-made objects from those of nature. Morehouse said man-made objects almost always deal with combustion technology and were easily distinguished by the viewers. It was closer examination of other types of flying vehicles that they began to classify as alien in nature.

He added that the Psi Spies have not been able to closely study all of the vehicles that they have encountered in their psychic travels because there are just too many of them. Morehouse described remote viewing as very hard work. You look at one thing at a time. You don't get interested in the surroundings. Like a pilot on a bombing mission, the viewer is intensely thinking about the target.

As the Psi Spies continued to work with the Enigma Files, their fascination with these issues increased, and they began to differentiate between the various types of beings they encountered. They admitted to making mistakes in their interpretations of Enigma data and said the entire subject of these vehicles and their occupants is much more complex and subtle than first thought. It apparently concerns potential contact between species not only from other worlds but from other dimensions.

All of the Psi Spies seem to take the idea of alien cultures and other dimensions as a matter of fact. Riley described it this way:

> I guess when you deal with it so long, you stop thinking of it as something wondrous. This is just part of the overall cosmos. They've always been here, and they will be here after we've gone.
>
> We just kept looking at these various things and we found out that UFOs were for real—that there were real vehicles and real abductions. But it was all so esoteric that we just did not understand. I began to see how complex the picture was and I wasn't making any inroads in understanding their agenda.
>
> All this has just become part of my view of the universe. I'm pretty hard to convince. I don't take anything on someone's say-so. Now I have had my own experiences and nothing out there surprises me anymore.
>
> What most people would take as outrageous, we just take for granted. We know that it is within everyone to perceive this. Now if they don't choose to follow this, than that's their problem.

Lyn Buchanan's first bi-location or Perfect Site Integration experience was out of this world. It was also a complete surprise. He recalled:

> I went to the Operations Building one day to work a practice session.... This Training Officer was to be

the monitor, so...I knew ahead of time that it was probably going to be an ET target.

He said, "I think that I've uncovered the location where the aliens have stashed thousands of their young in hibernation. They're waiting for the day to come when they will wake up and begin taking over. I'll give you the coordinates and you are to describe what you find there. I've already worked it, and found everything, so this is just to check your work for accuracy. I think you'll be amazed at what you find."

That was an insurmountable amount of pollution. I should have walked out of the room at that point. I don't know of a single remote viewer of any kind who can work a session under such circumstances, with ease. But, it was a practice session and I had work at my desk I didn't want to do, so I decided, take an hour's vacation, to give him what he wanted and get it over with.

During the beginning part of the session, I toyed with the "perceptions," not really working a session. I was mainly feeding him what he wanted to hear, and watching him react. It was entertaining. At those times during the session when I said anything that didn't confirm what he felt the target to be, he would correct me and tell me what I really meant to say....Pretty soon, the whole farce became boring, and I wanted to end it. His excitement had reached a peak, though. I had created a monster. I finally got the idea to intentionally pretend to "go blank." That is a time in a CRV session when the impressions just dry up for seemingly no reason, and you can do nothing about it. It is rare, but maybe if I faked it, it would work. I looked up and said, "Uh-oh. I just went blank."

"No problem," said my monitor, his enthusiasm undaunted. "You're underground, in the hive chamber, and I need you to move 100 feet higher and begin describing what I've found up there."

I sighed and wrote down the move command, thinking, *Will this never end?* He said something else that I did not quite hear, and when I looked up, I could not see him any longer. I saw a very dark and cold corridor stretching forward, with light streaming into the far end of it.

I did not realize it at the time, but my desperation to get away from the painfully fake session had driven me to mentally escape to the actual tasked geographic location. I had spontaneously "bi-located" to the actual coordinates he had given me—just to get away from the misery of what was going on. To his credit, none of the massive pollution he had given me included the name of the actual location....I had no idea where I was.

I walked forward along the corridor. I always work sessions in my stocking feet, and at the site I could feel sand piled up on stone flooring under my feet. At the other end of the corridor, I stepped out onto an extremely small porch-like structure about 100 feet up the sloping side of a building. It overlooked a vista of land stretching out to the horizon. The sloping side of the building was to my left and right behind me. I turned a little and looked at it. It sloped backwards as it went up. I looked up and saw that the slanted side of the building rose many hundred feet higher and came a point above the place where I stood.

I looked back at the vista before me. Something was wrong with it. The sun was out and the skies were devoid of clouds. But the sky looked strange. It was much too dark for daytime, and the sun was much dimmer than it should be. The land looked very rocky and rough, and had no vegetation at all. There were some other things which looked like possible ruins of other buildings, but they were far away and hard to make out. They looked as though they were as worn and old as the building on which I stood. I turned again to look at the building which held the ledge on where I stood. Then, the sudden realization struck me that I was someplace else other than the viewing room. How had I gotten here? What had happened? As soon as the realization came, I found myself looking across the table at my monitor again. The very act of realizing that I had bought completely into the virtual reality had destroyed it.

The monitor asked me where I had been and I answered, "That's what I'd like to know!"

"Mars," he answered with a smile. "That's where they are."

"That's where who are?" I asked.

"The hibernating aliens!"

Then I remembered what had driven me to mentally leave the room in the first place. "Oh, yeah," I lied. "I guess that's where they are."

So that no one will misunderstand, I usually enjoy working targets such as UFOs, prehistoric events, the surfaces of other planets, and such other esoteric things. I even have a good amount of faith in the results I get, simply because I have a track record in a database which gives me a dependability rating on my work. In that session, though, right up until the time of the bi-location, I was simply telling the monitor what he wanted to hear. It had become boring and painful. It was not excellent site contact which drove me into the Perfect Site Integration. It was the need to escape.

To be totally honest, I had serious doubts about the whole session, and actually convinced myself that I had gone to sleep during the session and dreamed it all. It was about two years later, when I was at Stanford Research Institute, in California, that I happened to see a picture on the wall of "The Face on Mars." I had never seen that before. As I looked closely at it, I saw what looked like a pyramid far off to one side. I thought back to the Perfect Site Integration incident to remember the locations of the buildings I had seen off in the distance, their shapes and sizes. Studying the photograph even closer, I saw that the coordinates I had been given had corresponded to this location on Mars. Further, my perceptions had had the correct features in the correct places. I can't really say whether or not there were any aliens hibernating there. However, right before I received the move command, I had already bi-located to a place in which I did perceive a form of alien life much like a large segmented worm. They were very active and not at all in hibernation. I had just looked up and realized that there was a way out of the chamber I was in when I received the move command to "move up 100 feet and describe." How much of that part of the bi-location was accurate, I do not even guess.

There is no feedback, and probably will not be within my lifetime, so I do not even want to guess as to the accuracy of those perceptions. I still imagine that most of that part of the experience was due to the pollution I had received from my monitor. But what I did see, and get feedback on, was enough to convince me that at one time in my life, I experienced what it is like to stand on the surface of another planet. Some time later, pictures got sent back from the [*Viking*] Mars Lander, and when I saw them on television, my first reaction was "been there, done that." Too bad the Army never gave us travel pay for these sessions.

As amazing and unbelievable as all this must seem to many, there is now feedback on at least one of the Psi Spies' Enigma cases that strongly corroborates their claims.

This case concerned the *Mars Observer,* a joint venture between the Russian, American, and European space agencies, which vanished on August 20, 1993, just as it was about to go into orbit around Mars. Both scientists and laymen had high hopes that the *Mars Observer* would transmit photographs back to Earth, which might solve some of the Martian mysteries—such as the human-looking "face on Mars" and the three symmetrical pyramids seen in NASA photographs.

The 5,672-pound *Mars Observer* spent 11 months traveling to our neighboring planet and was scheduled to go into orbit around Mars on August 24. The $980 million satellite was to begin a two- to six-year mission to map the planet in greater detail than ever before. It was to be the vanguard of several spacecraft from the United States, Russia, and Japan.

But contact was broken and the craft hasn't been heard from since. What happened?

NASA officials initially theorized that the probe's timing clock malfunctioned, making the onboard computer unable to process commands being radioed from the Jet Propulsion Lab. But as the days passed and communication was never resumed with the craft, hopes dimmed of ever knowing precisely what happened to the *Mars Observer.*

But the Psi Spies knew.

Less than a week after the Mars probe was lost, the Psi Spies reported that the fate of the *Mars Observer* was identical to that of the Soviet *Phobos II.*

In March 1989, the unmanned Soviet probe *Phobos II* was lost just as it too was about to move into orbit around Mars. Communication was lost as the *Phobos II* passed into the vicinity of Phobos, its namesake and one of the two Martian moons. The Soviets issued a communiqué, suggesting that the craft had spun out of control due to an erroneous ground command.

There the matter rested until mid-1991, when former Psi Spies were commissioned by officials within the Russian space program to study the cause of *Phobos II*'s disappearance.

Six remote viewers were asked to view what really happened in the space near Mars in March 1989. Their final report, entitled "Enigma Penetration: Soviet Phobos II Space Craft Imaged Anomaly," was issued on September 29, 1991.

The report stated that:

> Sometime after entering Martian orbit, the Phobos II space craft appears to have entered an "ADIZ" [Air Defense Interrogation Zone, an electronic zone which protects national boundaries] of sorts, triggering an ensemble of actions in response to its presence: A disc-shaped object (Object 1) arose from the planet's surface to meet the probe, briefly perused it, then returned to the surface. Another object, already in space, was also attracted. Object 2 moved into close proximity and, in an act having some similarity to an "IFF" [Interrogation, Friend or Foe aircraft transponder] query, directed a very powerful, wide, and penetrating particle beam into the interior of the spacecraft. Shortly afterwards, Object 2 departed. The directed energy was neither reflected nor absorbed by the probe's skin. However, the beam inflicted serious damage upon the space craft's electronic components, altering or rearranging their material structure at the molecular level to such a degree that circuits became paralyzed, in turn rendering many systems dysfunctional.
>
> Phobos II attempted to "fix itself," but became even more paralyzed in the process, creating short circuits

and locking up servo mechanisms. Continued ground commands caused chaos, exacerbating the already hopeless situation. Subsequently, Phobos II underwent a radical course change, after which—in a totally random event—a small meteoroid administered the coup de grace, effecting catastrophic damage to the spacecraft.

At no time did the viewers detect hostile intent in connection with the (re)actions of Objects 1 and 2. Moreover, unintentional damage notwithstanding, Phobos II—an "alien" object—seems to have merited merely passing interest and cursory inspection. There are certain perceptions attendant with viewing Objects 1 and 2 that persuade one to label them as "escort vehicle" and "navigational buoy" respectively.

A parallel idea is connected with yet another object that viewers detected on the Martian surface during this project. This takes the form of a tall, pyramid-shaped edifice, which serves as a type of "corner reflector" or "glide path homing transponder," a passive navigational aid. It designates a site around which much or all of this activity seems to focus. In the vicinity of this marker, beneath the Martian surface, something is existing—something living—that is periodically visited by "others" on "caretaking" missions. Perceptions that are strongly connected with this resident life form include: ancient, marooned, and desperation combined with associated ideas of tremendous tragedy, grief, and pathos.[14]

Once again the Psi Spies had produced a report that read as though it were a science fiction story. Again, the question of feedback arose. Was there anything to prove the validity of what the viewers saw?

Ingo Swann, the father of remote viewing, urged caution when he stated:

> In the case of the ET thing, there may never be feedback.
>
> The public gets very excited....''Oh gee, a highly trained remote viewer is going to try to view the extra-terrestrials.'' I mean, there's a lot of sensational interest in that! But there is a bottom line. The bottom line says ''feedback,'' and without that [the whole thing] could be a waste of time.[15]

Swann's caution is well founded, but in this instance there was feedback—astounding feedback—from the Soviets themselves. It first came from Alexander Dunayev, chairman of the Soviet space organization responsible for the *Phobos II* project.

Dunayev announced that the doomed probe had photographed the image of a small odd-shaped object between itself and Mars. He suggested the object might have been ''debris in the orbit of [the moon] Phobos'' or even jettisoned parts from the spacecraft. His tone was anything but certain.[16]

More detailed—and exciting—news came in December 1991, when Soviet cosmonauts visited the United States. Retired Soviet Air Force colonel and cosmonaut trainee Marina Popovich displayed to newsmen in San Francisco one of the last photographs received from the *Phobos II.* She said the photo was given to her by Cosmonaut Alexei Leonov, a high official in the Soviet space program. She said the object could very well have been an alien spacecraft.

The photo showed the silhouette of an odd-shaped object approaching the spacecraft. Popovich said the picture was taken on March 25, 1989, in deep space near the Martian moon Phobos, shortly before contact with the craft was lost. The shape and size of the object matched the drawings of alien objects made by the remote viewers.

"The reasons for its disappearance are unknown," commented Popovich, "The photo is only information for thinking...information for all kinds of decisions."[17]

Although several theories about the object were advanced—some thought it might be a small undiscovered Martian moonlet or simply a product of a *Phobos II* camera malfunction—Professor Emeritus James Harder of the University of California at Berkeley and former director of research for the Aerial Phenomena Research Organization stated, "No one can answer precisely what it is."[18]

The Psi Spies viewed the photo as confirmation—feedback—of what they had reported months earlier. And if their account of the demise of *Phobos II* is correct, then serious attention must be given to their statement that the same fate befell the *Mars Observer.* "It appears that whoever is up there does not want us to know about them," commented Riley.

A micrometeorite was described by two separate remote viewers as delivering a coup de grace to the *Phobos II.* This may have been no accident.

The Psi Spies said it seems that all of the technology we put into space is scrutinized closely. If it would reveal the

Martian activities, then it is decommissioned. They noted the similarity of fates between the *Phobos II,* the *Mars Observer,* and the *Titan 4* rocket, which blew up carrying a super-secret spy satellite in August 1993.

That same month, we lost our newest weather satellite. The weather satellite, NOAA-13, was lost shortly after its launch on August 9, 1993, according to the Associated Press. The polar-orbiting satellite, designed to permit a view of the entire Earth during the course of one day, had been operating successfully until contact was suddenly lost, said officials of the National Oceanic and Atmospheric Administration.[19]

Later, on October 5,1993, a new *Landsat 6* satellite was lost after being released off of a *Titan 2* rocket 180 nautical miles from Earth. No one knows what happened to it.

An article in *Science News* said the loss of the *Landsat 6* would force both private companies and government agencies to rely on the *Landsat 5* satellite for images of Earth. The *Landsat 5,* which had lost part of its ability to transmit data, was launched in 1984.

A *Titan 4* rocket, carrying top-secret military cargo, exploded moments after takeoff on August 2, 1993. According to *Space News,* the cause of the explosion was thought to have been linked to a solid rocket motor segment that had undergone repairs by the manufacturer.

A less mundane cause was noted in the same article:

> But in a strange twist, [U.S. Air Force colonel and the *Titan 4* program manager Frank] Stirling said he has been told that the Air Force video of the launch shows an unidentified object apparently striking the Titan at

an altitude of about 110,000 feet, shortly before the rocket blew up. Stirling is not a member of the Air Force investigation team and has not seen the official Air Force video of the launch and the explosion. His office, however, is conducting its own investigation.[20]

Remote viewers believe all of these mysterious space losses may be attributable to the same cause: small, faceted objects that remote viewers have seen dipping out of an Earth orbit and striking man-made spacecraft.

One remote viewer who has seen these small objects is George Byers, who was trained by Army remote viewers.

In December 1993, four months after the *Titan 4* disaster, Byers took a mental look at that event. He recalled:

> I ended up identifying what destroyed the missile. It was something like a small projectile, about fist sized. It was shiny and hit the missile. It was definitely not a natural object. It hit and burst apart like a grenade. I did get the very distinct impression that it was not made on Earth and that it was directed at the *Titan 4* for the purpose of destroying it. Whoever made this thing knew what they were doing. In other words, it accomplished the job for which it was intended.

The viewers saw that something illuminated the *Titan 4* and that one of these little devices detected that illumination. It then swung out of orbit in a downward manner, accelerated, and punched through the *Titan 4*. There was no sign of a propulsion system.

Byers said it certainly appears as if this planet is being kept in quarantine for some reason.

Other forays into Earth's mysteries by the Psi Spies produced even stranger accounts.

Several sessions targeting the famous Loch Ness monster revealed physical traces of the beast—a wake in the water, movement of a large body underwater. Their drawings even resembled a prehistoric Plesiosaur, often identified as matching descriptions of Nessie. But when the viewers tried to discover where the object came from or returned to, they hit a dead end. The creature seemed to simply appear and disappear.

Considering that reports of human ghosts date back throughout man's history, the Psi Spies seriously considered the possibility that the Loch Ness monster is nothing less than a dinosaur's ghost.

Another strange session involved the mysterious explosion over Siberia on June 30, 1908. On that date, something streaked across Russia's skies and exploded high above the ground just east of the Stony Tunguska River, creating shock waves, a firestorm, and black rain. The object, described by some witnesses as a cylinder, reportedly changed course slightly before exploding. The aerial burst was recorded by seismic monitors as far away as Washington, D.C., and flattened a whole forest of fir trees, but failed to make any crater.

Theories of the cause of the explosion have ranged from a falling meteor or comet to a small mobile black hole or even a spaceship crewed by aliens. None of the theories have been unanimously accepted by the scientific community.

According to the Psi Spies, the Tunguska explosion was caused by a nonhuman craft, which appeared to combine the attributes of both machine and sentient being. It was under the control of distant humanoid beings.

In this scenario, this self-aware craft accidentally penetrated Earth's atmosphere and became desperate as it neared the ground. Meanwhile, its controllers feverishly attempted to correct the problem and were successful at the last moment. The being/ship was snatched back into its proper dimension, but its sudden departure created an energy explosion comparable to a nuclear detonation.

As far-fetched as this story seems, it does explain the reported last-minute course change and why no appreciable radiation has been found at the Tunguska site.

Much wider public knowledge may be coming in the near future as man's comprehension of the universe continues to expand. Recent scientific discoveries have broadened the public consciousness and seem to support some of the contentions of the Psi Spies.

When the Psi Spies returned from their mental voyages and described multiple dimensions, distant planets, stars, and travel through time, even their own bosses were so skeptical of their claims that they refused to pass such information along to higher authorities.

But in a series of recent books, sober-minded physicists are now claiming to have found evidence of a "top quark," which they take to be a key element in the current view of our physical universe. According to some scientists, "It is a universe where space exists in 10 dimensions, where one can travel through time into the past, where holes in the fabric of space and time pop up and serve as shortcuts to other parts of the universe, and where the visible universe may be only one of myriad mini-universes that coexist like so many soap bubbles in a cosmic froth."[21]

The claims of the Psi Spies and scientific knowledge appear to be converging.

For now, though, all we have are the psychic insights of the remote viewers—visions that will be accepted by some, scoffed at by others, and viewed with a mixture of skepticism and keen interest by most.

The remote viewers themselves were not concerned with whether or not their experiences are met by belief. "We have direct knowledge," Morehouse said. "And with direct knowledge, belief doesn't enter into it. It's there. It's real. We've seen it."

It is up to those of us without this direct knowledge to decide for ourselves how much credence we wish to give to the remote viewers.

But even the most ardent skeptic must seriously consider the claims of the Psi Spies, especially when viewed in light of the rigorous scientific study involved as well as the feedback now available to support some of the information gained by remote viewing.

If even a small portion of what the Psi Spies are claiming is true—and the preponderance of evidence suggests that it is—then mankind is facing a whole new world in the 21st century.

The new frontier will be the human mind, where we may explore the reaches of space, the history of olden times, and even other dimensions through the medium of remote viewing.

Remote viewing may finally provide the curious with "direct knowledge" of the immortality of his soul, the "truth" of historical events, and a view of the universe in all of its majesty and diversity. It undoubtedly will be a humbling experience for the ego of humans, but truth always has proven stronger in the long run than any myth or delusion.

Most importantly, if remote viewing is accepted and practiced by a significant number of people, it may prove to be the true liberator of the human spirit. After all, who would need fallible leaders and authority figures to frame the context of our reality if we could all gain "direct knowledge" through personal remote viewing?

The army's Psi Spies may have found the techniques that might propel the human species into a future of heightened consciousness, knowledge, and hope.

It would certainly be ironic if the United States military proved to be the innovating force that leads a fearful and hesitant public into the mind-expanding and hopeful 21st century.

The new information "superhighway" may be in our minds, but whether remote viewing becomes widely used or is replaced by other mental abilities—or even if we continue to rely on electronics rather than our own senses—one thing appears certain: Our lives will never be the same.

Epilogue

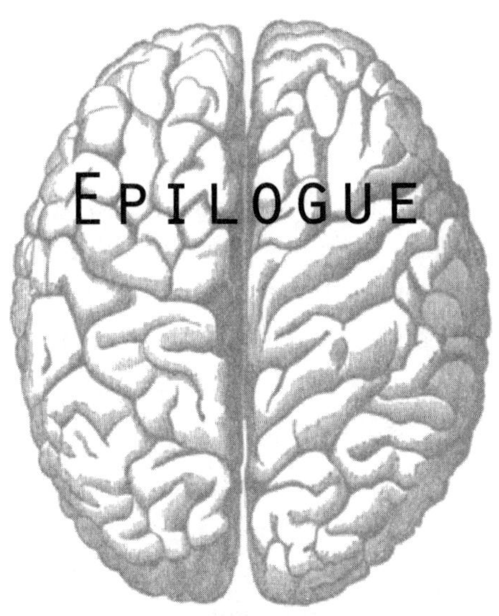

By the year 2007, the phenomenon of remote viewing was still known only to a small number of Americans, those who had taken the trouble to view materials outside the mainstream, corporate-controlled mass media.

But the techniques and potential of RV were not lost on the Psi Spies. Many of the military-trained remote viewers had turned to teaching RV in civilian life. Some continued to speak out concerning their experiences with military remote viewing, while others moved on to other pursuits.

One of the first Psi Spies to retire from the military and begin speaking out about remote viewing was Joseph W. McMoneagle. Since leaving the Army, McMoneagle has authored a number of books, including *Mind Trek: Exploring Consciousness, Time, and Space Through Remote Viewing*; *The Ultimate Time Machine*; *Remote Viewing Secrets*; and *The Stargate Chronicles: Memoirs of a Psychic Spy*.

Mel Riley retired from the military but never lost his interest in either remote viewing or Native Americans. "My time with the unit was a real experience," he said. "But no one took us seriously. We were orphans."

Riley said he continues to remote view. "I use it for everyday life. It heightens your awareness." He also said he sometimes participates in RV studies by the Physics Intuition Applications Corp. (P-I-A), a remote viewing organization that includes workshops by former psi spy officer Skip Atwater and RV pioneer Russell Targ.

Due to his work with Native Americans, by 2007 Riley had been accepted as a fully adopted member of the Ho-Chunk tribe, formerly known as the Winnebagos. He danced at tribal powwows and used remote viewing to access details of Indian history. Voted Vice-Commander of the Mohigan Veterans organization, Riley was honored by becoming the bearer of the Eagle Staff, a pole adorned with eagle feathers, which is the flag of the First Nation. "Not too shabby for a white boy," quipped Riley.

Ed Dames left the military with the rank of major and continued his remote viewing work through his company, PSI TECH. In 2000, Ed Dames broke with his fiancée and PSI TECH President Jonina Dourif and left the company. Dane Scotts, who had done media work for the firm, became the company's Chief Executive Officer. Later that year, Scotts and Dourif were married. PSI TECH continued to promote itself on the Internet as the "Founders of the Remote Viewing Industry."

Dames, who modestly describes himself as "one of the most distinguished military intelligence officers in recent United States history,"[1] by the mid-2000s was offering the public a game based on remote viewing entitled "Mind Dazzle." He continued to promote RV and offered a complete "Learn Remote Viewing" DVD course for $299.95 as well as live RV training workshops.

Paul Smith, who received his RV training from Ingo Swann, retired from the military and in 1997 became a founder and president of Remote Viewing Instruction Services (RVIS), Inc. In 1999, Smith joined with others to form the International Remote Viewing Association. By 2007, he was serving as vice president of the association.

Another psi spy trained by Swann was Bill Ray, who joined RVIS, Inc. after teaching remote viewing in Europe for several years.

Gabriella Pettingale, a member of the Psi Spies unit from 1987 until 1991, delighted in demonstrating remote viewers to members of Congress. While serving as director of operations for RVIS, Inc., she tragically was killed in a 2002 auto accident.

Smith's company teaches both Coordinate Remote Viewing and Extended Remote Viewing. ERV, or Extended Remote Viewing, is a term coined by Frederick "Skip" Atwater when he served as training officer for the Psi Spies. The name came from the fact that an EVR session always took longer than the shorter Coordinate Remote Viewing ones.

In 2007, Ingo Swann was still living in New York City but thinking of moving. His comfortable brick home in the Bowery was still filled with his artwork and cigar smoke.

Hal Puthoff's work on remote viewing led him into gravitational physics, and by the early years of the 21st century he was director of the Institute of Advanced Studies in Austin, Texas. He was one of the leaders in the search for Zero Point Energy (ZPE). He published a number of scientific papers with titles such as "Engineering the Zero-Point Field and Polarizable Vacuum for Interstellar Flight" and "Searching for the Universal Matrix in Metaphysics."

Dale Graff, a former commander of the Psi Spies unit, retired from the military and became a lecturer and talk show guest. Trained as a physicist, by 2007 he established Psi International Alert, Inc. (PSIA), a psychic activity designed to use precognition to avoid negative events in the future.

During his years of RV training, Morehouse was encouraged by many military people, both active and retired, to challenge his Army discharge. In March 2006, he appeared before an Army Discharge Review Board in Washington, D.C. The five Army colonels who constituted the board considered whetherMorehouse's 1995 discharge was fair and represented his service to the nation.

Morehouse quoted his attorney, Gary Myers, telling the board that "the charges drafted in the original documents were an embarrassment to the military legal profession. In fact, they are an embarrassment to any legal profession," and that "most are baseless, all without merit, and none are supported by credible evidence."

After reviewing the evidence, the board unanimously agreed and recommended to the Secretary of the Army that Morehouse's discharge be upgraded to "Honorable." This was done, and Morehouse witnessed "a full vindication of a record wronged over 11 years ago."

Morehouse has moved on to teaching spiritual values along with remote viewing in venues around the world. By late 2005, Morehouse had trained more than 23,000 persons in remote viewing, including both CRV and ERV. By 2007, Morehouse was director of training and education for an international firm specializing in medical advice for military personnel deployed by several nations.

Lyn Buchanan also has continued to teach remote viewing through his firm, Problems, Solutions, Innovations, headquartered in Alamogordo, New Mexico.

Buchanan deplores what he sees as "in-fighting" amongst today's remote viewing practitioners. "The greater part of the RV community is still trying to have their 'improved methods' become superior to everyone else's, fighting for the next paying student, etc. In this respect, very little has changed since the early days when it became public."

He said he and some few others, such as Courtney Brown of the Farsight Institute, offer free remote viewing database services via computer. "So far, the other instructors have not allowed their students to know about the free services, nor have they used it themselves. Such is the present state of the community," he noted.

An apprenticeship system, in which a mentor professional guided a newcomer's training, such as was practiced in the guild system, could be a way of educating a new generation of remote viewers, Buchanan said.

Buchanan and his firm already have provided remote viewing services to a variety of clients, including archaeologists, businessmen, corporate executives, police and investigative agencies, and the government. An interesting example of such work was a query to Buchanan from a moon-exploration company. They wanted to know the most cost-effective way to build a base on the moon. Buchanan said:

> What we found was that a crater makes for already-built walls. If you then stretch a plastic cover over it, you have a contained area. You only need to fill it with 16 psi of air (that's what Earth's atmosphere is at sea level), and any plastic sheeting will hold that much. If a meteorite hits it, it won't break, but will only punch a hole. Go up and cover the hole with duct tape, and you have a safe environment again. So, all it takes for a start-up moon base is a large roll of plastic and a bunch of duct tape. The customers were ecstatic over that, and more than likely, the first moon bases you see will consist of only that.

Buchanan and other former Psi Spies all wish that remote viewing could gain respect and a professional status.

The fact that virtually all of the Army's Psi Spies have continued to work with remote viewing in one way or another, attests to the legitimacy and importance of the phenomenon.

John Kovacs,at 43 years of age, represents a new generation of remote viewers, most trained by former Psi Spies.

Here is his story in his own words:

> In 1998, while sipping water following a long summer bike ride, I happened to catch a program called "The Real X-Files" on TV. Little did I know that this program would launch me into the world of Controlled Remote Viewing.
>
> I sat spellbound as this show revealed how the U.S. government spent millions of dollars training intelligence officers in the art of psychic spying. The hour-long show flew by and I sat stunned. Had I been lied to my entire life? After all, I was told over and again that psychic functioning does not work. There's no such thing. Yet, here was a documentary telling me the opposite thing.
>
> The next morning I went straight to my local book store and found...Joe McMoneagle's *Mind Trek.* I read the book quickly and then considered if McMoneagle, who had served the U.S. government for more than 20 years, was also lying to me. I began to think not. I then began to ask, "Could I be trained to remote view?"
>
> I learned that McMoneagle lived near and worked closely with the Monroe Institute [located in Faber, Virginia]....Our meeting lasted about 45 minutes with Joe doing most of the talking. He warned me that there had been remote viewers that needed psychological counseling after undergoing RV training. I said I had heard this before but when I asked him if he would train me, he answered, "No." But he did give me the phone number of Lyn Buchanan. He said, "This is a man who will train you."

I finally reached Lyn and this time made an appointment to attend an October class. I was surprised. There were only three others in my class. I was expecting between 15 and 20 in a class. I was surprised how personalized the training could be.

On the first day, we went over remote viewing terminology and had some discussions on the nature of time. The next two days we actually attempted some remote viewing.

An envelope was placed on the table in front of me and I was asked to describe the object or place depicted in the envelope. Usually, I am not one to brag, but I excelled in all of my attempts. For example, my final target was an individual parachuting. For my description, I wrote "an individual parachuting."

Lyn gave me a standing ovation and said, "Congratulations, John, you stayed in structure. Always stay in structure and you will make a great viewer."

...I cannot tell you how laughable I find individuals who dare call themselves remote viewers after one three-day course on the subject. Sure, they may get lucky now and then, but only through hard work and serious contemplation can one evolve into a viewer who can begin to understand the complexity and interaction between the conscious and subconscious mind in relation to time and space....

I soon began to explore the technique of Associative Remote Viewing. This is how one can predict binary future outcomes, perfect for stock trading and sports betting. I would use two photo images to represent one future outcome and the other another. For example, if the Yankees were playing the Red Sox, I would associate each team with a different photo. I would then ask myself to describe the photo of the winning team after the game. Since a viewer can breach the space/time continuum, if done correctly, he would be able to see the photo representing the winning team. This may sound easy, and sure, sometimes it works like a charm. However, there are many nuances that one must deal with to make this work correctly over time.

I trained with Lyn for a few years and took his basic, intermediate, and advanced training courses. Just like everything else in life, if you practice a discipline you will get better at it. But even after hundreds of sessions and years of training, I still had good days and bad. Sometimes the simplest everyday things, such as a headache, tension, or a skipped meal, can affect the viewing.

I started to attend remote viewing conferences and listen to other ex-military viewers. I met Paul Smith, who was trained by the world-famous Ingo Swann and went on to become the U.S. Army's remote viewing theory instructor. He also operated a remote viewing instructional service like Lyn....

I told Paul about my interest in Associative Remote Viewing and he suggested I come back and meet with his vice president of training service, Gabriella Pettingale.

I found her fun and witty, and she knew her remote viewing in and out. We hit it off instantly. Before I left this training, she suggested that we work together investigating Associative Remote Viewing. I was excited about this opportunity. It was just a few years past that I was watching the TV show about remote viewing and now I was invited to join in with ex-military viewers.

We began working together and were making great progress. Paul Smith joined in, and the three of us worked for more than a year. Then on June 7, 2002, Paul Smith called and informed me that Gabriella had been killed in a car crash. I was stunned. In a way, I am still stunned today. What could have been? What knowledge could we have gained?

Another ex-military viewer that I met was Mel Riley. He was part of the Army's remote viewing unit for 17 years. Anyone who knows Mel knows that he is soft-spoken and a man of few words. He only speaks out when he has something to say and when he does, it is usually important and thought provoking. Mel invited me to his home and we became friends. I have a deep respect for Mel and his lovely wife, Edith. I have never been trained by anyone better.

Mel is kind of my opposite. I am a Type A personality that always wants the answer right now. Mel would constantly remind me to ponder a situation, think, and wait for the answer to come....Being honed in RV by Mel was invaluable.

Mel also introduced me to Native American ways and even escorted me to Indian powwows where he would explain to me what was unfolding before my eyes.

Other RV instructors charge thousands of dollars for their ear. Mel charged me nothing. His lessons bled deeply into my life and, dare a recovering Catholic say, I became more of a spiritual person because of him....

But one's life does change with remote viewing. I have spoken with former students who tell the same story of their lives being changed after going through the training process. This may sound strange and conspiratorial, but some of them claim to have been visited by strange-shaped beings and that weird symbol-like downloads occur in their heads. I have to admit that I had had similar experiences. Has my brain been altered somehow, my hard wiring modified, so that it allows me to see these things? Certainly my dream world has been altered, and to say the least, it is very strange.

Ingo Swann believes that remote viewing is 400 years too early for humanity and that it will be both suppressed and taken advantage of by certain elements. Through RV, I believe that somewhere on this planet there exists gigabytes of individual data concerning how the human mind interacts with space and time. Who possesses this information? Those individuals with unlimited budgets and no constraints as to what pharmaceutical chemicals may be introduced into the viewer as they are simultaneously monitored by the latest hyper brain-body mapping computer systems.

Unfortunately, you will never hear of this as this information is highly compartmentalized. You have no clearance for this data, which could lead you to the ultimate prize: untainted truth.

In June 2002, I was privy to one of the most extraordinary examples of remote viewing I had witnessed. It occurred within five minutes in a crowded and noisy hotel bar. The viewer was John Kovacs.

The following notes are my original notes made at the 2002 International Remote Viewing Association Conference on June 14–16, 2002.

As a Civil War buff of sorts, I had always been puzzled by the famous "Rebel yell." Growing up in Texas, I always had heard the Rebel yell as a loud "Yeehaa!" sort of a cowboy whoop. I was puzzled why this boisterous yell would have caused shivers to run up Yankee spines, often resulting in flight, as recorded in numerous history books.

With the advent of the Internet, I visited a site that provided a recording made in the 1920s of one of the last of the Confederate veterans giving the Rebel yell. It was a strange wailing cry, similar to the howl of a coyote or wolf, which rose and fell in tone and intensity as if a wailing siren.

I suddenly saw the fear and apprehension that could be stirred by 12,000 men advancing with fixed bayonets while uttering this haunting wail. But, how was I to find confirmation of this?

Soon, I [would be] attending a conference of the International Remote Viewers Association. *Here was my opportunity,* I thought. But no one would accommodate me when I asked several viewers if they would take a look at the Rebel yell.

On the final day of the conference, I was seated next to John Kovacs in the hotel bar. It was crowded and noisy on this evening. There was standing room only. Patrons were almost shouting to be heard over the loud music and blaring TVs.

Offhandedly, I mentioned that I had a remote viewing target but no one would conduct a viewing for me. I asked if John would do it, and he shrugged and agreed.

For more than two days I had been carrying around a conference program with my question accompanied by a coordinate that I made up and attached to my question.

The question I had written down was, "Describe the sound of the Rebel yell as uttered at the battle of Gettysburg, July 1863." The coordinate number I had assigned to this question was 4281/2468.

I sat looking around at the crowd while John placed a stack of hotel notepaper in front of him and began staring off into space. Quickly, he began to scribble on the small note sheets, first one and then another. Within five minutes, he handed me seven note sheets, filled with letters and crude drawings.

With a sigh, I told him that I could not decipher the sheets, and I asked him to simply write down a summary. I handed him a paper bar napkin. He wrote, "Target is man made...silver, spinning, in constant motion, yet airy and open w/ site that is larger than it appears, motion is akin to that of a cyclotron. There are gray-dressed soldiers, the concept of the object [target] is to propel and land on target."

I was amazed. In his first line, I could clearly imagine the 12,000 men of Gen. George Pickett moving with fixed, silver bayonets moving across the open, airy, and sunny field in front of Cemetery Ridge, the whole spectacle much grander than portrayed in sketches and photographs.

My question—and verification of the old veteran's recording—came next with his words *akin to that of a cyclotron.* A cyclotron is an apparatus that charges atomic particles by an alternating electric field while in circular motion. This is the basis of a siren, such as the hand-cranked air raid sirens. The old veteran's wailing cry was confirmed by remote viewing.

The words *gray-dressed soldiers* confirmed to me that Kovacs was right on target. His description of the object of the session or target—the Rebel yell—as a means "to propel and land on target" again was dead on. The yell was to bolster the men's courage while demoralizing the enemy to help win success in achieving their objective or target.

I was stunned. Here was a near-perfect remote viewing session done under the most distracting circumstances and within five minutes.

This then is the wonder of remote viewing. And remember: The SRI tests showed that RV is not limited by either time or space, and that we all have within us the ability to contact planes of existence other than our own.

But be warned. It will change your life.

Appendix
U.S. Government Remote Viewing (RV) Chronology

1970—Shiela Ostrander and Lynn Schroeder's book, *Psychic Discoveries Behind the Iron Curtain*, concerning Soviet psychic research is released.

1971—Ingo Swann and Dr. Janet Mitchell coin the term *remote viewing* to describe an experiment, not a psychic ability.

1972—The CIA becomes concerned with Soviet research and hires Dr. Hal Puthof for studies at Stanford Research Institute (SRI). He is soon joined by Ingo Swann.

1973—(May 29)—Project SCANATE (SCANning by coordiNATE) is initiated at SRI. According to Ron McRae, it was "the most severely monitored scientific experiment in history." True geographical coordinates were used.

1974—Psychic Pat Price named target 20 minutes before researchers arrived, proving that RV is not limited by either time or space. Price performed such feats seven out of nine tests against odds calculated at 100,000 to one.

1975—The CIA, plagued by scandals, dropped SCANATE following Price's death.

1976—Army Chief of Staff for Intelligence Gen. Edward Thompson forms "black" unit, detachment G or GRILL FLAME, to study RV for intelligence use.

1977—The unit moves under the Army's newly formed Intelligence and Security Command (INSCOM) and continues SCANATE research.

1980—Col. John Alexander publishes "The New Mental Battlefield" in *Military Review.* He later said he was aware of the psychic studies and that it is "real and effective."

1981—Brig. Gen. Albert Stubblebine heads INSCOM. The unit commander reports to Stubblebine, who reports to the Secretary of the Army. The short chain of command assured secrecy.

1983—Military Intel officers begin training under Ingo Swann at SRI.

1984—Gen. Albert Stubblebine, "Spoonbender," is replaced by Gen. Harry E. Soyster.

1985—Defense Intelligence Agency (DIA) takes over the unit, which is supervised by the DIA's Scientific and Technical Intelligence Directorate.

1995—Report by Ray Hyman and Jessica Utts prompts a press release from the CIA. The U.S. government's official connection to remote viewing ends.

APPENDIX: IMAGES

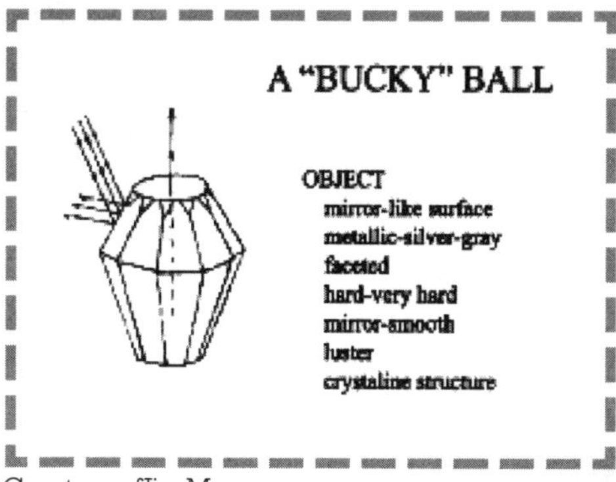

Courtesy of Jim Marrs

AN ET ENFORCER?

Named after the geodesic designs of Buckminster Fuller, several of these "Bucky Balls" have been seen in orbit around the Earth by remote viewers. About the size of a hand grenade, the multifaceted objects reportedly have dropped from orbit, causing several space setbacks, such as the loss of the 1993 *Titan 4* and the *Mars 96* rockets.

Courtesy of Jim Marrs

GRUNT RANGER

Army Maj. David Morehouse, who said he was nothing more than a "shaved-head, high-and-tight, grunt Ranger," nevertheless became an accurate remote viewer for the Psi Spies. His mental faculties were broadened some years before when he was struck by a bullet to his head while serving in the Middle East.

Courtesy of Joe McMoneagle

THROUGH TIME AND SPACE

Joe McMoneagle, one of the original Psi Spies, also was one of the first to retire from the military. McMoneagle went on to write a series of books detailing his remote viewing experiences, which ranged from looking at the origins of humankind to the John F. Kennedy assassination.

Courtesy of Skip Atwater

ALIEN BASES ON THE EARTH

Army Capt. Frederick "Skip" Atwater was operations and training officer of the Psi Spies. As a test, he once tasked viewers to look at four extraterrestrial bases on the Earth previously identified by Pat Price. To his amazement, the viewers confirmed Price's information concerning the alien bases.

Courtesy of Jim Marrs

NATIVE AMERICAN VIEWER

Army Master Sgt. Mel Riley, one of the original Psi Spies, was introduced to remote viewing as a young boy when he experienced an apparition of an ancient Native American village while hiking. Incredibly, one of the Indians appeared to acknowledge his presence. The experience set Riley on a lifelong quest for the greater meaning of life.

Courtesy of Jim Marrs

PSI SPIES HQ

These two wood-frame buildings on the grounds of Fort Meade, Maryland, served as headquarters for the Psi Spies for almost two decades. Formerly used as a bakery school during World War II, these structures were torn down in the mid-1990s. It was here that military intelligence officers used laboratory-tested methods of remote viewing to seek out military secrets behind the iron curtain.

Courtesy of Jim Marrs

A VARIETY OF UFOS

Although not all of them will speak openly about it, every single one of the military-trained remote viewers experienced firsthand knowledge of unidentified flying objects. Some were tasked to seek out UFOs, but most ran across them in their psychic searches. They reported a variety of types as well as a variety of beings crewing them. These are sketches of some of the vehicles they observed.

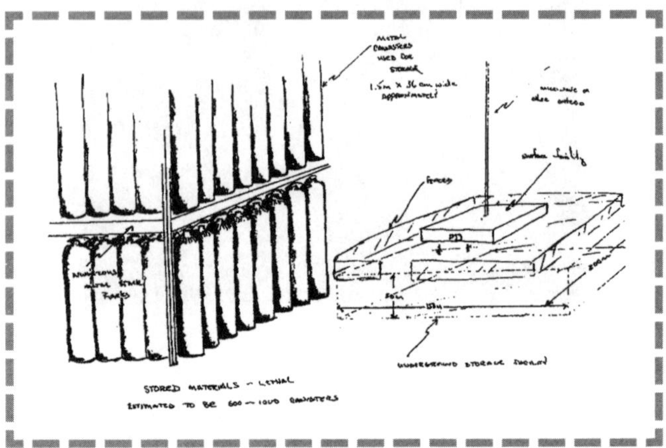

Courtesy of U.S. Government

CHEMICAL WEAPONS IN IRAQ

This drawing from the Psi Spies files depicts a chemical weapons stockpile belonging to Iraq's Saddam Hussein. Government officials, fearful that Saddam may have left weapons of mass destruction behind in Kuwait City following the first Gulf War, sent Psi Spies to look for hidden nuclear or biochemical weapons. None were found.

Courtesy of Jim Marrs

THE DISINTEGRATED MAN

Lyn Buchanan, a former trainer of the Psi Spies, today teaches remote viewing from his New Mexico home. During one mission against a Soviet secret weapons testing facility, Buchanan placed himself in the trajectory of a particle beam weapon. Psychically, he felt the effects of losing solidarity and becoming a streaming mass of particles, an experience that perhaps no other human has encountered.

Courtesy of Jim Marrs

THE FATHER OF REMOTE VIEWING

Both scientist, psychic, and painter, Ingo Swann was involved from the inception of remote viewing, even coining the term. A naturally gifted psychic, Swann applied scientific standards to study the phenomenon and even devised Coordinate Remote Viewing as a testing method. Swann's mental travels reached from the Earth to the stars.

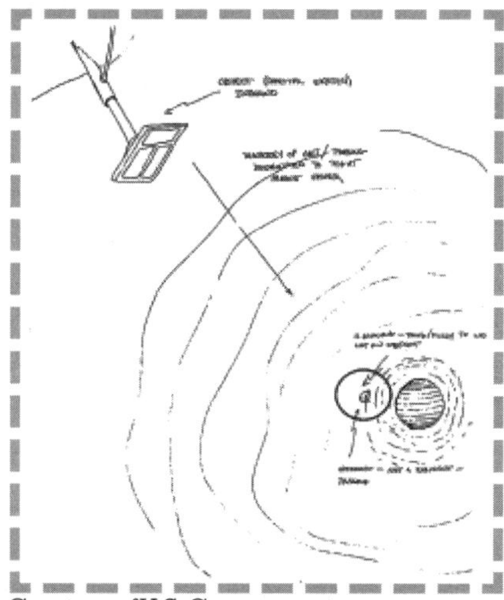
Courtesy of U.S. Government

MARS OBSERVER INTERCEPTED?

When the *Mars Observer* was lost in August 1995, military-trained remote viewers quickly stated that it had suffered the same fate as the Soviet *Phobos II*, lost in March 1989, as it entered orbit around Mars. In this viewer's sketch, an array or antenna of the *Mars Observer* is shown in the upper left corner, and the planet Mars is depicted as the globe in the lower right with rings representing layers of atmosphere. A strange oblong object is shown moving from Mars toward the *Mars Observer*. Astounding feedback came in 1991, when a visiting former Soviet cosmonaut displayed one of the last photos transmitted back to Earth by the *Phobos II*, which showed a similar object approaching that spacecraft.

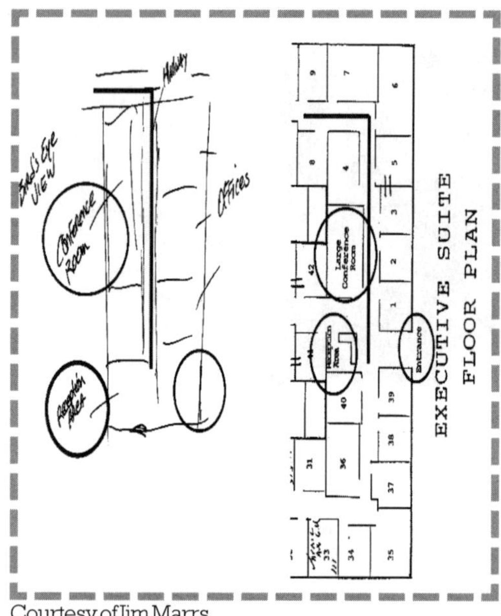

Courtesy of Jim Marrs

REMOTE VIEWING FEEDBACK

When author Jim Marrs was invited to New Mexico in October 1992, to visit the office of a remote viewing company, he decided to try his hand at this government-studied psychic phenomenon. At left is his sketch of the floor plan of a single-story office complex he envisioned before his trip. Arriving in New Mexico, Marrs was disappointed to find the "office" actually was someone's ranch-style home. More than a year later, though, he was flabbergasted to learn that the firm had indeed taken offices in a new one-story office complex and that the official floor plan, at right, matched his previous drawing 100 percent—right down to naming the "reception area" and "conference room." Incredibly, this office space had been built after Marrs's 1992 viewing attempt. He had remote viewed something in the future.

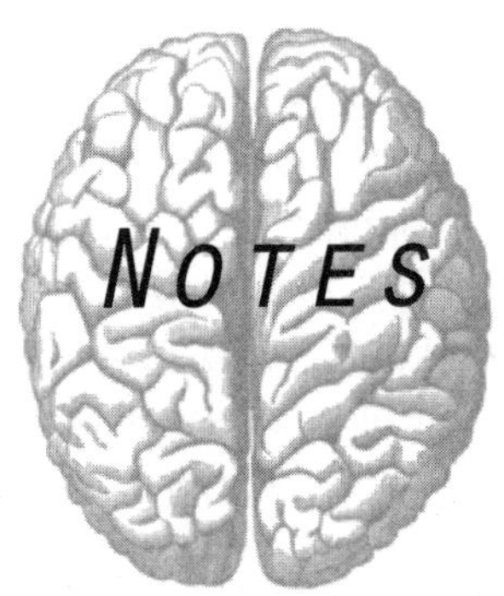

Notes

Preface

1. R. Jeffrey Smith, "Pentagon Has Spent Millions On Tips From Trio of Psychics," *The Washington Post* (November 29, 1995), p. A1.
2. Ibid.
3. Ibid.
4. J. Antonio Huneeus, "UFO Chronicle," *Fate*, Vol. 46, No. 9 (September 1993), p. 32.

Chapter 1

1. David Morehouse, interviews with the author, spring and summer, 1993.
2. U.S. Army records. Officer Record Brief, David Allen Morehouse. March 2, 1989.

Chapter 2

1. Richard S. Broughton, Ph.D., *Parapsychology: The Controversial Science* (New York: Ballantine Books, 1991), p. 103.
2. Ibid.
3. Trent C. Butler, gen. ed., *Holman Bible Dictionary* (Nashville, Tenn.: Holman Bible Publishers, 1991) p. 1142.
4. Broughton, op.cit., pp. 50–1.
5. Brad Steiger, *American Indian Magic: Sacred Pow Wows & Hopi Prophecies* (New Brunswick, N.J.: Inner Light Publications, 1986), p. 114.

6. Steve Wall and Harvey Arden, *Wisdomkeepers: Meetings With Native American Spiritual Leaders* (Hillsboro, Oreg.: Beyond Words Publishing,1990), pp. 32–33.
7. Arthur C. Parker, *The Indian How Book* (New York: Dover Publications, 1975), p. 286.
8. *The Missionary Society of St. Paul the Apostle in the State of New York, Native North American Spirituality* (Mahwah, N.J.: Paulist Press, 1979), pp. 92–3.
9. Frederick W. Turner III, *I Have Spoken: American History Through the Voices of the Indians* (New York: Pocket Books, 1972), p. 153.
10. Justine Glass, *They Foresaw the Future: The Story of Fulfilled Prophecy* (New York: G.P. Putnam's Sons, 1969), p. 86.
11. Stephan A. Schwartz, *The Secret Vaults of Time: Psychic Archaeology and the Quest for Man's Beginnings* (New York: Grosset & Dunlap, 1978), p. 207.
12. Glass, op cit., pp. 32–5.
13. David Wallechinsky, Amy Wallace, and Irving Wallace, *The Book of Predictions* (New York: Bantam Books, 1981), p. 346.
14. Ibid.
15. Glass, op. cit., p. 95.
16. Ibid., pp. 96–8.
17. Ibid., pp. 352–55.
18. Erika Cheetham, *The Prophecies of Nostradamus* (New York: G.P. Putnam's Sons, 1974); Edgar Leoni, *Nostradamus and His Prophecies* (New York: Bell Publishing Co., 1982 edition).

19. Ibid.
20. Ibid.
21. Ibid.
22. Ibid.
23. Ibid.
24. Ibid.
25. Ibid.
26. Time-Life, *The PsychicsPsychics: Mysteries of the Unknown* (Alexandria, Va.: Time-Life Books, 1992), p. 74.
27. Broughton, op. cit., p. 55.
28. Colin Wilson, *The Supernatural* (New York: Carroll & Graf, 1991), p. 69.
29. Broughton, op. cit., p. 56.
30. Wilson, op.cit., pp. 81–8.
31. Ibid., p. 83.
32. Ibid., p. 87.
33. Ibid.
34. William Denton, *Soul of Things: Psychometric Researches and Discoveries* (Wellesley, Mass.: Mrs. E.M.F. Denton, Publisher, 1873), pp. 345–46.
35. Ibid., p. 273.
36. Broughton, op.cit., p. 64.
37. Ibid., p. 65.
38. Ibid., p. 67.
39. Wilson, op. cit., p. 215.
40. Broughton, op. cit., p. 294.
41. Ibid., p. 72.
42. Michael Colmer, Anglo American Spiritualist Ministries, *clearlight.com.*
43. Tim Rifat, *Remote Viewing: The History and Science of Psychic Warfare and Spying* (London: Century, 1999), p. 66.

Chapter 3

1. Broughton, op cit., p. 98.
2. Ibid.
3. Ibid., pp. 102–5.
4. Ibid., p. 279
5. Ibid., p. 296.
6. Ibid., p. 286.
7. Ibid.
8. Ibid., p. 287.
9. Ibid., p. 288.
10. Hal Puthoff, interview with the author, July 23, 1993.
11. Ingo Swann, interview with the author, August 27–28, 1993.
12. Ingo Swann, *To Kiss Earth Goodbye* (New York: Dell Publishing, 1975), pp. 118–19.
13. Ibid., pp. 218–19.
14. Ibid.
15. Ibid.
16. Peter Tomkins and Christopher Bird, *The Secret Life of Plants* (New York: Avon Books, 1973), p. 27.
17. Editors of Time-Life Books, *Psychic Voyages, Mysteries of the Unknown* (Alexandria, Va.: Time-Life Books, 1987), p. 39.
18. Swann, op.cit., pp. 135–36.
19. Ibid.
20. Ingo Swann, "On Remote-Viewing, UFOs, and Extraterrestrials," *Fate,* Vol. 46, No. 9 (September, 1993), p. 76.
21. Swann, loc. cit., p. 75.
22. Ibid., p. 78.
23. Ibid.

24. Ibid.
25. Russell Targ and Harold E. Puthoff, *Mind-Reach: Scientists Look at Psychic Ability* (New York: Delacorte Press, 1977), pp. 18–9.
26. Ibid., p. 20.
27. Ibid., pp. 22–3.
28. Ibid., p. 24.
29. Ibid., p. 25.
30. Time-Life, *Psychic Voyages,* op cit., p. 41.
31. Targ and Puthoff, op. cit., p. 26.
32. Ibid., pp. 26–7.
33. Ibid.
34. Ibid., p. 27.

Chapter 4

1. Ronald M. McRae, *Mind Wars: The True Story of Government Research into the Military Potential of Psychic Weapons,* (New York: St. Martin's Press, 1984), p. 32.
2. Time-Life, *The Psychics,* op. cit., p. 71.
3. Shiela Ostrander and Lynn Schroeder, *Psychic Discoveries Behind the Iron Curtain* (New York: Bantam Books, 1970), p. 6.
4. Ibid., p. 9.
5. Ibid., pp. 417–18.
6. Ibid., pp. 253–54.
7. McRae, op. cit., pp. 33–4.
8. Ibid.
9. Ibid.
10. Ingo Swann, Letter to Dr. Alex Imich, November 8, 1992. Copy in author's files.
11. Editors, *The New Encyclopedia Britannica, 15th ed. rev.* (Chicago: 1991), Vol. 9, p. 147.

12. Martin Ebon, *Psychic Warfare: Threat or Illusion?,* (New York: McGraw-Hill Book Co., 1983), pp. 257–260.
13. Time-Life, *The Psychics,* op. cit. p. 76.
14. Ibid., pp. 79–80.
15. Jack Anderson, "Psychics Kept on U.S. Payroll for Secret Studies," *Washington Merry-go-round,* August 12, 1985.
16. Time-Life, *The Psychics,* op. cit., p. 81.
17. McRae, op. cit., p. 99.
18. Ibid.
19. Kenneth A. Kress, "Parapsychology In Intelligence: A Personal Review and Conclusions," *Journal of Scientific Exploration* (January, 1999), p. 71. This report originally was published in the Winter 1977 issue of *Studies in Intelligence,* a classified CIA internal publication, released to the public in 1996.
20. Targ and Puthoff, op. cit., pp. 2–4.
21. Ibid.
22. Ibid.
23. Swann, loc. cit., p. 79.
24. Ibid.
25. Ibid.
26. Targ and Puthoff, op. cit., pp. 34–5.
27. Ibid.
28. Ibid., p. 36.
29. McRae, op. cit., p. 98.
30. Ibid.
31. Targ and Puthoff, op.cit., p. 37.
32. Ibid.
33. Ibid., p. 44.

34. Ibid., p. 47.
35. Ibid., pp. 47–8.
36. Ibid.
37. Ibid., p. 50.
38. Ibid.
39. Ibid., p. 50.
40. Russell Targ and Keith Harary, *The Mind Race: Understanding and Using Psychic Abilities,* (New York: Villard Books, 1984), pp. 57–8.
41. Editors of Time-Life, *Psychic Powers: Mysteries of the Unknown* (Alexandria, Va.: Time-Life Books, 1987), p. 61.
42. Targ and Puthoff, op. cit., p. 69.
43. Ibid., p. 71.
44. Ibid., pp. 74–5.
45. Ibid., p. 79.
46. Ibid., p. 84.
47. Ibid., p. 90.
48. Time-Life, *Psychic Voyages,* op. cit., p. 32.
49. Targ and Puthoff, op. cit., p.1.
50. McRae, op. cit., p. 102.
51. Ibid., p. 103.
52. Time-Life, *The Psychics,* op cit., p. 82.
53. McRae, op. cit., p. 111.
54. Ibid., p. 109.
55. Alan Vaughan, "Remote Viewing: ESP for Everyone," *Psychic Magazine,* July–August, 1976, p. 32.
56. Kress, op. cit., p. 79.
57. Russell and Harary, op. cit., p. 58.
58. Ibid., p. 103.
59. *The Chicago Tribune,*August 13, 1977.

Chapter 5

1. Mel Riley, interview with the author, spring and summer 1993.
2. Kress, op. cit., p. 69.
3. Ibid.
4. Lyn Buchanan, interviews with the author, 1993–94 and 2007.
5. Jim Schnabel, "Tinker, Tailor, Soldier, Psi," *Independent on Sunday* (London), August 27, 1995, pp. 10–13.
6. Riley's military records. Copies in author's files.
7. Joseph McMoneagle presentation at Project Awareness Conference, Clearwater, Florida, November 14, 1999.
8. Joseph McMoneagle, *The Ultimate Time Machine* (Charlottesville, Va.: Hampton Roads Publishing Company, Inc., 1998), p. 37.
9. Lt. Col. John B. Alexander, "The New Mental Battlefield: 'Beam Me Up, Spock'," *Military Review* (December 1980), p. 47.
10. Col. John B. Alexander, interview with the author, August 16, 1993.
11. Col. John B. Alexander, Major Richard Groller, and Janet Morris, *The Warrior's Edge: Frontline Strategies for Victory on the Corporate Battlefield* (New York: Avon Books, 1990) p. 205.
12. Alexander, Groller, and Morris, op. cit., p. 48.

Chapter 6

1. Broughton, op. cit., p. 103.
2. McMoneagle, op. cit., pp. 20–1.
3. Time-Life Editors, *Psychic Voyages,* op. cit., p. 32.
4. Paul Tyler, M.D., Capt. U.S. Navy (Ret.), interview with the author, August 16, 1993.

5. Daniel Druckman and John A. Swets, editors, *Enhancing Human Performance* (Washington, D.C.: National Academy Press: 1988) p. 22.
6. Ibid., pp. 170–71.
7. Ibid., p. 171.
8. Ibid.
9. Ibid., p. 173.
10. Ibid.
11. Ibid.
12. Broughton, op. cit., p. 323.
13. Ibid., p. 324.
14. Col. John B. Alexander, "A Challenge To The Report," *New Realities,* (March/April), 1989, p. 10.
15. Ibid.
16. Ibid., p. 11.
17. Ibid., p. 12.
18. Ibid., p. 13.
19. Ibid., p. 12.
20. Ibid., p.13.
21. Ibid.
22. Druckman and Swets, op. cit., p. 252.

Chapter 7

1. Test reports in Morehouse's files.
2. J.M. Davis Arms & Historical Museum promotional piece. *www.state.ok.us/~jmdavis/*
3. GRILL FLAME "Working Paper," August 1, 1980.
4. Ibid.
5. Ibid.
6. Ibid.
7. Ibid.

8. "Session Summary," February 6, 1989. Copies in David Morehouse's files.

Chapter 8

1. *www.trv-psitech.com/flash/topbar_menu.swf.*
2. Mark Sauter, "Special Assignment: Psychic Spooks," KIRO News, Seattle, Washington. Aired fall 1990.
3. Ibid.
4. From PSI TECH company literature.
5. McMoneagle, op. cit., p. 29.
6. PSI TECH Report Titles. Copies in author's files.
7. Ibid.
8. Ruth Sinai, "U.N. enlists psychic firm to find Iraqis' weapon sites," The *Washington Times,* November 19, 1991.
9. PSI TECH report "Clandestine Iraqi Biological Weapons Facilities," November 9, 1991.
10. Ibid.
11. Ibid.
12. Sinai, op. cit.
13. George G. Byers, interviews with the author, May 19, 1994 and August 29, 1994.
14. McMoneagle, op. cit., p. 72.

Chapter 9

1. Howard Blum, *Out There* (New York: Simon and Schuster, 1990), pp. 33–8.
2. Swann, op. cit., p. 149.
3. B. Humphrey, "Swann's Remote Viewing Probe of Jupiter," *SRI International Report* (Menlo Park, Calif., March 17, 1980).
4. Targ & Puthof, op. cit., pp. 210–11.
5. *Time,* March 19, 1979, p. 87.

6. Targ & Puthoff, op. cit., p. 211.
7. "Science News of the Week: The Strange and Cratered World of Mercury," *Science News Vol. 105* (April 6, 1974) p. 220.
8. McMoneagle, op. cit., p. 34.
9. Courtney Brown, *Cosmic Voyage* (New York: Dutton, 1996), p.76.
10. Final Project Report, "Atmospheric Ozone Depletion—Projected Consequences and Remedial Technologies," PSI TECH (March 12, 1992).
11. Ibid., pp. 1–4.
12. Ibid.
13. Author's notes made during Atwater's speech, Annual International UFO Congress, February 5, 1998.
14. Final Report, "Enigma Penetration: Soviet Phobos II Space Craft Imaged Anomaly," PSI TECH Report (September 29, 1991), pp. 1–2.
15. Vicki Cooper, "The Business of Remote Viewing," *UFO,* Vol. 8, No. 3 (1993), p.27.
16. Patrick Huyghe, "Martian Mystery: Is the Red Planet host to a third lunar body or UFOs?," *Omni,* May 1993, p. 79.
17. Jack Vlots, "Soviet Photo of a UFO Near Mars," *The San Francisco Chronicle,* December 7, 1991.
18. Ibid.
19. Associated Press, "New Weather Satellite Lost," *Los Angeles Times,* August 23, 1993.
20. Ben Iannotta, "Titan 4 Motor Is Prime Suspect," *Space News,* August 23–29, 1993, p. 1.

21. William F. Allman, "Alternative Realities: Beyond the top quark lies a bizarre new realm of theoretical physics," *U.S. News & World Report,* May 9, 1994, p. 59.

Epilogue

1. *www.learnrv.com/eddames.cfm.*
2. John Kovacs, correspondence with the author, March 2007.

Appendix A

1. Ronald M. McRae, op. cit., p. 99.

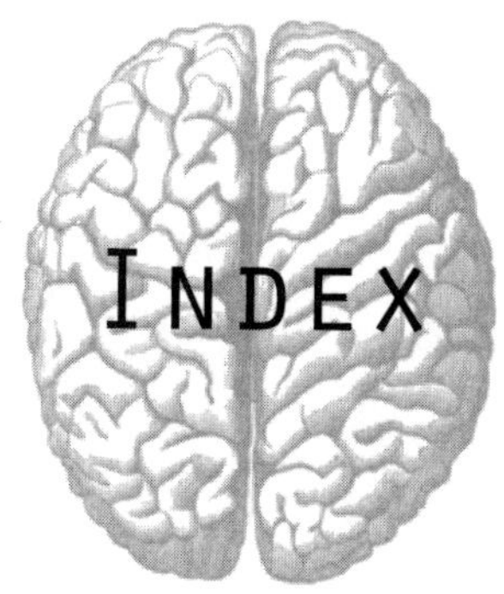
INDEX

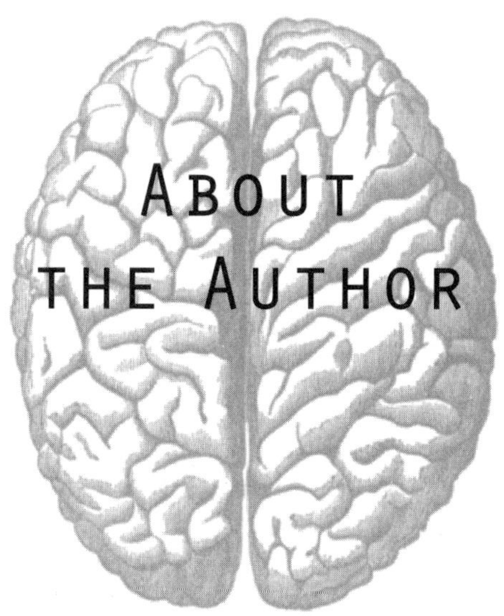

About the Author

Jim Marrs is a native of Fort Worth, Texas. He earned a B.A. in journalism from the University of North Texas and attended graduate school at Texas Tech before pursuing a career in journalism. Since 1980, Jim has been a freelance writer, author, and public relations consultant. He also published a rural weekly newspaper, along with a monthly tourism tabloid, a cable television show, and several videos.

An award-winning journalist, Jim is listed both in *Who's Who in the World* and *Who's Who in America*, and has won several writing and photography awards.

He has appeared on major television networks and cable channels, as well as numerous national and regional radio and TV shows. Jim is a current member of the Society of Professional Journalists, Sigma Delta Chi, and the Investigative Reporters and Editors.

His other books include *Alien Agenda, Rule by Secrecy, The Terror Conspiracy,* and *Crossfire,* which served as a basis for Oliver Stone's movie *JFK.*